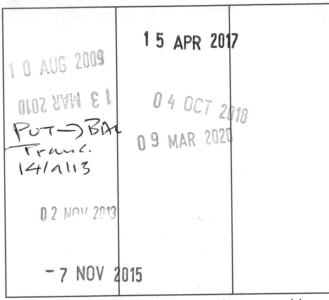

Soffritto

Soffritto

A DELICIOUS LIGURIAN MEMOIR

Lived by **LUCIO GALLETTO**
Written by **DAVID DALE**
Photography by **PAUL GREEN**

First published in 2007

Copyright text © David Dale and Lucio Galletto 2007
Copyright photographs © Paul Green 2007

Allen & Unwin
83 Alexander Street
Crows Nest NSW 2065
Australia
Phone: (61 2) 8425 0100
Fax: (61 2) 9906 2218
Email: info@allenandunwin.com
Web: www.allenandunwin.com

National Library of Australia
Cataloguing-in-Publication entry:

Dale, David.

Soffritto : a delicious Ligurian memoir.
1st ed.
Bibliography.
Includes index.
ISBN 978 1 74175 076 8 (hbk.).
1. Galletto, Lucio - Travel - Italy - Liguria. 2. Galletto
family. 3. Cookery, Italian - Northern style. 4. Liguria
(Italy) - Description and travel. I. Galletto, Lucio. II.
Green, Paul (Paul Evan). III. Title.
914.51

Map on case and page 207 by Luke Sciberras
Edited by Karen Ward
Designed by Pfisterer + Freeman
Typeset by Pfisterer + Freeman
Printed in China through Colorcraft Ltd,
Hong Kong

10 9 8 7 6 5 4 3 2 1

We shall not cease from exploration
And the end of all our exploring
Will be to arrive where we started
And know the place for the first time.

T.S. Eliot
'Little Gidding' (the last of his *Four Quartets*)

Contents

Introduction

There are a lot of books in here. It began as a psychological investigation and ended up a love story, travel memoir, war adventure, eating guide and portrait of modern Europe.

I was curious about some key questions of our age: How did the Italians conquer the English-speaking world without firing a single shot? How did their food, their art and their attitude become so influential on 21st-century life? Does Italy hold the secret of human happiness?

I'd been a visitor at Lucio's restaurant for years before we started discussing these sorts of issues. He wasn't even sure they were the right questions, but thought his cousin Mario would have something to say on the subject. The next time I was travelling in Italy, I went to see Mario in the seaside town of Bocca di Magra. And there I discovered the restaurant called Capannina Ciccio, the area called Lunigiana and the tale of two families.

Mario, like Lucio, was a reluctant restaurateur. Young Mario intended to make movies. Young Lucio intended to design buildings. Fate intervened while they were making other plans. And it turned out that something in their upbringing had equipped them perfectly to become successful hosts at opposite ends of the planet, and to realise, much later in their lives, that this was what they were meant to do.

When I got back to Sydney, I found that my urge to explore the questions about Italy coincided with an urge in Lucio to understand his origins – to bring to his conscious mind the concepts and skills his younger self had absorbed unconsciously. Lucio put his self-analytical mood down to a midlife crisis, but I suspected it came from a realisation that his children were on the verge of adulthood, examining their own career options after growing up in a totally different environment from their father. He was wondering what he could pass on to them that might help make their lives as enjoyable as his had been.

So Lucio and I decided to go back to Lunigiana in search of his *soffritto* – the local word for the base of a sauce, the ingredients that give a dish its identity: oil, garlic, herbs, celery, family, locality, tradition … This wasn't the first time Lucio had returned home in the

26 years since he 'ran away for love'. He'd made brief visits so his children could get to know their grandparents. But during those trips he'd paid no attention to his surroundings.

This was his first opportunity to examine his territory with the eyes of a stranger, talking to the farmers, cooks, artisans, fishermen, winemakers, shepherds, waiters and scholars who produce the fundamentals of the Italian food repertoire – parmesan, olive oil, pasta, prosciutto, balsamic vinegar, truffles, pesto and much more.

It was the first time Lucio had spoken to family members about how his aunt and uncle eloped to make ice-cream, how his father fought the fascists, how four friends built a shack on a beach and how his cousins saved the restaurant when his uncle died. And it was his first chance to meet a new generation of young Italians who are seeking authenticity in peasant traditions which embarrassed their parents.

Of course, one visit was not enough. There were too many people to see, and too many meals to eat. With photographer Paul Green, we ended up travelling through the north-west of Italy three times – in the spring of 2002, the autumn of 2003 and the summer of 2004. Lucio came back to Australia a rebuilt man.

You may judge whether we answered the bigger questions.

David Dale, August 2007

A NOTE ON LANGUAGE

You don't need to speak Italian to understand this book, but a few clues on pronunciation might help the flow of reading. The key proper nouns are pronounced 'Looch-oh', 'Cheech-oh' and 'Loo-nidj-ah-nah'.

In Italian, any time the letter *c* is followed by *i* or *e*, it is pronounced like the 'ch' in church. The rest of the time it is pronounced like the k in cake – 'zukini', 'kianti', 'rah-deek-ee-oh', and so on. So the beef dish *carpaccio* is 'kar-pah-chee-oh' and the fish soup *cacciucco* is 'ka-choo-koh'.

Same principle with the letter *g* – soft as in 'sage' before *i* or *e*, hard as in 'got' before other vowels and before h. Thus Via Francigena, the pilgrim trail from France to Rome, is pronounced 'Fran-chidj-enuh' and *cinghiale*, wild boar, is 'chin-ghee-ah-leh'. But when *g* is followed by *l*, it is not pronounced at all – so *tagliatelle* is 'tal-ya-tel-eh' and *grigliata* is 'greel-yata'.

'POTESS'IO SOSTENERTI NELLA MANO, TERRA DI LUNI, COME UN VASO ETRUSCO!'

Arrival

This story begins, as everything does, with a meal. You could eat a meal like this anytime you happened to be passing through a village called Bocca di Magra (which means the mouth of the Magra River) on the north-west coast of Italy, if you went to a restaurant called Capannina Ciccio (which means 'Chubby's hut'). This particular meal was consumed in the spring of 2002 by Lucio Galletto.

To eat the dinner, Lucio had to travel for 28 hours – or 26 years, depending on how you look at it. He boarded a plane in Sydney, Australia, landed in Rome 24 hours later, spent a moment changing his currency and lamenting the replacement of the lira with the euro, then took a half-hour flight to Pisa, where he hired a car, ignored the Leaning Tower, and got on the autostrada going north.

Driving towards the town of his birth, with the sea on his left and the white-topped Apuan Alps on his right, past the quarries where Michelangelo sourced the marble for most of his sculptures, Lucio has a lot on his mind, which is why his left leg won't stop jigging up and down.

He is about to turn 50, and has been diagnosed with diabetes, an occupational hazard for restaurateurs with erratic eating habits. He's thinking that if he hasn't had a midlife crisis yet, he's entitled to one now.

He's wondering what he would have been doing if he'd stayed in Italy, instead of moving to Sydney when he fell in love with an Australian girl 26 years ago. Probably, he reflects, he'd be working as an architect instead of a restaurateur. He doubts if designing buildings would be as satisfying as feeding people, but then again, he would not have been subject to the whims of food critics.

His restaurant, Lucio's, has just been downgraded from two-hat status ('Kitchen alchemy') to one-hat status ('Consistently very good') in the latest edition of Sydney's *Good Food Guide* (wherein the maximum score, three hats, is defined as 'world class'). Lucio is wondering what he did wrong. Has he drifted too far from the traditions of his homeland in an effort to modernise, or should he have changed even more to meet twenty-first-century tastes? Has he been distracted from the main game by opening a second eating house, Arte e Cucina, designed to be a trattoria with simpler food and service than the ristorante, Lucio's? Should he close number two in order to bring number one back to its former glory?

Issues of identity are plaguing him. He recently became an Australian citizen, swearing allegiance to a new flag after deciding that the country in which a person has spent more than half his life really should be defined as his home.

In what Lucio now thinks was a misguided attempt to behave like a typical Australian, he voted for the conservative prime minister, John Howard, in the first election after his naturalisation ceremony. That decision would have horrified his father, who was always a passionate supporter of the Left in Italian politics. If he could have discussed it with his father, Lucio would have said that John Howard is not the same as Silvio Berlusconi, and that when you own a business, you value a stable economy. But Mauro Galletto died last year, and his expatriate son couldn't get back in time for the funeral.

Lucio now holds two passports, and for the sake of speed he leaves Sydney's border control as an Australian and enters Rome's border control as an Italian. But what does being an Italian mean? As a nation, Italy is younger even than Australia. It was stitched together from a diverse bunch of territories only in the 1860s. Italians are notorious for what they call *campanilismo*, which translates literally as 'belltower-ism' and means they are loyal only to the neighbourhood they can see from the top of the local church.

Lucio has been crossing borders all his life. During his teenage years he woke up each morning in the region called Liguria but spent the day in Tuscany, at a high school where lessons were conducted in a national language with only a passing resemblance to the dialect he spoke at home.

His family felt neither Tuscan nor Ligurian. They thought of themselves as citizens of a land called Lunigiana, a territory based on the ancient Roman colony of Luna but not recognised in modern Italian geography. Lunigiana stretches along the Magra River from the mountains to the sea, overlapping the bottom right of what is now Liguria, the top left of Tuscany and the bottom left of Emilia-Romagna. Lucio thinks of it as a land of *pastori* (shepherds), *contadini* (farmers) and *pescatori* (fishermen).

He's recently become Treasurer of an organisation called CIRA (pronounced 'cheeruh'), the Council of Italian Restaurants in Australia, which is dedicated to preserving regional recipes and cooking techniques before they are lost in the rush towards Mod Med (con) fusion. As part of CIRA's community education program, Lucio wants to present a Lunigiana dinner in his restaurant, and he hopes, during this trip, to find inspiration in the homes and trattorias of his neighbourhood.

The view of Tuscany from Liguria, Punta Bianca from the sea and Ciccio's from the river.

Driving towards the town of his birth, with the white-topped Apuan Alps on his right, past the quarries where Michelangelo sourced his marble

But he'll be observing local customs as both an outsider and an insider. He has been reading some examples of that genre of literature we might label 'Anglo goes to Europe and patronises the peasants'. The trend started with Peter Mayle in the south of France and progressed to the experiences of American divorcees in Tuscany and English ingénues in Liguria. Lucio wonders if he has become so Anglicised that the people of Lunigiana will look like quaint eccentrics rather than simply his friends, relatives and former neighbours. He hopes he won't find himself telling his Sydney customers that Lunigiana is the new Tuscany.

He's remembering a story his father told as Lucio was packing for the trip to Australia, about a young fellow we could call The Rake Boy. The boy had grown up on a farm in Lunigiana, then went off to work in an office in Rome. When he came home for his first holidays a few months later, his family was surprised to find him talking in high Italian, using it to answer all questions put to him by his parents in local dialect.

After dinner, the boy went out into the yard and in the darkness trod on a rake, which sprang up and whacked him in the face. He yelled: '*Ki 'glă miso ki 'stă rastelo?*' (local dialect for 'Who put this bloody rake here?'). If he'd stuck with his high Italian, he'd have said, '*Chi ce l' ha messo qui questo rastrello?*' but pain had brought him down to earth. Lucio's father said: '*Ne fare come quelo dar rastelo*' – 'Don't do what the rake boy did', or, more loosely, 'Don't forget your roots'.

So Lucio is watching out for rakes as he bumps up the steep narrow track that leads to the pink two-storey home of his sister-in-law Wendy and his cousin Mario. Tall, blonde and elegant, Wendy emerges, does the two-cheek kiss, and apologises that Mario is away working on his Latest Project.

With Mario, there is always a Latest Project. People say of him that he has *un marcia in più*, an extra gear. Jet-lagged and short on sleep, Lucio is secretly relieved not to have to face his former mentor at full acceleration just yet.

Wendy is the older sister of Lucio's wife, Sally. Travelling in northern Italy in the late 1960s, she fell in love with a charming Italian restaurateur named Mario Guelfi, and married him. A couple of years later, Sally came to visit her sister, and met Mario's cousin, who was working in the restaurant while training to become an architect. So Lucio has Wendy to thank for the joyous upheaval of his life.

Wendy serves a snack of dense bread, pecorino cheese (from sheep in the Lunigiana mountains) and slices of *cinghiale* (wild boar meat). Boars are a nuisance in the forest behind Wendy's house, wandering down the hill at night to nibble the vegetables in her garden, so she wishes the local hunters well, even when their shotgun blasts wake her early in the morning. But this meat came in a pack from the local supermarket. Lucio is amused to reflect that there's a good chance it originated in Australia, which supplies 20 per cent of Europe's wild pig requirements.

He showers, takes a 30-minute nap and, emerging from the house, looks up at the hill town of Ameglia, which he'd always thought of as pink, in the style of Liguria, but which today has more of a Tuscan gold colour in the late afternoon light. Like him, Ameglia is perpetually on the edge of two identities.

He drives to the local cemetery. This is the first time he has seen his father's grave,

which was designed by Lucio's brother, Aulo. The headstone displays a colour photo of a bespectacled man with a strong jaw, and the name Gerolamo Mauro Galletto. Mauro hated his first name, and when he wasn't calling himself Mauro, enjoyed the nickname Merigo, which was given to him in 1943 when he escaped from a Nazi prison camp and joined the partisans in the nearby hills.

The grave is covered with smooth orange pebbles. Aulo has apologised to Lucio for failing to find pebbles of a deeper red colour, which the boys had wanted on the grave to signal Mauro's allegiance to the communist faction of the partisans. Lucio can look up from the cemetery to the forest behind the town of Castelnuovo Magra, from which members of Mauro's Garibaldi brigade conducted their raids on the Nazis and the Fascists.

When Lucio was five, his father called him and ten-year-old Aulo into the parental bedroom, and opened a drawer. He took out something wrapped in what looked like a large red handkerchief. The something turned out to be a revolver, which looked surprisingly small and square to kids who had only seen guns in cowboy comics.

Mauro said the boys were never to touch this revolver, even though there were no bullets in it. It was a souvenir of his war service, he said. He knotted the red handkerchief round his neck and explained that it was the scarf he wore, fluttering in the wind, as he rode on an American tank to help liberate the city of Sarzana in April 1945.

Until that moment, Lucio had thought of his father as a man who chopped up tomatoes and carried demijohns of wine in the restaurant that belonged to Zio Ciccio (Uncle Ciccio). It was exciting and scary to think that Mauro was also a man who might have killed people in a heroic cause. He'd asked his father if he had ever killed anybody, but Mauro would only reply, 'In war, if there is a fight, somebody has to die'.

In the cemetery 45 years later, Lucio is wondering what happened to the gun and the scarf, and pondering what his father thought he was fighting for, back then. It wasn't to

The mountains of Carrara from the promenade outside Ciccio.

Following pages, Ameglia in the afternoon light.

the hill town of Ameglia, which he'd always thought of as pink, in the style of Liguria, but which today has more of a Tuscan gold colour in the late afternoon light. Like him, it's perpetually on the edge of two identities.

On the river bank, two men are repainting a red fishing boat. But the nets are no longer hung out to dry on racks in front of Capannina Ciccio.

restore Italy to the way it was before the war, because that was a Fascist dictatorship which came to power before Mauro was born. Apparently he was fighting for an ideal in his imagination of Italy as it might become.

Finally Lucio heads for his dinner date. He's driving beside the river along Via Fabbricotti and wondering which of the houses on his right were the holiday homes of the writers who started escaping city life in the 1940s to find inspiration in a tiny northern fishing village. But he's forced to turn off the road by a sign which diverts cars around to what is apparently the local carpark. Bocca di Magra has grown from a village to a town with a traffic problem.

Lucio recognises the carpark as the piazza where the fishermen's wives used to do their washing when he was a kid. With no running water at home, they'd bring buckets to a fountain built over a spring, and they'd scrub their clothes in marble basins set up around the piazza. The teenage boys would accumulate there too, to look at the fishermen's daughters.

Now the square is full of cars and the fountain is dry. Lucio walks back to the river down a lane between three-storey apartment blocks which have sprung up in the past 20 years.

Back on Via Fabbricotti he glances at the fenced-off ruins of a Roman villa, which he remembers being excavated when he was ten. The kids asked the archeologists why they were digging. 'There's a villa under there,' they replied. 'It must have been a holiday home for a family from Luna, across the river. It had hot running water 2,000 years ago.' The kids were fascinated. How come the Romans could do what modern people couldn't?

On the river bank, two men are repainting a red fishing boat. But their nets are no longer hung out to dry next to the tablecloths on racks in front of Capannina Ciccio. They've been replaced by bronze sculptures showing a small boy sitting restlessly on a high-backed chair and an older boy holding a stick for measuring the depth of the river.

The boys could be Mario and Lucio, dreaming of a different life while their parents were inside cooking. The sandy foreshore on which Mario and Lucio played has been replaced by a tiled promenade, and there's a crane on what used to be a sandbar, part of a project to build a marina for launches.

Two sides of Ciccio's: fishermen and sculptures on the river bank, and gelateria on the street

Lucio faces the restaurant entrance, with people queueing to buy coffees and icecream at a counter on the street. Icecream was the way it all started. If the archaeologists were to excavate Capannina Ciccio as if it were the site of Troy, they would find at the lowest level a cabin where Lucio's aunt Anna and uncle Ciccio started making gelati to sell to daytrippers climbing off the buses on their way to the beach in 1951.

At the next level the archaeologists would find the brick walls built by Anna's brother Mauro, when Ciccio's gelateria spread onto the sand to become a café serving fish soup and spaghetti. It had wooden columns made from old telegraph poles, supporting a roof made of the long leafy canes that grew by the river. Anna in the kitchen was joined by her three daughters and by Lucio's mother Bruna, while Ciccio in the dining room was joined by his son Mario, who worked the record player when Ciccio installed a dance floor for Saturday night socialising.

Ciccio's hut kept adding layers, not only of property but also of people, as cousins and aunts and uncles and friends rushed to supply its needs in wine, olive oil, vegetables, meat, cheese, fruit and fish. As Ciccio's grew in popularity, the neighbourhood grew in prosperity.

Half a century later Lucio walks into a riverside bungalow which seats 250 people in two big rooms, a wide verandah and a sprawling courtyard. The entrance is an obstacle course of sculptures and bookcases displaying wine bottles and publications by local and visiting writers. The walls are covered with paintings donated by visiting and local artists. In the middle of the first room is a huge fish tank, with lobsters crawling over each other.

From the wall, Ciccio Guelfi surveys his legacy

Lucio has put only one foot inside when he is enveloped by a flock of women fluttering from behind the bar and the cash desk and the kitchen. They're the daughters and granddaughters of Ciccio, kissing, hugging and pinching. These women hold Capannina Ciccio together 40 years after the death of its founder – doing the welcomes, the seating, the cocktails, the coffee, the gelati, the bills, the administration, but never the table service, because that is the province of men.

Cousin Rosangela takes Lucio by the arm and leads him towards the inner sanctum, where he will pay his respects to Zia Anna (Aunt Anna), still in residence at the age of 80. They pass the toilets, wherein Lucio locked himself on the first day he was expected to don waiter's uniform. No combination of threats and inducements from Mario could persuade shy 14-year-old Lucio to emerge and face the customers, and eventually his mother had to be brought to the door to embarrass him out with the power of tears.

They pass the portrait of Ciccio on the wall, still observing the room, and beneath it a photo of Ciccio carrying two roast chickens to a wedding party and a framed poem, perhaps a haiku, typed in the restaurant by the art critic Giorgio Soavi. It says: '*Qualcosa vorró sempre anche per dopo*' ('I will always want something else for afterwards'). It was the response of the loyal customer to Ciccio's habit of asking, as he took an order, '*E per dopo?*' – 'and after that?'

Cousin Rosi leads Lucio through the kitchen, now full of white-uniformed chefs who work for wages instead of love, past the deep-fryer where Lucio's mother Bruna presided for 30 years. Everyone said she had the eye for the perfect moment, hovering to scoop out any piece of flour-crusted fish or crumbed meat just as it turned golden and before it

The dining room at Ciccio's observed by the new generation of professional chefs.

could turn brown and bitter. These days she'd be called a master of the art of tempura.

They pass the big table where Lucio and his cousins had to chop garlic and parsley with a *mezzaluna* (two-handled knife with a half-moon blade) every summer afternoon before they were allowed to go swimming. The *aglio e prezzemolo* (garlic and parsley) mixture was for Zio Ciccio's *soffritto*, the base of his sauces. With his plump fingers, he'd toss a handful of garlic-parsley pulp and a splash of olive oil into a frying pan, get it sizzling, and then add the other elements.

With some dishes he'd wipe a sprig of rosemary through the oil; with others a bundle of sage and thyme called a *mazzetto odoroso* (fragrant bunch). In the last few seconds of cooking, he'd sprinkle on another handful of aglio e prezzemolo. So his kitchen used vast quantities of the stuff. One of Lucio's earliest memories is the voice of Ciccio shouting 'Aglio e prezzemolo!' from the kitchen, summoning any family choppers who happened to be around.

They pass into a comfortable parlour where Zia Anna, the last survivor of Lucio's parents' generation, rises from her chair with the help of her stick and embraces the nephew who hopes he's not the Rake Boy.

He isn't sure if Anna knows that her nephew was conceived in Ciccio's storeroom, as Mauro and Bruna enjoyed a few moments of passion on a bed set up amongst the boxes of onions and flasks of oil. But certainly she watched him grow from a baby in his basket near the gelato machine to a toddler hanging onto his mother's skirts near the fryer; from an embarrassed teenager refusing to leave the bathroom to a lovestruck waiter announcing he was moving to Australia.

Anna is the window into Lucio's past and into the Lunigiana traditions he is trying to understand. He asks if they can arrange a time to talk about the early days: how she changed from farmer's daughter to gelato maker's wife to restaurant matriarch. She says she's always here, and if he likes, they can start the history lesson tomorrow morning.

And now Lucio is ready to eat. Coming back into the dining room, he encounters an old friend, Sandro, eating a steak and salad at a table by himself. Sandro is a candidate for the *Guinness Book of Records* as 'World's Most Loyal Restaurant Customer'. He reckons he has eaten at Ciccio's every day it has been open for the past 30 years – apart from a few occasions when he had to go to Milan for medical treatment. Sandro's job description used to be 'playboy'. From a wealthy family in Parma, he was a devotee of fast women and fast cars. It was the second of those that broke his spine in 1969 and put him permanently in a wheelchair.

For his convalescence, he bought a cottage in Bocca di Magra, because he liked the sea air, and started eating at a little trattoria on the beach, which proceeded to expand into a national institution. Long ago Mario stopped charging Sandro for meals, because his money ran out and he became part of the Ciccio family – and an entertainer of the other regulars.

Sandro insists on updating Lucio about Italian politics. 'Let me explain about Berlusconi,' he says. 'He is like the Roman emperor Caligula, only stronger.'

Lucio: 'Wasn't Caligula the mad one?'

Sandro: 'Yes, that's the point. Caligula only took his horse into the Senate. Berlusconi took a whole herd of donkeys.'

Lucio looks up, laughing, into the beaming boyish face of head waiter Giuseppe. The sight fills Lucio with a mixture of joy and guilt. With Giuseppe there, he knows he'll get great service. But he wonders how Giuseppe feels about the night Lucio nearly killed him, 30 years ago.

It was the middle of August, when everyone in Italy is a little crazy. About 2 am, after the last customer had left, the waiters were playing a game of chicken in the street outside the restaurant. Lucio rode towards Giuseppe on his Lambretta, intending to swerve away at the last second. But as Lucio swerved to his right, Giuseppe jumped to his left. The impact put Giuseppe in hospital for three weeks and off work for three months. Lucio, his brother Aulo, and another waiter pooled their wages and tips and gave a quarter of the total to Giuseppe for those three months.

Lucio was relieved when Giuseppe's wife produced two children a couple of years later, because an important part of Giuseppe's anatomy had borne the brunt of the scooter's impact. So maybe Lucio is forgiven. There seems to be only delight in Giuseppe's welcome now. He says Aulo is waiting in the next room.

Aulo is sitting alone at a table for six, spacious enough for many dishes to be laid out as the night proceeds and for many passing friends to sit and pick and sip and chat. Aulo is thin and thoughtful, with a neat beard that would usually be the uniform of a university professor in Italy.

Lucio envies his brother his thinness, his scholarliness and his palate – which earned him the role of 'official taster' in the kitchen at the age of 15, after Ciccio's sudden death. Lucio doesn't envy Aulo's current job, which involves driving around the neighbourhood selling clothing to fashion stores.

Lucio thinks Aulo is the family member most qualified to run a restaurant – or to write an encyclopaedia of food. Aulo gave up the job of head waiter at Ciccio's when his second son was born, because he wanted to spend time with his family. He also gave up his university studies in geology. He won't admit to any regrets.

These women hold Capannina Ciccio together, doing the welcomes, the seating, the coffee, the gelati, the administration, but never the table service, which is the province of men.

The brothers get the family details out of the way and fall into discussion about how Lucio can understand the real Lunigiana. 'We must walk in the mountains,' says Aulo. 'And we must eat testaroli. Let's go by donkey, like the pilgrims.'

Aulo launches into a dissertation about the Via Francigena, the pilgrim trail from France to Rome that passed through the Lunigiana mountains in the Middle Ages. Aulo is nicknamed 'Google' (pronounced goo-gleh) by his grownup sons (who still live with their parents) because he can answer any question on any subject.

But Lucio isn't listening. The word 'testaroli' has sent him into one of the daydreams that kept getting him into trouble at school. He can picture his mother cutting a potato in half, stabbing a fork into it, rubbing the flat surface of the potato in olive oil and then smearing it over a black skillet, called a testo. Then she'd pour on a mixture of flour, water and salt, put the skillet on the stove, and produce savoury pancakes to be served with pesto sauce. Lucio hasn't thought about testaroli – let alone eaten one – for decades. He just hopes Aulo is joking about the donkeys.

He has no trouble settling into the dialect, and then shifting to Italian when Giuseppe (who was born in the south) asks what they'll drink. Aulo reminds Lucio that he left Italy a teetotaller. As a child he'd been required to help an uncle clean wine barrels. Lucio was small enough to crawl inside with a brush and hose to scrub out the crust that formed from the previous vintage.

The smell was so powerful he felt like vomiting, so when his friends started drinking wine during his teenage years, the idea nauseated him. It was only in his forties, in Sydney, that Lucio developed a taste for light whites such as pinot grigio, 'which don't smell like wine – the more like water it is, the better I like it'.

Giuseppe recommends a vermentino from the Colli di Luni (which means the hills around the Roman ruins just across the river). It's precisely to Lucio's taste. 'The wine around here has improved so much,' says Aulo. 'We used to get rough stuff in demijohns, and the waiters had to put it in bottles before the lunch service.'

Now for the food. Lucio wants to try the classics he was rarely allowed to eat when he worked as a waiter (because the best dishes were only for customers). Giuseppe wants to show off the creations that prove Ciccio's has moved from a trattoria to a modern restaurant in the years since Lucio left. They compromise on a mixture of old and new, which accumulates on the table as a spectacular degustazione, sampled by visiting conversationalists.

The women of Ciccio's: Anna, centre, and from left, granddaughters Roberta and Annalisa, daughters Graziella, Giovanna and Rosi, granddaughter Silvia. Below, head waiter Giuseppe and his team, and loyal customer Sandro.

THE 'NEW' DISHES

Carpaccio di branzino. The slices of raw sea bass, splashed with olive oil and lemon, start Lucio thinking about the origins of the word 'carpaccio'. Harry's Bar in Venice named a plate of finely sliced raw beef in honour of the deep red colours favoured by the sixteenth-century painter Vittore Carpaccio. Now the word has come to mean any raw food, even the white fish Lucio is currently consuming. Ciccio's is right up with modern menu terminology, even if the etymology is wrong.

Gamberi e fagioli. Grilled prawns sitting on cannelini beans and topped with roe has

Lucio wants the classic dishes he served but was hardly ever allowed to eat during his time as a waiter at Ciccio's.

Giuseppe wants to show him the new dishes that prove Ciccio has become an imaginative modern restaurant

been a signature dish at Lucio's for years. Lucio is delighted to find it at Ciccio's, and he wonders if Mario got the idea from him during a visit to Sydney.

Frittelline di bianchetti. These are deep-fried fritters of baby sardines or anchovies, called neonata in southern Italy, in the shape of golden spheres, with a sauce which seems more Asian than Italian. Giuseppe says it's just an evolution of the classic Venetian *agrodolce* (sour-sweet), made with pineapple, capsicum, onion, chilli, vinegar and a tiny bit of tomato.

Grigliata. This includes pieces of three local fish – triglie, cicale and seppioline – barbecued with zucchini slices. Giuseppe explains that the old standby, zucchini, has come back into fashion as a way of lightening dishes.

Rombo al vermentino. This is whole flounder baked in the oven with pine nuts, sultanas, garlic, basil, cherry tomatoes and white wine. Italians like their fish served whole, to be shared around the table. Australians like their fish to arrive already cut into fillets.

Lucio is watching Giuseppe deftly deboning the rombo, so he doesn't realise that someone is creeping up behind him, and Aulo, smiling, gives him no warning. It's Mario. A pair of hands go around Lucio's neck and he's back in the mock strangling game that started when he was a kid and Mario was a teenager with the task of mustering his junior cousins to chop garlic and parsley.

With his bald pate surrounded by a fringe of long hair, Mario could be a medieval monk – or more precisely an archbishop, given his status in Lunigiana. He's wearing the navy blue sweater that seems to be a uniform in the neighbourhood – half the men in the room are dressed the same way. Mario bounces into a seat, stares at the rombo, and sighs: 'Our food used to be simple'. But he's joking. It's Mario as much as Giuseppe who has been driving the modernisation process.

He asks if Lucio has tried Ciccio's most popular dish of the moment: *zuppa di farro e moscardini* (soup of baby octopus and farro). Farro, sometimes translated into English as 'spelt', is an ancient grain between wheat and barley, beloved by the Romans. It's a hearty mountain ingredient, said to keep the men of Lunigiana fertile until their nineties, and only Mario would have thought to reinvent it for the twenty-first century.

Opposite, from top left: rombo al vermentino; the first room; gamberi e fagioli; local fish dentice, branzino and scorfano; zuppa di farro e moscardini; frittelline; carpaccio di branzino. Above: left, brother Aulo, right, cousin Mario.

Mario whispers a detailed order to Giuseppe, who returns a couple of minutes later with a plate of hot potato chips that Mario proceeds to scoff, a small jug of olive oil in which chillis have been marinated, and a bowl of live scampi. Mario starts pulling the scampi meat out of the carapaces and popping it into his mouth while it is still wriggling. 'This is how the Japanese like them,' he says gleefully.

Mario has always been a risk-taker. Seeing Lucio's wariness, he says, 'Let's get some steamed ones and compare the taste'. When the steamed scampi arrive, the cousins agree they taste better than the raw ones. Sometimes the Italians know better than the Japanese.

Now Lucio learns what the chilli oil is for. Giuseppe delivers terracotta bowls filled with the farro soup. It's the ultimate comfort food, but a splash of chilli oil lightens it and enhances the flavour. Mario says, 'At the moment this is our secret, but within two years it will be in every restaurant along this coast'. It's the ideal bridge between the new creations and the traditional favourites that are finally emerging from the kitchen.

THE CLASSICS

From top left: *fritto misto*; *spaghetti alla Ciccio*; *cacciucco*; *spaghetti service*; *tartina*; serving the *pesce al sale*; *muscoli*.

Tartina alla Ciccio. A slice of white bread is soaked in fish stock, dipped in egg and deep-fried, then topped with a salad of finely sliced prawns, calamari and mussels, and a spiral of mayonnaise. Eight-year-old Aulo was watching wide-eyed in the kitchen when Ciccio invented it, trying to use up some slices of yesterday's bread and some beaten eggs left over from making crumbed veal. It became an instant hit, relying for its success on Bruna's deep-frying skill – too little sizzling, the bread would be soggy; too much, it would be dry and bitter. Lucio reflects that tartina, which the Tuscan customers preferred to call crostino, is a creature of its time – no chance of the words 'deep-fried' and 'mayonnaise' appearing together on a twenty-first century menu – but he still loves its contrasts of flavours and textures.

With it, Giuseppe brings two fine slices of prosciutto, from nearby Parma, knowing that's the meat Lucio misses most in Sydney. The importation of raw ham is forbidden in Australia on health grounds (even though the United States permits it) and the Australian version lacks the lusciousness of the Parma variety.

Muscoli alla marinara. Mussels (known as *cozze* elsewhere in Italy) are Lucio's favourite seafood. When he went swimming as a kid, he'd take a penknife and a lemon, ready to eat the shellfish raw off the rocks. Tonight he wants them cooked as simply as possible – piled into a deep pot with a little oil, parsley and garlic (no wine, no water, no tomato), heated just till they open and start to expel their juices. He eats with his fingers, using an empty shell in a pincer movement to pluck the mussels out of the other shells.

Cacciucco. Every settlement around the Mediterranean coastline makes a soup out of sea creatures considered too ugly or too bony or too tiny to be sold on their own. The French call it bouillabaisse, the Spanish call it zarzuela, the Greeks call it kakavia, and the Italians have at least ten dialect names. Cacciucco is the north Tuscan word for a mixture of up to 15 fish, molluscs and crustaceans with onion, white wine and tomato. Ciccio's version used to be served with little pieces of fried bread. Nowadays Mario serves it with slices of toast for dipping, which makes a lighter meal but disappoints traditionalists.

Ciccio's shack kept adding layers, not only of property but also of people, as cousins and aunts and uncles

and friends rushed to supply its needs in wine, olive oil, vegetables, meat, fruit and fish.

Fritto misto. Prawns, sardines, calamari and grongo (a long fish that looks like an eel) are tossed in flour, deep-fried for a few seconds, and served on brown paper. This was another of Bruna's specialities. The current kitchen professionals do a passable job.

Spaghetti alla Ciccio. Mario's older sister Graziella arrives with a huge pan, from which a waiter proceeds to dollop spaghetti and seafood onto six plates. She takes credit for developing this dish, from a local speciality with fewer ingredients. She explains that you partly cook calamari, scampi, prawns, clams and mussels in a big pan (with garlic and a bit of chilli, but no tomato), throw in partly cooked spaghetti and stir them so they finish cooking together and the pasta absorbs the seafood juices.

It was the first of what she calls 'the tossing dishes' for which Ciccio's became famous – as in, tossing the ingredients in front of the customer to make the experience more theatrical. In 1959, she says, it became *il piatto che* ... (literally 'the plate which ...'). Lucio thinks this would translate into English these days as 'flavour of the month', though the month turned into decades.

Mario remarks that Australians have odd ideas about spaghetti. The first time he came to Australia, on his way to meet Wendy's parents in the countryside west of Sydney, he stopped at the town of Lithgow for lunch. The café at the railway station sold him a tinned spaghetti sandwich. It was not, he observes, al dente.

Graziella says Ciccio's menu now is very different from 40 years ago, but the family never noticed it changing. 'One day we would just think of a new way of doing something, and after a while it felt like that was how we always did it,' she recalls. 'When it was just the family, there were about ten dishes we used to do all the time. Nothing was written down. Ciccio would go around the tables and then come back in the kitchen and yell out what people wanted. Most people just had the spaghetti and the fritto misto. Now the chefs do hundreds of dishes.'

Mario laments: 'You have to keep adding new things or the regulars will get bored. The trouble is we can never take anything off. There are people who travel across Italy for the tartina. They had it when they came for holidays to the beach as children, and 30 years later they bring their children to try it. Or somebody comes in and remembers a dish my father put together just for them one day. We have to work out what it was.'

Looking around the room, Lucio realises he recognises about a quarter of the customers – some of whom he last saw as teenagers. Reflexively, he feels an urge to go around and greet them, as he would do in his own place in Sydney, but his old shyness has returned. In any case, working the room is Mario's job, which he now proceeds to do, shaking hands, slapping shoulders, answering questions.

Graziella observes Mario fondly and says: 'It's so different from when he first took over, after Dad died. He hated it. He wanted to be somewhere else. Now he's a natural. The place comes alive when he's here, but he's away most of the time now. The regulars keep asking "*C'é Mario?*" ("Is Mario here?") and we have to tell them he's doing his new project.'

When Mario returns to the table, Lucio has to ask: 'So what's this new project?'

'I'm building a second restaurant,' says Mario. 'It's at the docks in Carrara, with a nightclub underneath, so the top people from the marble quarries will bring their clients, have dinner and stay on drinking afterwards.'

Lucio marvels again at how events in his second life in Sydney seem to parallel events in his old home. 'You sound like me, with this second restaurant idea,' he tells Mario. 'Did you want to prove to yourself that you still had the imagination and the strength to do it all again?'

'No, no,' says Mario. 'It's because the family is growing so big. This place supports about 30 people – my sisters, their husbands, their children, their grandchildren. I needed another activity for them, somewhere for the young ones to go and work, or even just sit around. We're running out of space here.'

Giuseppe arrives with the most spectacular dish on a trolley ...

Pesce al sale. This is a whole sea bass buried in rock salt and baked at high temperature so the salt fuses into a thick hard shell which can be lifted off. Lucio occasionally serves it in his restaurant (using whole snapper) but not this way – here, flames are issuing from the salt crust. The flames are another piece of theatre, nothing to do with the cooking process. He contemplates trying this in Sydney, but suspects his customers would consider it over-the-top.

The feast is almost done. Giuseppe offers the trolley of desserts, most of which he has made himself, but Lucio, as a newly diagnosed diabetic, opts for pecorino cheese and some slices of pear.

He takes his coffee in the bar, which he remembers as the first place he saw the gorgeous blonde who became his wife Sally (in the mid 1970s) and the first place he ever saw television (in the late 1950s). Ciccio the innovator installed the amazing gadget in 1956. When *la tivú* arrived, the local fishing families brought chairs from their homes and set them up in the bar, treating it as a mini-cinema. Now the coffee drinkers barely give the screen a glance – unless it's Sunday and there's a soccer match.

It's only 11 pm, the restaurant is still half full, and the family is keen to keep chatting over grappa, but Lucio must head back to his bed at Mario and Wendy's house. Tomorrow he's talking to Zia Anna. He'd better be alert.

'CA' RÓSA: ERIMO TANTI FRADEI.'

Anna

This part of the story begins, as few things do these days, with a dance. This was When Anna Met Ciccio – except that when he came up to ask permission from Anna's mother, sitting among a row of mothers along one wall of the dance hall, he introduced himself as Gino (he wasn't called Ciccio till he joined the partisans in 1943). Better say When Anna Met Gino, and save the name Ciccio for later chapters. It was the summer of 1938, and Anna had just turned seventeen.

Anna's mother was doubtful – this short plump fellow was clearly a few years older than her daughter, and a *cittadino* (city boy), while skinny, bespectacled Anna was a *contadina* (peasant girl), who had rarely stepped outside the farm. And their landlord was not going to be pleased if he learnt that Anna was dancing with someone other than the neighbour's son he'd picked out as a future husband, so that Anna would continue the line of tenant farmers who'd worked for his family for centuries.

But to hell with the landlord. It was just a dance. And away they shuffled around the floor, to the sound of piano, guitar, accordion, and saxophone. As they shuffled, they chatted – or rather, Gino chatted and Anna listened. Anna was vaguely aware of the Guelfi family. They lived in the middle of the town of Sarzana, four kilometres from Anna's farm. Gino's father had run a small printing house which published a weekly newspaper. The family name suggested an aristocratic background (in the thirteenth century, the Guelfi were the Tuscan faction which supported the Pope in a power struggle with the Ghibellini, who supported the emperor).

Anna didn't know – but soon learnt, because Gino was a better storyteller than he was a dancer – that the Guelfi family money had been gambled away at Monte Carlo by Gino's uncle, who had then committed suicide. Now Gino worked in a gelateria in Sarzana, run by some Jewish people from Switzerland. They had kept their recipes a secret, but as he served customers at the front of the shop, Gino could see in the mirror how the owners made their icecreams at the back.

They were thinking of moving back north, because they were uneasy about the growing ties between Italy's leader, Benito Mussolini, and that weirdo Adolf Hitler in Germany, where Jews were having a terrible time. Gino thought he'd learnt enough in the mirror to run the shop if they left – although he would have to remember to do their movements in reverse. Anna laughed.

In the winter when people didn't buy icecreams, Gino used to go into the mountains of Lunigiana to collect mushrooms and buy cheeses and hams and sausages from small producers, and then sell them in the villages around Sarzana. He was a natural salesman. 'I like travelling and I like eating and I like talking and I like dancing,' he told her. 'Can I come and visit you tomorrow?' She said he would have to ask her mother.

Gino seemed an exotic creature to Anna, whose life on the farm, though happy, followed the same pattern every day. She'd had three years' schooling, which was considered enough to provide all the skills in reading, maths and Italian history that a future farmer's wife would need.

Gino was talking about a world she only glimpsed on Sunday mornings when she and her parents and her ten brothers and sisters, plus assorted nieces and nephews, went into Sarzana to go to church and chat with the other families in the town square.

When Anna's father, Giovanni, arrived in the cart to take her home that night, it felt terribly early. But then, she had to be up at five o'clock next morning to get the water from the well, light the fire, set the coffee boiling, help her brothers milk the cows and help her mother make breakfast for the 16 people who lived in the farmhouse.

Anna was a little surprised the next afternoon when Gino appeared in the courtyard in front of her house, pedalling his icecream *carretto*, which was a three-wheeler bike with a tall wooden box on the front. Anna's brothers took to him immediately, and not just because he handed around gelati. He had a way of getting onto everyone's wavelength – the word for it is *simpatico*. He was fascinated by how the farm worked, interrogating everybody on every detail of their specific roles.

Gino had worked out that Giovanni, though short and balding, exercised absolute power in matters concerning the farm, while Angela, taller and bonier, exercised absolute power in matters of the household. If Gino had failed to charm either of them, it would have been the end of the relationship.

Anna's family were *mezzadri*, from *mezzo*, meaning 'half', because they were required to give the landlord half of everything they grew. The farm produced milk, eggs, wheat, corn, grapes and a vast array of vegetables and fruits. Even half of it was plenty to go around, as long as all the family members pulled their weight. And any surplus they could sell at the markets in Sarzana, using that money to buy what they couldn't make themselves – tools or furniture, mostly, or sometimes a piglet they could fatten up for Christmas.

The Gallettos lived in a two-storey house, which had redwashed walls and green shutters. From the colouring they had gained a nickname in the neighbourhood – Ca' Rósa (Red House), which Gino loved to use. 'Buona sera, Anna dei Ca' Rósa,' ('Good evening, Anna of the Red House People') he would say, making her feel like nobility.

Upstairs were four bedrooms – one for Anna's parents, two for her married older sisters and their husbands and babies, and one big space for the kids, with the floor taken up by nine canvas mattresses stuffed with dried leaves from corn cobs. (As Anna told Lucio: 'Erimo tanti fradei' – 'We were so many brothers and sisters').

Downstairs was a vast kitchen with a red-brick floor that served as dining room and living room, adjoining a barn where the cows and steers lived. In the middle of that kitchen was a table big enough to seat 16. But it could squeeze 17 whenever Gino turned up.

There was, of course, no television. Nor was there radio, phone, or books – luxuries with which Gino was a little more familiar in his family's apartment in Sarzana. Instead of manufactured entertainments, there was conversation, mostly about food, because planning, growing, making and looking forward to the next meal was what kept the Galletto family going. As it happened, these were Gino's priorities too.

The men would start the day dipping a chunk of bread into milky coffee and rushing out the door to the fields. At 8 am Anna and the other women would put rectangular baskets on their heads and carry breakfast out to the men – bowls of baccalà (dried cod marinated with water, vinegar, tomato and onions), stewed liver, cheeses, bread and polenta.

The women would join the men in the fields for breakfast, then scurry home to start work on lunch. Anna and her mother were responsible for planning, creating and serving a total of 48 meals every day – a figure that often rose to 60 when friends and relatives dropped by. It was as much a feat of management logistics as it was a cooking marathon. Although she didn't know it at the time, Anna was being perfectly trained to run a restaurant. Anna's mother spent most mornings making bread, while Anna spent most mornings making pasta, both of them shovelling flour onto the kitchen table from a square bin in the corner.

The flour came from their own wheat, cut once a year by the men and taken to the local mill, where it would be ground and some of the flour kept as payment. Half of the flour went to the landlord, and the other half waited in sacks in the storage barn to be transferred to the kitchen whenever the flour bin was empty – which was every week.

Angela was a good cook and a good teacher, but Anna had surpassed her mother in the making of a pasta called, in local dialect, tajarin (taglierini or tagliolini in Italian). It is probably the second oldest pasta style in the world. The first pasta was lasagne, called lagana by the Romans, who apparently got the idea from the Etruscans. That was sheets of dough rolled out thin, layered with stewed meat and cheese, and baked in the oven. Some time in the next 1,000 years somebody thought of cutting the sheets into strips and boiling them when needed. They were called taglierini if they were thin, or tagliatelle if they were a bit wider, from the word tagliare, to cut.

The principle is simple, but the trick is in the time you spend working the dough. Anna would pile a mound of flour on the tabletop, create a well in the middle of it, and break eggs into the well. Then with her hands she'd mush the flour and eggs together, kneading until she had a dense sphere.

Then she'd roll the dough out into a flat sheet, fold the sheet over and roll it out again, and keep doing that until the sheet had a springy consistency and was translucent when held up to the light. Then she'd roll the sheet into a cylinder, and slice the cylinder into discs. When she pulled the discs apart, she had a handful of fine ribbons. It was very satisfying for Anna to do and, apparently, for Gino to watch. (Later in post-Roman history, someone thought of pushing the dough through holes to make rounded noodles, or spaghetti. But it didn't have the texture of tajarin.)

Anna would drape the ribbons over a broom handle resting between two chairs, so they'd dry a bit. When lunchtime came, she'd simmer olive oil and onions and tomatoes in a frying pan, or, in the autumn, fry the small pioppini mushrooms which grew in the old trunks of poplar trees, or big porcini mushrooms the kids had found in the forest. Then she'd sprinkle the noodles into a pot of fiercely boiling water for just two minutes, strain them and pour the sauce over them. Depending on the season, the pasta might be preceded by a vegetable soup or followed by a mixed salad.

After lunch, everyone would rest or do household chores until after 3 pm, when the men would return to the fields until sundown. Dinner might be more pasta or more soup or, occasionally, stewed rabbit or stewed chicken with vegetables and polenta.

On most Sunday mornings they'd put on a lump of beef to simmer with tomatoes, and when they got back from church, they'd extract the now tender meat from the ragú surrounding it, and end up with two courses. They'd layer the sauce of meat juices and tomato between ravioli made with ricotta and *erbi* (wild greens), and they'd serve the meat later with boiled potatoes and onions.

From flour, eggs and salt come the noodles Anna called tajarin.

When Gino came to eat, he usually brought a big piece of parmesan or pecorino, which he'd picked up on his travels. Occasionally he'd bring a fish caught where the Magra River entered the sea, which the Gallettos found very strange, because theirs was the cooking of the countryside.

After the evening meal or the Sunday lunch the men would sit around the table and play card games called scopa or briscola, in which Gino cheerfully joined. Anna wondered if he was there to talk to her or to talk to her brothers. When he chatted with the boys, she worried that sometimes their conversation drifted into politics – a dangerous topic in this neighbourhood.

Sarzana had been the last town in Italy to fall to Fascism. The year Anna was born was the year Benito Mussolini was making his move to power. Gangs of his supporters roamed from town to town, picking fights with people they branded socialists or communists, inspired by Mussolini's declaration: 'The socialist party is a Russian army encamped in Italy. Against this foreign army, Fascists have launched a guerrilla war, and they will conduct it with exceptional seriousness.'

When the *squadristi* got to Sarzana, the local mayor had the police aim machine guns at them, and as they ran away through the fields, the mezzadri chased them with pitchforks. The socialists won that battle, but the war was lost the following year.

Once Mussolini took power in Rome, Sarzana got special attention from the Fascist bosses. And there were enough opportunists in the neighbourhood who were prepared to join the 'Voluntary Militia for National Security', wear the black shirt, and report their neighbours for any talk that might be construed as anti-Mussolini.

There had been riots in Sarzana after a socialist member of parliament, Giacomo Matteotti, was kidnapped and murdered in 1924. Matteotti had the nerve to suggest that the election that year, in which the Fascist party apparently gained 70 per cent of the votes, was not legitimate.

Mussolini used the protests to reinforce his proposition that the nation needed discipline, and emerged from the controversy more determined than ever: 'Italy requires a government. A man. A man who has when needed the delicate touch of an artist and the heavy hand of a warrior. A man who is sensitive and full of willpower. A man who knows and loves the people, and can direct and bend them with violence if required.'

That was certainly required in red Sarzana. Discipline was maintained by *manganello e olio* – baton and castor oil, which was poured down the throats of people brought to the local Fascist headquarters for expressing antisocial opinions. The biggest troublemakers would be sent to 'internal exile' in other parts of Italy, unable to contact their families.

For the mezzadri, loose talk brought a more enduring punishment. Most of the landlords were enthusiastic supporters of Fascism, so any hint of rebellion in a peasant family could see them thrown off their land without notice.

The revolutionary zeal that burned in the peasants during the 1920s had been thoroughly suppressed by the late 1930s. But in the evenings after dinner, in the privacy of the family, Anna had been disturbed to hear her younger brother Mauro railing against the brutality of the system. He was only one year old when Matteotti was murdered, but somehow he'd absorbed the reformist values of that time.

Mauro had been expelled from school at the age of eight for throwing an inkwell at a teacher who, Mauro thought, had treated another student unfairly. Now he couldn't see why the landlord was entitled to so much of the produce from the farm when he never did any work for it.

The local Fascist bullies steered clear of Mauro because he was tall and strong and short-tempered. A story had gone around about the occasion he knocked down a charging bull with one fist. In fact, the bull hadn't been all that big, but Mauro enjoyed his reputation as a character not to be messed with. Gino found him highly entertaining.

Anna's father and brothers were delighted to hear that Gino had never bothered to obtain a Fascist party membership card – supposed to be compulsory for anyone who worked in town. He seemed to have the knack of getting away with things through sheer charm.

One night, just after dinner, the landlord arrived. He was looking very serious, but for once, it wasn't to do with Mauro and his habit of earning pocket money by working for other farmers. Anna's father sent her upstairs, but she crept out onto the staircase to hear raised voices, and she realised they were talking about her.

The landlord had heard rumours that she was going out with a city boy and showing no interest in the excellent farmer's son he'd picked out for her. How could her parents allow this – were they anarchists?

The next time she went walking with Gino, she told him about it. 'How did your parents take it?' he asked. 'They didn't like it,' she replied. 'They seemed to be saying that it was none of his business, and that I should do what *they* thought was best for me, not what he thought would be best for his farm. He stomped out.'

Anna and Gino (centre) celebrate their wedding anniversary; below, a hand of briscola.

After the evening meal the men would sit around and play card games.
Anna wondered if Gino was there to talk to her or her brothers.

Gino was delighted. 'So we've got nothing to worry about. Now let me try out an idea on you. Maybe I'm joking and maybe I'm not – you tell me.

'We could save your parents a lot of trouble if we ran away together. It wouldn't be their fault. It would be us being naughty, and they wouldn't be defying the *padrone* [master]. You could come and live with me above the gelateria in Sarzana and I'll teach you how to make icecream.'

Anna thought about this disgraceful proposal for five seconds, and realised she wasn't shocked. Really, she'd be doing her parents a favour. And she was eager to see the wider world from which Gino was an ambassador. But these were rationalisations. She loved him.

And so they eloped. When they married a year later, Anna's parents attended the ceremony and Gino's didn't, saying that would look as if they condoned the months the couple had spent living in sin. Gino cooked his own wedding feast. Their first child, Graziella, was born in 1941, delivered by Anna's aunt at Ca' Rósa farmhouse.

Anna found she enjoyed making gelato almost as much as she enjoyed making tajarin. She'd boil the milk in big pots on the coal stove in their big apartment on Piazza Grande, then carry the milk downstairs and pour it into the gelato tub, which was surrounded by a mixture called *salamoia* – salt and ice delivered every morning by horse and cart.

You simply added flavourings and the secret thickening ingredient called 'neutro' (made from egg whites at the time, but later from carob seed flour). Then you had to turn a handle to stir the mixture, stopping every so often to scrape the frozen stuff off the sides of the tub with a wooden paddle. As with pasta, the quality depended on how much shoulder muscle you put into it.

Anna sliced the cylinder into discs. When she pulled the discs apart she had a handful of fine ribbons.

Served in bowls or sandwiched between biscuits, the flavours were vanilla, chocolate, hazelnut, lemon, banana, strawberry and a creamy concoction called *fior di latte*. For the strawberry and banana gelati, Gino used real fruit, pulped by pushing through horsehair mesh, because he'd found that metal sieves tainted the flavour.

In the winter, Gino turned the place into a cheese shop and a butchery, specialising in tripe, since classier cuts were hard to get in this period of war. What they didn't sell, they took to the family at Ca' Rósa.

In 1943, their second child, Mario, was born. Hardly had Anna moved back into the Sarzana flat when she had a visit from a very solemn Mauro. 'I've got some big news,' he said.

Anna thought he was going to announce his engagement to Bruna Martini, the cute girl he'd met while unloading trucks at the local tile factory. But it was something else. 'I've been called up. Here's the letter. I have to go to Rome next month and start training for the army.'

Anna was alarmed but also amused. As she told Gino: 'Mussolini doesn't know what he's in for if he thinks Mauro is going to fight for the Fascists. With Mauro in your army, you don't need enemies.'

'NON SI PUÓ INGANNARE A LUNGO LA GENTE CON L'ARIA FRITTA AL PROFUMO DI NIENTE … QUI, POI, LA SEQUENZA DELLE STAGIONI, PER LA CUCINA E IL PAESAGGIO, HA ANCORA UN SENSO.'

Bocca di Magra

Ameglia, the tiny hill town one kilometre from Mario's house, has a belltower that tells the time twice every hour. In case you lose count when it chimes midnight, it waits a minute and dongs you 12 times more. That's what happens just after Lucio has closed his eyes at the end of his first day in Lunigiana.

He sleeps through the next few time calls – the combination of a 24-hour flight and a ten course dinner can be a powerful sleeping potion. But after the fourteenth chime in the morning, he's ready to accept Mario's suggestion of a walk to Ameglia for a coffee and a closer look at the bloody tower.

DAY TWO

Mario's two-storey pink house, built into a hillside, has nine double doors opening onto gardens that are currently sprouting lettuce, artichokes, basil, rocket, asparagus, broad beans, baby eggplants, cucumbers, peas and what Mario calls *erbi* – not herbs but green plants, some like watercress, some like baby asparagus, which go into the vegetable pie called *torta d'erbi*. Lucio remembers as a child seeing local women scavenging in the fields and forests for the wild form of these greens. There are also hens wandering around, but Mario says he never seems to be able to find their eggs. In a few weeks, says Mario, he'll get tomatoes, chillis, strawberries, raspberries and peaches.

It's the first time Lucio has considered the notion that when the Romans arrived in his area, it was not terra nullius.

He's keen to show Lucio a discovery he made last year after a big tree behind his garden fell over in a storm. It's a rectangular hole in the ground that turned out to be an ancient tomb. Lucio knows Mario's house is built on what was once a Roman road, so he assumes Romans must have been buried in there.

Mario: 'Hah, everybody makes that mistake. The archaeologists have been here and dated the tomb at around 500 BC. So it was the people before the Romans. Under this ground was their necropolis.'

Lucio: 'What people? The Etruscans?'

Mario: 'No, it's more likely the Liguri, the ones the Romans defeated.'

It's the first time Lucio has considered the notion that when the Romans arrived in his area, it was not *terra nullius*. These people Mario is calling the Liguri were already in residence. What did they look like, Lucio wonders.

'Supposedly they had more of a square-shaped head and kind of flattened features,' says Mario. 'You sometimes see people like that up in the mountains, past Pontremoli. If you want to know more about all this, you should go over to the ruins of Luni. They've got a museum there now.'

Lucio remembers the ruins only as a quiet place where he used to go as a teenager to rehearse with his band (acoustic 12-string guitar, acoustic six-string and bongos), and where local people would scavenge bits of marble to use as ornaments or doorstops. Now that he's exploring Lunigiana, he really ought to learn something about its origins. He phones Aulo and arranges to meet him at Luni later that morning. Aulo is glad of any excuse to postpone his morning deliveries.

Mario and Lucio walk up the Roman road to Ameglia, past a slope on which Mario has recently planted 100 lemon saplings. Lucio remembers that Ameglia was famous for its ships' cooks, ships' stewards and lonely wives, because their husbands would spend months of every year away at sea.

'It's not like that now,' says Mario. 'When the cruise ships faded away, most of those people sold their houses to rich types from Milan or Parma, and went to live in the valley. The Milanesi renovate the houses and use them as holiday homes in the summer, so they're empty nine months of the year.'

The town is quiet – just a few old ladies sitting chatting in the main square, which is dominated by the stump of a tower built in the year 1100, and a monument to 15 Americans who died fighting the 'NaziFascisti' in 1944–45. Mario's preferred coffee place is closed for renovations, so they go to Locanda dei Poeti, which Mario correctly predicts will serve terrible macchiato. Not every Italian can make great coffee.

Through narrow cobbled lanes and under low porticos, they make their way to the church with the noisy campanile. The piazza in front of it has a view across to Mario's house and then the sea.

The cousins assemble in Mario's garden and take the Roman road (above) to Ameglia

The crumbling porticoes, facades and doorways of Ameglia

Mario remembers that a poet named Roberto Pazzi wrote that to predict the weather when you were in Bocca di Magra, you looked south, over the sea. If you could see the island of Elba, it would be fine tomorrow. But to predict the weather when you are in Ameglia, you look across to the hills terraced with olive trees. If they have a white look, the weather will be bad. If green, it will be fine. The colour change is to do with the way the wind turns the leaves.

'Do you remember Pazzi – he was a customer of Ciccio's in the early 1970s?' Mario asks. 'Yes,' says Lucio, 'but he didn't look like a poet. He wore a jacket.'

There's a smell of minestrone and baking bread in the air, so not every house is empty. But the church is deserted, even though today is Sunday. In a glass case, Lucio can see three skulls and assorted bones supposedly belonging to Saints Vitale, Clemente and Modesto. Maybe they're the ones who ring the bells all night.

They cross back to Mario's house, and Lucio sets off in his car. As he reaches the end of the lane from Mario's, he stops to let a stooped old man cross the road, and realises it's Dantin, a fisherman who used to bring his catch to Ciccio's 30 years ago. He wants to call out to Dantin, but the car behind is tooting, so he turns onto the highway towards the bridge over the Magra.

He is remembering the words of a song he wrote one day after he saw Dantin mending his nets on the sand in front of Ciccio's. The song was an image of country life, comparing the movements of Dantin's hand with the movements of a grapegrower tending his vines. It described a bucolic scene of women with sacks of grass on their heads (to take home and feed to their rabbits), and children chasing dogs through the vines and the cornstalks, and continued:

The man looks up and gives a quick greeting, then turns back towards the silent hills, pruning the branches with the same close attention that a fisherman pays to his nets when he hangs them and pierces them with the wooden needle … I was watching this as in one of those half

dreams that settle the busy mind as you're going to sleep, when everything becomes peaceful and hopes seem real. But there will always be a morning with its bitterness.

Trying to recall why he wrote that jarring last line, Lucio thinks the song reflected his 'angry young man' stance at the time, during the social upheavals of 1968–69. He was part of student protests about redistribution of wealth, and he thought the life of the contadino or the pescatore was too often romanticised, when it was really a grinding struggle for survival. It certainly seems to have bent Dantin's back.

Lucio was expecting to drive up to the ruins in the same way he used to ride his bicycle over them as a kid, but now he finds a tall wire fence, and a gatehouse demanding three euros to let him in. Clearly the years of local souveniring are over.

Aulo, in Google mode, explains that the land on which the Luni ruins stood was owned by the Fabbricotti family, who lost most of their money during the 1930s because they were anti-Fascist. They recently donated the land to the museum at nearby La Spezia, and the archaeologists moved in to protect what little remained of the glory that was Luna.

They've done a brilliant job of reconstructing the mosaic floor of a typical house in the city. It displays a boy on a dolphin using a trident to hunt fish which Lucio can recognise as local favourites still served at Ciccio's.

As Aulo and Lucio discuss the fish, a guide appears, introduces herself as Sara, and gives them some background on the place: Luna was a wealthy city because of the marble trade from Carrara, and an important naval base from which the Romans launched invasions of Sardinia and Spain.

The town was apparently named in honour of a moon goddess, symbolised by the crescent shape of the bay. It started in 177 BC with a population of 2,000, but must have grown tremendously, because the wide amphitheatre, built around 100 AD, had two tiers of seating and could hold 7,000 spectators.

The reconstructed mosaic floor of a first century mansion in Roman Luna; following pages, the amphitheatre

named in honour of a moon goddess, symbolised by the crescent shape of the bay. It started in 177 BC with a population of 2,000, but must have grown tremendously, because the wide amphitheatre, built around 100 AD

When she speaks about the Romans, Sara uses a tone of contempt. 'You don't seem to like the Romans much,' Lucio observes.

'I hate them because of what they did to my race,' she says. 'They were worse than Milosevic.'

Her vehemence comes as a surprise. Like most Italians, Lucio was taught to admire the Romans as brilliant engineers, lawmakers and military tacticians who spread civilisation across barbarian Europe. The landscape he grew up with was moulded by the Romans. They spread the chestnut forests, established the grapevines, terraced the hills for olive groves. Now he's hearing from someone who presents them as invaders and oppressors.

He asks: 'What do you mean, your race?'

Sara: 'The Liguri-Apuani. They had a civilisation here for thousands of years. The Romans tried to make them slaves, and when they couldn't defeat them, they shipped thousands of them down to the south. It was ethnic cleansing. But a lot of the Liguri-Apuani went to live in the mountains.'

She makes the Romans in Lunigiana in 200 BC sound like the Americans in Vietnam in the 1960s, rumbling in with heavy weapons to impose their ideology, but unable to cope with guerrilla warriors familiar with the terrain. The difference, of course, is that the Romans triumphed – at least until an earthquake brought down most of their glorious city in the fourth century. When Luna rebuilt itself as a Christian city, its name changed to Luni.

Sara looks nothing like Mario's description of the Liguri-Apuani. She's skinny, with dark curly hair and pointy features, and reminds Lucio of young Anna Galletto in the black-and-white family photos.

Lucio is fascinated that Sara can hold a grudge that's more than 2,000 years old. He has to ask: 'But how do you know you're from that race?'

Sara: 'Because I feel it in myself. I identify with them.'

Lucio and Aulo decide to discuss this over lunch at La Chioccia (pronounced key-otcha) d'Oro, a trattoria where they used to grab snacks and coffee when they were teenagers. Back then it was right next to the ruins, but a museum now occupies that spot, and the trattoria has been rebuilt outside the fence. These days Chioccia d'Oro is calling itself an *agriturismo*, which, according to Aulo, makes it an agricultural tourist attraction and entitles it to government assistance to maintain the surrounding orchard. Nearby there's an enclosure displaying ostriches, deer and peacocks.

Lucio worries that Chioccia d'Oro might have gone upmarket, but is reassured when he sees bristles still on the pieces of pork in a dish called *cotenna*. Mixed with olives and mushrooms, it's salty, vinegary and fatty, but delicious. The tajarin noodles are hand-made, and served with an asparagus sauce. And there's a huge platter of barbecued vegetables. At the end the brothers get complimentary glasses of a home-made *digestivo* liqueur called *nocino* (walnuts fermented for three months with sugar). The Romans might have eaten this entire meal two millennia ago.

Lucio notes the absence of seafood. La Chioccia d'Oro would have been on the shore of a half-moon bay 2,000 years ago, but now the silting up of the river mouth has put it 3 kilometres inland. So it does country cooking, not coastal cooking. Italians are strict about these distinctions, while Australians eat prawns at Uluru.

The rise of Luna, the fall of Luni

A QUICK HISTORY OF THE BAY WHERE THE RIVER MAGRA ENTERS THE SEA: FIRST THERE WERE THE LIGURI PEOPLE, THEN THE GREEKS, THEN THE LIGURI, THEN THE ETRUSCANS, THEN THE LIGURI, THEN THE ROMANS, THEN THE CHRISTIANS, THEN A WHOLE LOT OF INVADERS, THEN THE MOSQUITOES AND THEN THE SCAVENGERS.

Speculation about the name reveals much of the history. When the Greeks sailed there, as part of their expansion around the Mediterranean before 500 BC, they found a crescent-shaped bay, and named it Selene, in honour of their moon goddess. Scholars later assumed that the Romans, when they started exploring the place around 300 BC, simply translated that concept into the name of their moon goddess, Luna. But the Etruscans had already been there, and their word for 'port' was 'luna'. So the name's origins may be less poetical and more practical. Or an elaborate pun.

Certainly we can say that the Romans did the most with the place. The Greek geographer Strabo, writing in Rome around the year 10 AD, said Luna was 'both very large and very beautiful, since it includes within itself several harbours, all of them deep right up to the shore, just such a place as would naturally become the naval base of a people who were masters of so great a sea for so long a time'.

The Romans used the marble of Carara to build a city so magnificent that various geographically-challenged seafaring barbarians thought they'd reached Rome. Although Pompeii got more publicity, Luna was Italy's second city between 100 and 300 AD: a military base, an economic power-house, and a gourmet centre.

Pliny, the writer of the world's first encyclopaedia around 50 AD, gave this part of 'northern Etruria' his Palm award for its wine, fruits, figs and prunes of 'incomparable grace'. The poet known in English as Martial (Marcus Valerius Martialis) wrote around 80 AD: 'On the cheese with the stamp of Etruscan Lunae your children will snack a thousand times'. The Luna cheese, he said, was made in huge wheels, which suggests it was the forerunner of parmesan.

One of the earliest popes, Eutichiano, came from Luni and in 275 AD introduced the custom of blessing fruits and vegetables because they were evidence of God's goodness. (Another Lunigiana Pope, Nicolo V in the 1450s, is credited with preserving the manuscript of the Roman writer Apicius, who produced the first recipe book in the fourth century.)

In the 400s, the city suffered an earthquake, converted to Christianity, and changed its name to Luni. Presumably the timing was coincidental. The marble was stripped off the Roman temples and used as facades for churches. Luni managed to fight off invasion by Vikings, Saracens, Goths, Lombards and Normans, but not by mud, which turned the whole area into a malarial swamp by the year 900.

In the 1940s, writing with a power that survives translation into English, Corrado Martinetti, the librarian of Sarzana, described the fate of the city by the bay:

Luni lost its maritime importance and was a land of incursions, made red with blood, sacked by savage hordes in flashes of flame. Its port, which had seen the flourishing traffic of Roman triremes, was exposed to the raids of the Saracens and the Normans and began to fill with enormous quantities of debris, fragments of broken rock, and the remains of tree branches that entered the Magra from the Cisa landslides. Deep changes in the soil allowed the formation of squalid stagnant ponds and swamps that brought death with their spread. Malaria kept the country under its power. The population of the Luni valley, impoverished and depressed, driven out by the barbarian hordes, fearful and feverish, found refuge in the villages that appeared on the hills along the sides of the Apuani alps.

The silting of the Magra had turned the Luni area into a malarial swamp by the tenth century, forcing the citizens to flee uphill and start towns such as Ameglia and Castelnuovo. The Bishop of Luni moved 10 kilometres inland to Sarzana, so this afternoon Lucio and Aulo will do the same.

'Remember how, when we were kids, going to Sarzana was like going to New York for us?' Lucio asks Aulo as they drive through the main gate. Aulo laughs and says 'And like New York, its population is so big – 22,000'.

Country cooking at La Chioccia d'Oro: *cotenna*, tajarin with aspargus, barbecued vegies.

Sarzana is a walled city, guarded by a massive fortress and surrounded by a moat which is now full of flower gardens and chicken runs instead of water. It has never looked back since it replaced Luni as the local capital in the twelfth century – clearly still a centre of wealth, its main street lined with boutiques and foodstores full of well-dressed people.

When the Sarzanese have finished shopping and strolling each afternoon, they must go for coffee and cake to a café called Gemmi, which opened in 1929. Its speciality is *spungata*, a tart of fruit pulp, honey and spices inside crispy pastry. Spungata supposedly originated with the Romans, and would have moved with their descendants from Luni to Sarzana. It's a local tradition that landlords must give spungata to tenants for Christmas.

Lucio isn't allowed to eat spungata any more, but he wants to buy a family-size one to take home to Wendy. He recognises Fiammetta Gemmi, granddaughter of the founder, standing behind a glass case crammed with pastries and sweets. Rumour around Ciccio's is that she is the first girl Mario ever kissed, when they were both about ten and lived in adjoining apartments on Sarzana's main square.

Now Fiammetta (which means 'little flame') is a tall, thin woman with severe features and half-glasses on a chain around her neck. She greets Lucio warmly when he introduces himself.

He remembers a trick his gang used to play on Fiammetta's father, who would ask everyone as they left the shop, 'Have you paid, have you paid?' The naughty boys would eat their cakes, pay their bill, get a receipt, and then run out of the shop as if they were guilty

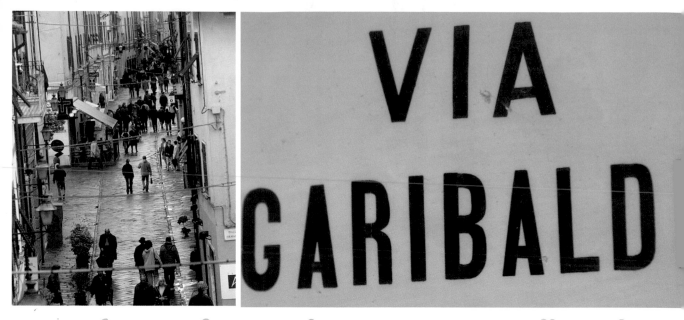

A stroll around Sarzana, past Anna's old home and the cake shop of Fiammetta Gemmi.

of something. Silvano Gemmi would chase them into the street shouting, 'Have you paid?' They would turn around with shocked expressions and calmly produce their receipts.

Fiammetta is keen to show how she has expanded the café since Lucio's day, taking him upstairs to display a richly decorated restaurant section. Business is booming. People will always want pastries. Her only concern is that there's no next generation to continue the Gemmi legacy – a common complaint in Italy now, as couples have fewer or no children.

As they part, Fiammetta asks to be remembered to Mario. Clutching their bags of pastries, Aulo and Lucio look at each other meaningfully.

Lucio drops into a nearby shop to fortify himself with Sarzana's other speciality – focaccia bread stuffed with farinata (chick pea fritter) – and in a local bookshop he buys a video of a 1980 melodrama called *The Lost City of Sarzana*, about the locals' fight against Fascism in 1921.

The brothers decide they should see what became of the old Galletto farmhouse, which was in the country in Anna's day but is now in the suburbs of a spreading town.

When Lucio was a child, the snobbish social division in Sarzana was between people who lived *de sovre* – north of the railway crossing – and *de soto*, south of the crossing (which was semi-rural 'peasant' land). Now the brothers discover that de soto has become yuppie renovator territory. The old Galletto farmhouse is a handsome home, painted a lighter pink than before, with gleaming dark green shutters. A middle-aged man in an expensive cardigan is mowing the lawn.

The surrounding farmland has been subdivided for new cottages, and across the road the old well, where Anna got water for the family every morning, has become part of a children's playground maintained by the council.

On the new outside wall, the inhabitants have stuck colourful letter-tiles that spell out the words 'LA CA' ROSA'. Lucio and Aulo don't know whether to be flattered or offended that their old family nickname has become a piece of retro chic.

For dinner, Aulo is recommending a restaurant called Il Cantinone, which does both new food and traditional food. Its owners are Mario Musetti, an architect turned chef, and Sabrina Tendola, daughter of a local winemaker.

Cantinone's speciality is beef from the white cattle called Chianina, which are fed on special grasses in central Tuscany. Musetti puts slabs of the beef into an open oven next to burning logs, thus charring the outside and leaving the inside rare. Then he cuts the slab into cubes and serves them with exotic salts and condiments.

That might earn his place the label of Tuscan restaurant. But then he also makes testaroli, the pancake of Lunigiana, and half-moon ravioli stuffed with leeks, a classic Ligurian ingredient. He knows the Sarzanese are sophisticated diners, with diverse tastes.

Aulo introduces Lucio and explains that he's researching the foodways of the area. Musetti says, 'You have to meet my father-in-law. He'll talk your head off. I'll get him to come down.'

Despite their protestations, Musetti phones Giorgio Tendola at his winery in the Colli di Luni, and 20 minutes later the maestro bursts through the door, his face almost the colour of the two bottles of red he's carrying. Most of the tables in Cantinone are empty, but with Giorgio in the room, the place seems full.

In the manner of these conversations, they begin by establishing common ground. In this neighbourhood, it's never a case of six degrees of separation, it's usually three. Giorgio says his father used to deliver wine to Ciccio's in demijohns. Lucio has a flash: 'Was he called Tomalon? I remember as a kid hearing Anna looking forward to Tomalon arriving. They loved him, or his wine at least.' In fact, Giorgio says, his father's name was Luigi. Tomalon was a nickname he used with customers.

Mario Musetti presents the specialties of Il Cantinone: testaroli pancakes and chargrilled beef with spiced salts.

Initially Giorgio didn't join his father in the winemaking business. He went off and became an executive with Shell Oil, only returning to the family farm when his father died in 1990. That's why Lucio hasn't met him before.

Giorgio speaks in a vigorous local slang. Asked about a schoolfriend of Lucio who supposedly went into the restaurant business, Giorgio dismisses him as a *figaiolo* (addicted to women). Instead of doing his work, says Giorgio, '*sempre n'ziro per moza*' ('he's always going around looking for pussy').

Lucio finds he is even enjoying Giorgio's red wine. It takes Giorgio only a minute to decide that Lucio is simpatico, and then he invites him to come for a meal at his winery. 'We must talk more. My wife will make *tagliolini fatti in casa alla contadina con i fagioli borlotti* (home-made noodles in the style of the farmer's wife with borlotti beans). And I might shoot some birds for us to eat afterwards.

'You better come for lunch, because if you come for dinner you'll be tossing and turning all night from all the food.'

DAY THREE

Mario has arranged a media lunch to celebrate the fiftieth anniversary of Capannina Ciccio. In fact, the fiftieth anniversary was last year, but Mario never got around to it then. Now he has published a book of black-and-white photos of the restaurant over the decades, and he might as well coincide its launching with the anniversary party.

While Mario organises the restaurant, Lucio takes a stroll around Bocca di Magra. For him, every bit is coloured by memories, and he wonders how it would look to a newcomer. He's been reading some guidebooks, which mostly dismiss the town simply as the beginning (or the end, depending on where you're coming from) of the Italian Riviera.

The *Cadogan Guide* describes Bocca di Magra as 'a fishing village favoured as a summer resort after the war … now given over to tourism and boating under the parasol pines'. The *Rough Guide to Italy* describes it as 'an important day habitat for birds', which Lucio had never noticed, while David Downie's *Enchanted Liguria* overstates it as 'the chic pleasure port where Tuscany begins'. That title should really go to Fiumaretta, across the river. There's a small yacht marina outside Ciccio's (where the fishing boats used to chug in) but there are no grand hotels – just the modest Sette Archi and The Garden.

Lucio heads up the hill into the pine forest where he and Aulo used to dump the human waste products from Ciccio's. Bocca di Magra wasn't connected to the sewer system until the mid 1960s, and in the summer, the night cart collections weren't frequent enough.

When there was risk of overflow, the brothers had the job of scooping the stuff out of the septic tank with a giant ladle, putting it in a wheelbarrow, pushing the barrow uphill and emptying it behind a tree. 'Talk about starting at the bottom,' he thinks. Perhaps Lucio can take some credit for the lush greenery of the forest, which produces a healthy crop of pine nuts to go into pesto sauce.

He passes the ruins of a private zoo where he first saw lions as a child, and emerges onto a promontory called Punta Bianca. Here are the remains of the massive gun emplacements built by the Germans in 1943 and bombarded by the Allies throughout 1944. From here, cannons repelled Allied ships approaching the coast, and lobbed shells onto the hills to the south where Lucio's father and uncle were hiding as partisans.

He drops in on the partly restored Monastero del Corvo (Monastery of the Crow) where, according to a plaque on the wall, Italy's greatest writer Dante once stayed. This is not so remarkable. The poet slept around during his period of exile from Florence in 1306, and many places claim to have sheltered him.

In the chapel is a blackened wooden sculpture of Jesus on the cross, which is the subject of a local legend. One morning in the eleventh century, a crewless ship floated ashore in the bay of Luni. It contained a wooden statue of a crucified man with a remarkable face. The English writer Aldous Huxley, who holidayed near here in the 1930s, described it thus:

The face is not the face of a dead or dying or even suffering man. It is the face of a man still violently alive, and the expression of its strong features is stern, is fierce, is even rather sinister. From the dark sockets of polished cedar wood two yellowish tawny eyes stare out, slightly squinting, with an unsleeping balefulness.

The locals summoned the local bishop to examine it, and he concluded that the ship must have floated from Palestine, the statue must be made of wood from the original cross, and the face must have been sculpted by somebody who had actually seen Jesus – most likely the disciple

From here, cannons lobbed shells onto the hills to the south where Lucio's father and uncle were hiding as partisans.

Nicodemus. This information came to the bishop in a dream, so it was bound to be right. The statue, now called the Volto Santo (Holy Face), was quite a prize, and it was instantly claimed by both the city of Sarzana and the city of Lucca. The bishop decided to let God determine where Jesus should rest, so he loaded the statue onto a cart pulled by two white oxen without reins, and said, 'Whichever direction the oxen take it, that's where it will belong'.

Perhaps you are now under the impression that the steers chose Bocca di Magra. But Huxley will correct you: 'The oxen were divinely inspired to take the road to Lucca. And at Lucca the Face has remained ever since, working miracles, drawing crowds of pilgrims, protecting and at times failing to protect the city of its adoption from harm.'

So what is this dark wooden face Lucio is now examining? Ah well, such is God's generosity, he caused a second Volto Santo to float ashore a few years later to placate the disappointed residents of Luni, and that is what now stares down from the wall above the altar in the chapel just up the hill from Ciccio's. It's striking, even if it is second best.

Back down on the river, Lucio is delighted to see a man in a boat hurling a net out over the water. He hasn't seen a *razzaglio* for 30 years, and assumed the net fishermen who crowded the river during his childhood had all died out. The net blossoms from the man's hand, sprawls over the water like a tablecloth being spread over a table, settles gently down and, as it sinks, gets pulled back into the boat. The man is young and obviously just learning how to do it, but Lucio hopes this is part of a movement in Italy to recapture traditional skills before they vanish.

All this sightseeing makes him late for lunch, and speeches by local dignitaries are already underway as he slips into his seat. He is delighted to see that Mario has been able to find a rare local delicacy to serve to the dignitaries and media – big clams called *tartufi di mare* (sea truffles). They were standard fare at Ciccio's in the 1950s, but now they are almost fished out. The other delicacies of the time – dolphin meat and the shellfish called *datteri* – are banned.

He finds himself sitting between Alex Muzi-Falcone, an environmental activist who earns his living arranging summer rental houses for rich English, American and Australian travellers, and Salvatore Marchese, the restaurant critic for *L'Espresso* magazine. Alex is small, neat and bald, while Salvatore is big, expansive and afro-topped.

Mario comes over to Salvatore, who has always worn very thick glasses and recently had an eye operation, and this conversation, in a mixture of dialects, ensues …

Opposite, the river mouth from the hill behind Ciccio's, the wooden statue that miraculously floated ashore, and the German fortress at Punta Bianca.

Above, the not-quite-lost art of net fishing on the Magra.

Mario: '*Come I van I oci?*' (How are your eyes going?)

Salvatore: '*J'en li.*' (They are still there.)

Mario: '*Te vedi m'po mei?*' (Do you see better?)

Salvatore: '*Si, ma anche e cose brute a gi vedo mei.*' (Yes, but I also see ugly things more clearly.)

Mario: 'Sometimes it's better not to see very well. I heard about an ugly man who had a beautiful wife who was blind. He didn't want her to have the operation. She had it, saw him and left him.'

Lucio is not currently well disposed towards food critics, having suffered at their hands in the latest *Good Food Guide*, but Salvatore is different. He also functions as a kind of administrative officer in the town of Castelnuovo and officiated at Lucio's wedding in 1977. In the time Lucio has been in Australia, Salvatore has developed an Italy-wide reputation as an *enogastronomo*, a scholar of food and wine.

Lucio is keen to hear his sense of current restaurant trends in Italy, and Salvatore is happy to pontificate. 'Now is a time of confusion. The demand for tradition is growing but supply can't meet demand. There is not enough local produce, so ingredients are sourced from all around the world, but cooked to traditional recipes. Some cooks are experimenting with serving ingredients raw, or as tempura.'

'If you want to see how it's possible to get the balance between tradition and modernisation just right, you have to come up to my town, Castelnuovo, and have lunch with me at Armanda's Trattoria.'

At the fiftieth
anniversary lunch,
Salvatore Marchese
praises the sea truffles
and Super Mario.

Lucio went to junior high school in Castelnuovo and remembers Armanda's as a snack bar that happened to be at his bus stop. 'I used to get my *panini* [bread rolls] there on my way to school,' he says. 'And on the way home I'd play pinball until the bus came.'

'Oh, it's much more than panini and pinball now,' says Salvatore. 'It's one of the best places in the area. They are evolving the food without making it silly. And they do the best *panigacci*.'

There's a word Lucio hasn't heard in a while. Panigacci is another name for testaroli, which are made (and spelled) in all sorts of ways in the mountains of Lunigiana. He makes the lunch date with Salvatore.

Alex the environmentalist agrees with Salvatore that Italians have started celebrating ancient foods and customs. 'It's because people are thinking about the good old days, trying to recuperate that spirit before it is lost. They want something to attach themselves to, and with the fading of religion, this interest in traditional foods and customs is almost a return to paganism.'

In the neighbourhood, Alex is known as Il Barone (the baron), and not just because of his impeccable manners, dress and mode of speech. His father was a hereditary aristocrat who worked as a diplomat during the Mussolini period, and if such titles had not been thrown out, along with the king, in the referendum of 1946, Alex would have inherited a baronetcy. He finds this impresses the Americans who were, until September 2001, his main customers for the villas he rents out.

Alex has been eating at Capannina Ciccio since his mother, known as La Baronessa, moved into the area in 1960. 'The essence of Ciccio is not in the food, it's in the people who run it,' he tells Lucio. 'You're not eating in a restaurant that is run by big business.

With the fading of religion, this interest in traditional foods and customs is almost a return to paganism

You're visiting a family. Mario has a special touch. His humanity, his love for the arts, his overall view of life – people notice that and come back for more.'

Alex says the river outside Ciccio's became badly polluted ten years ago, because there were no controls on the factories upstream, and that killed the local fishing industry. Most of the fish are now caught by much bigger boats which go far out to sea towards Sardinia. Finally the government started imposing controls and the river is returning to its old clarity.

The problem now, he says, is likely to be overdevelopment of tourist facilities – boat marinas, big hotels, shops: 'There's a proposal that would increase the population on the river by 10,000. I am horrified about it.

'The councils of Sarzana and Ameglia have always been of the Left, and are keen on creating jobs, so they are inclined to let the developments go ahead. I stood as a Greens candidate in the local elections. We don't oppose all development, but we want to limit it, so the spirit of Bocca di Magra, the reason people want to come here in the first place, won't be destroyed. But I didn't win.'

By 3.30 pm the officials have finished their speeches, the journalists have done their interviews, and the chefs have cleaned up the kitchen and gone on their break. Now Ciccio's reverts to a family living room.

Anna's grandchildren toddle around, eating gelati and watching the fish in the tank. Graziella's husband, another Giuseppe, wanders into the kitchen with two rabbits he has just killed on his farm, and some wild asparagus he has picked in the forest. He throws oil, garlic and sage into a frying pan, and gets it sizzling while he skins and chops the rabbits, throws the pieces into the pan with some leftover vermentino, simmers it for a while, then throws in the asparagus and some olives. The restaurant fills with a delicious smell, but there is no customer to appreciate it. Giuseppe and Graziella eat the rabbit for a late lunch or an early dinner.

A family friend comes in with a big sea bass he caught that morning near the bridge over the Magra. Graziella weighs it and discovers it's a 5-kilogram beauty. She offers him

20 euros a kilo for it, and he agrees. That night, she tells Lucio, it will turn into 12 portions, each earning 15 euros. So everybody does well out of the deal.

Lucio meets up with Aulo, his wife Mariella and their two sons for dinner at Sarzana's trendiest restaurant, Taverna Napoleone. It's in a seventeenth-century stable, and displays its wines in the wall troughs where the horses consumed their hay. The host, Gianmarco Viscardi, is very casual, with designer stubble. When asked if he can recommend a mixture of the chef's specialities, he says, 'I'll give you some stuff I haven't been able to sell today'.

Lucio asks the wine waiter to recommend a white that is young, light and *non-barricato* (not aged in wood). He sends back three bottles that don't meet these specifications before settling on his old favourite vermentino.

The food proves to be a cheeky twist on local classics, adding Asian flavours such as sesame, ginger and star anise to sauces on gnocchi and duck, using curry-flavoured couscous instead of rice in a vegetable 'risotto', and using thin slices of zucchini instead of pasta to wrap 'ravioli'. This, it would seem, is 'the new Italian cooking'.

DAY FOUR

The morning papers have given a good run to the fiftieth anniversary of Ciccio's, and the return of its prodigal son. *Il Secolo XIX* reminisces about how 'the mythical Ciccio' built a *baracchetta* (yet another word for hut) on the mouth of the Magra where you could eat a fritto misto 'of unforgettable flavour' and 'the best cacciucco in the world', because of Ciccio's friends, the local pescatori. It continues …

> At the end of the meal, always a gelato. Guelfi had a son, Mario, who was thinking about art. In 1963, when he was 19, he went on a different course of life, going into his father's business … Then Mario transformed the architectural lines and the place became popular with artists and literati who had come to Bocca for a relaxed climate, a few fishermen's houses, silences, and an incredible view of the Apuane mountains. People like Vittorio Sereni, Marguerite Duras, Mary McCarthy, Ernesto Treccani, Marino Marini, Franco Fortini, Giovanni Giudici, Indro Montanelli. 'They were coming to my restaurant because you could eat fresh fish and talk about prose, poetry, cinema and art,' said Mario. 'Therefore Bocca was the ideal place for a holiday.'

Il Tirreno notes that Ciccio's is being visited by 'a nephew, Lucio Galletto, who, after breathing art – not just culinary art – at the capannina, migrated (because of a beautiful Australian woman) to the land of kangaroos. After doing it tough for a short while, today he is the owner of one of the most important restaurants in Sidney [their spelling].'

> 'I started very young,' said Galletto, 'and then when I followed my future wife I went to work in an Italian restaurant in Sidney to get experience. There I understood that I could do better, so I jumped. And today Lucio's is the reference point for people who love Italian food. In Australia, after Chinese, Italian is the most loved cuisine, and we still have room to grow.'
> Apart from the dishes, the greatest restaurant of Sidney will soon see wine from Colli di Luni. 'I got some contacts with local producers and I really think the vermentino will appear on my tables.'

Festa a «La Capannina da Ciccio», c'era anche Giudici

50 anni di buona cucina e ai tavoli grandi scrittori

di Federico Ricci

CASTELNUOVO M. Festeggia cinquant'anni di attività uno dei più noti ristoranti della zona, «La Capannina da Ciccio» di Domenico Guelfi, oggi nelle mani, sempre DI famiglia, del figlio Mario.

A testimoniare l'importanza del ristorante come luogo di incontro, anche il grande poeta Giovanni Giudici, testimone del fervore culturale che si respirava in passato in quel luogo, dove Einaudi, Fortini, Giudici, Moravia, Marguerite Duras, Mary Mc Carthy, Sereni, Pavese e altri ancora si incontravano e discutevano davanti ad un buon piatto di pesce e ad una bottiglia del buon vino dei Colli di Luni.

Festeggia il mezzo secolo di attività, oltre che con la pubblicazione di un bel libro di memoria fotografica, anche assieme a un nipote, Lucio Galletto che, dopo aver respirato arte (culinaria e non solo) alla Capannina, è emigrato (complice una bella donna australiana) nella terra dei canguri e dopo una breve gavetta è oggi il proprietario di uno dei più importanti ristoranti di Sidney.

A presentare la cerimonia l'enogastronomo Salvatore Marchese, e con lui lo scrittore Zeno Birolli, curatore del libro, il poeta Giovanni Giudici, il sindaco di Ameglia Francesco Pisani, il vice sindaco di Castelnuovo Magra Giorgio Baudone, la direttrice dell'Apt della Spezia Lucia Solaro (che ha evidenziato come i turisti provenienti dall'Australia verso la nostra provincia siano in forte aumento).

«Ho cominciato giovanissimo - ha detto Galletto - e poi, quando ho seguito la mia futura moglie, sono andato a fare esperienza in un ristorante italiano a Sidney. Lì ho capito che si poteva fare di più e meglio. Così mi sono buttato e oggi il mio "Lucio's" è il punto di riferimento per chi ama la cucina italiana. E in Australia, dopo quella cinese, è la cucina più amata ed abbiamo margini di crescita».

Al suo seguito un fotografo e un giornalista australiani che stanno raccogliendo materiale per scrivere un libro sulle origini della fortuna di Galletto. «Nel mio locale propongo una volta ogni tanto un menù tutto lunigianese, con le torte di verdura, la "Scarpaza" e altre specialità di questi posti. E poi tanta pasta fatta da noi».

E dopo i piatti, a breve nel maggior ristorante di Sidny sbarcherà anche il Vermentino dei Colli di Luni. «Ho avuto contatti con alcuni produttori e credo proprio che sulla mia tavola ci sarà anche il Vermentino dei Colli di Luni».

La Nazione takes liberties with the spelling of Lucio's surname:

How the local press reported Lucio's visit, and the eggplants flourishing in his old backyard

He's called Lucio Galletti. Maybe his name is not famous in our area, but it is in Sydney, Australia and is associated instantly with one of the most appreciated restaurants of the city – Lucio's.

After all, its art is a family thing, a family in Bocca di Magra who made history, having run Capannina Ciccio for 50 years. To mark the occasion, the heir of the mythical Ciccio, Mario Guelfi, who runs the restaurant with 25 other people, has published a volume, or better, an album …

The deputy mayor of Castelnuovo, being the representative of the birthplace of Lucio Galletto, praised him without hiding a certain pride, because Lucio arrived in Australia 25 years ago for love, and with the intention of staying only a few months.

After gaining experience in a restaurant for three years, Lucio decided to go on his own with typical Italian and Lunigianese cooking, because, he underlines, 'I make the scarpazza even if our speciality is fresh pasta.'

He is being followed by a journalist and photographer from Australia, gathering material for a book on the origin of the fortune of Galletto, to find out where and how a country kid (*ragazzo di provincia*) could have become so famous on a new continent.

To clear his head of this nonsense, Lucio sets off to visit the cottage where he grew up, in the village of Molicciara. His parents made the cement bricks themselves, and Mauro did all the construction work. The house is a fawn-coloured box surrounded by a small orchard, where Aulo still grows vegetables (although he lives in an apartment a kilometre away). Lucio is impressed with the fat black eggplants behind the house.

He walks down the road to a place he thinks of as his 'might-have-been' Lunigiana restaurant. It's a place called Maneccia, where his father used to play cards after dinner. Maneccia is an osteria, where the food is simpler than you'd find in a trattoria and the priority is drinking and socialising rather than eating. One night Mauro came home from

his card game and told the family the business was for sale at a very reasonable price. Here was a perfect opportunity for a family fascinated by food. Bruna could cook, Mauro could grow and buy the produce and maintain the property, and the boys could do the service. 'It could be a whole new start in life for us,' said Mauro.

Aulo, studying at university and effectively head waiter at Ciccio's, was keen. Lucio, still at school, was doubtful. And Bruna was absolutely opposed. 'What will Anna do without me?' she asked. 'Nobody else at Ciccio's can work that fryer. I could not let them down like that.'

Mauro and Aulo pleaded and cajoled. 'This is our chance to use everything we've learnt to build something of our own,' said Aulo. 'We can move out of the contadino life. We can stop working for other people.' But Bruna was implacable. She could never leave Ciccio's.

So Maneccia slipped into other hands. As Lucio looks at it now, it is temporarily closed, presumably waiting for the summer season, but even so, it smells of old smoke. Clearly it never moved from being an osteria, because there's a soccer machine on its front verandah. Lucio wonders if his family would have become local culinary heroes, or settled into suburban monotony there. He's glad his mother stood firm.

He has a big eating day ahead. Lunch will be at the once-legendary Locanda dell'Angelo, where Angelo Paracucchi created a world reputation in the 1980s. Dinner will be at Locanda delle Tamerici, where a hot new chef has just been given the Michelin star that Paracucchi lost. There will be lessons to learn today, as if Lucio needed an excuse to sample fine food.

When Lucio opened his restaurant in Sydney in 1981, Aulo sent him Paracucchi's book *La Cucina della Lunigiana*, inscribed '*A Lucio per ricordo delle origini. A Sally per conoscerle*' ('For Lucio to remember his origins, and for Sally to know them').

It was the first cookbook Lucio had seen which gave a regional identity to Lunigiana, and which resisted the Tuscany-mania that was growing at the time. Paracucchi, who was

A lost opportunity? The osteria that might have been the Galletto family's future.

born in Umbria and began his cooking career in Florence, chose to live in Lunigiana because of the produce and the opportunity to be close to the markets.

Aulo and Lucio had been to Paracucchi's place when he was first building his reputation, and had been impressed, first by the cutting-edge architecture of Vico Magistretti, and second by the rotund figure of Angelo Paracucchi coming to every table and saying, 'What can we make for you today?'

As Salvatore Marchese, in full *enogastronomo* enthusiasm, wrote: 'He can play anything on the keyboard of gastronomic tradition. You must watch him in the dining room – the fire comes out of his hands and lights his face to form a solar smile. The face becomes intense with tenderness when he sees people enjoy his creations.'

This set Lucio's definition of 'the host'. He often finds himself unconsciously imitating Angelo's posture when he greets his customers in Sydney. Every food magazine in the world wrote about Angelo, he got his own TV series, and he opened a second restaurant in Paris and a third in Japan.

Now the brothers are shocked to find only one other table occupied when they meet at 1.30 pm. Angelo's son Stefano is in charge, because his father is semi-retired and more concerned with his cooking school in Japan than his ties to Italy. When Lucio describes Angelo as his hero, and looks around the room sympathetically, Stefano confesses that he's been going through tough times.

'It's a problem of reputation, not reality,' he laments. 'People make an assumption that because my father is not here, it can't be as good, but our chef worked with my father from the age of 15, and he's doing a brilliant job of keeping the menu up to date. I think it will take us two more years to come back on top.'

But Lucio is thinking that excessive ambition can destroy the reason you were successful in the first place. With restaurants in three countries, Angelo could not do what he did best: ask the customers what he might make for them today. Lucio is wondering again whether he really should have opened his own second eatery.

When they try the food, the brothers think Stefano's optimism may be justified, athough there is no longer anything particularly Lunigianese about the menu.

They start with a tiny 'tempura' of prawn and zucchini flower in beer batter, served fastidiously on a white paper doyly. Then there's crisped eggplant with buffalo mozzarella, pieces of scampi sitting on a rosemary-flavoured bean puree, a seafood salad with mango and raspberry vinegar, tagliolini noodles with scampi and zucchini, wide black pasta strips with tiny squids and spinach, duck with porcini mushrooms and olives and, for dessert, a classic cassata made with ricotta cheese, raspberries and pistachios.

They conclude that the food is beautifully cooked and presented, but overworked. The lonely atmosphere does not make for a comforting experience.

A walk and a siesta puts Lucio back into condition to test the newest claimant for Angelo's crown that night. Locanda delle Tamerici (inn of the cherry trees) is a renovated farmhouse with its own private beach on the Tuscany side of the Magra River. The food guide published by L'*Espresso* raves about the food but describes its chef–owner Mauro Ricciardi as 'brontolone e narcisista' (complaining and vain). Lucio suspects the review was written by the ever-present enogastronomo Salvatore.

At Locanda dell' Angelo, Stefano and his headwaiter offer eggplant with buffalo mozzarella, tempura, and seafood salad. But where are the customers?

He can only indulge his cooking fantasies because the entry fees for the private beach subsidise the restaurant.

As if to compensate for this forthright description, the service, by young women in long black dresses, is shy and retiring. But when Lucio asks if he could speak to the chef, a bulky bald man emerges from the kitchen and, having established that Lucio is a fellow restaurateur, opens a bottle of rare rum from British Guyana and sits and chats for an hour.

He reveals that he's a businessman who learnt to cook by paying famous chefs – including Angelo Paracucchi – to let him work and observe in their kitchens. He'd opened Tamerici in the mid 1990s as a small hotel and piano bar, and found he couldn't get a chef to do the kind of food he wanted. So he spent two years teaching himself. He was then surprised at how quickly he became flavour of the month with the media.

The food is in a style sometimes called *ricca-povera* (rich poor) – a mixture of peasant ingredients with luxuries. Thus he tops a crescent of foie gras with a grilled prawn, and puts pieces of scampi on chestnut tagliatelle which has been tossed with bits of sausage and broccoli. He wraps slices of *lardo* (pork fat) around poached fish, and sits a mould of polenta with the breast of a tiny bird called *tordo*.

It's highly refined and yet every ingredient retains its flavour. Lucio is impressed again, although he doubts if he could afford to emulate Mauro, who reveals that he can only indulge his cooking fantasies in this way because the entry fees for the private beach in summer subsidise every other part of his operation.

DAY FIVE

After the *alta cucina* (haute cuisine) of the last three meals, Lucio is looking forward to the home cooking of Vanda Tendola at Il Torchio winery as much as to the conversation of her husband, and he's not disappointed. But before he eats, he must join Giorgio in a tour of the house and grounds. That marble fireplace came from the ruins of Luni, before they put the fence around them. 'It's better here than in a museum,' says Giorgio.

But really, this place is a museum. Giorgio keeps his olive oil in big terracotta jars that haven't changed since the days of the Romans. He has wooden ravioli moulds he thinks are 200 years old and a wooden device for holding stalks of wheat while they are cut 'so the women wouldn't ruin their hands'. His great grandfather's rusting rifle hangs on the wall, next to a hunting licence dated 1855 with the words '*Professione: contadino*' still visible.

Everything is old except the winery, which has state-of-the-art stainless steel equipment and flickering temperature gauges. 'Tradition doesn't work in everything,' says Giorgio. 'When I came back here in the 1990s, I threw away all my father's equipment, bought French machinery, and started doing wine in the modern way.'

Now he makes just one white – vermentino – and one red, a mixture of sangiovese and merlot which he calls Il Torchio. The wines keep winning prizes, which means a retirement hobby has turned profitable.

True to his promise, Giorgio has barbecued some small birds he shot himself – as proven by the pellets the lunchers have to spit out every couple of bites. As another appetiser Vanda has poached some *triglie* (red mullet) with white wine.

Then Lucio watches with fascination as she composes the main course. Normally pasta can be treated in two ways. The first is *alla macchia*: boiled, put in a bowl, then sauce

At Locanda delle Tamerici, Mauro offers foie gras with prawns and chestnut pasta with scampi and sausage.

dolloped on top (macchia means 'stain' and gives us the form of coffee called macchiato, as in stained with milk). The second is *strascicate*: partly boiled, then tossed in the frying pan with the sauce, which finishes the cooking of the pasta.

Vanda Tendola is taking a third approach. She has made strips of pasta, boiled them with kidney beans, and is now composing them meticulously in a big bowl. First she does a layer of pasta and beans, then a layer of sausage in tomato sauce, then a layer of parmesan, then another layer of pasta and beans and so on. In theory it's a soup, but it's really a kind of lasagne, except with tagliatelle instead of sheets. Lucio remembers watching his mother do this 40 years ago.

Ladled into a smaller bowl, the *pasta alla Contadina* roars with flavour and perfectly matches the red wine Giorgio serves in flasks. Lucio is remembering a remark by Salvatore: 'With the food of the rich, we talk and debate; with the food of the peasants, we fall in love'. Lucio feels like he's home again.

After lunch, Giorgio takes him for a walk to visit his neighbours – the Baracchini family. They live in a four-storey villa with vast gardens and a wrought-iron fence with their family crest woven into it.

Lucio: 'But I've been here before! When I was 13 I came here for our end-of-school party. I was at school with Mietta Baracchini. She was in my school class but not in my social class.'

Giorgio: 'She's still here. They used to be rich, but now they run an insurance company from the ground floor of their house.'

The door is opened by an office worker who phones upstairs and returns to a computer terminal in one of the front rooms. In the foyer, Lucio looks up a grand staircase to a ceiling with frescoes of Dante and his beloved Beatrice, somewhat obscured by washing on lines strung between third-floor doorways.

La Signora Mirella Baracchini, matriarch and oldest surviving member of the family, waves them to come upstairs and immediately begins reminiscing about the glory days with Giorgio, who winks at Lucio. She complains that nobody has respect any more. People have been stealing marble statues from the front garden, apparently lifting them over the fence with a crane late at night. 'There used to be four servants here all the time,' she says. 'They would have stopped the thieves.'

Giorgio reminds her that he used to sneak into her garden and hunt rabbits: 'You would come out on the balcony and shout "I know it's you, I'll tell your father".'

Mirella is talking about her father-in-law's First World War record and showing Giorgio the old man's sword when trim, blonde Mietta rushes in and kisses Lucio on both cheeks. He goes into another of his 'might have been' daydreams. Would Mietta and Lucio have become a couple if he'd been brave enough to pursue the relationship? And if so, would he now be one of those sad-looking people sitting in front of the terminals downstairs?

Mietta may be thinking along similar lines. 'So I hear you went away to Australia and became rich,' she says.

Lucio: 'I went to Australia but I didn't become rich. But I found the love of a good woman.'

Winemaker Giorgio and wife Vanda offer red mullet, *pasta alla contadina* (top right and bottom centre) and barbecued little birds (bottom right). Centre left and bottom left: the interior of Villa Baracchini.

'NON CONOBBERO

Mauro

Gino and Mauro are in a hole, although they are now calling themselves by the code names Ciccio and Merigo. It's dark down there. Also smelly, because it's a storage hole in which cow manure evolves into fertiliser. Merigo has a grenade in his hand. He has just pulled the pin and is holding his thumb on the safety lever. Above their heads they can hear the voices of German soldiers and the local Fascist militia known as *Maimorti* (never die).

One of the Fascists, Galli, has just shouted, 'If we catch Ciccio, I'll make sausages out of him'. He's attempting a joke based on Ciccio's background as a seller of meat, and on Galli's suspicion that Ciccio has been bringing food to the partisans who keep sabotaging the Germans from their encampments in the densely wooded hills behind Sarzana.

It was that joke which caused Merigo to pull the pin, reasoning that if Galli lifted the trapdoor, Merigo would have only a second to throw the grenade out and prevent the Fascists from shooting them.

Ciccio isn't sure this was such a wise strategy, but he's in no position to argue. He's wondering what the boys will do if the Fascists and Germans don't find them. Can you put the pin back into a hand grenade? And even if you can, how will they find the pin in the darkness? And how will Merigo get out of the hole without dropping the grenade?

The hole, in the backyard of a farmhouse in the village of Giucano, is one of many hiding places the partisans have made for themselves, and this is a time when hiding places are useful.

Ciccio and Merigo are on the run from a joint Nazi-Fascist operation called the *rastrellamento* – literally 'the raking'. Just after midnight on 29 November 1944, the ten German cannons at Punta Bianca started bombarding the top of the hills behind Sarzana to drive the partisans down towards the valley. At the same time, squads of German troops and Maimorti started moving up the hills to meet the descending partisans. As well as killing or capturing the men running down, the Germans set fire to the houses of anyone identified by the local Fascists as being sympathetic to the Resistance.

With 300 of their comrades killed, Merigo and Ciccio have made it as far as the bolthole, and are now waiting for the enemy to pass by – or be blown up.

How did Mauro Galletto get to this situation? We last encountered him as a 19-year-old boarding a train for Rome, where he was to join the Italian army. That was in 1943, the year everything changed.

Even Mussolini's supporters had doubts about his decision to enter the Second World War on Germany's side in 1940. They thought Italy could follow the example of Spain and Switzerland and stay neutral. Their doubts were confirmed when Italian troops suffered military disasters in Africa and Greece, when Allied troops landed in Sicily, and when German troops moved into northern Italy.

Mussolini kept conscripting every healthy young male he could find, even notorious troublemakers like Mauro, who learnt, on arrival in Rome, that he'd be getting three months' basic training in how to use weapons before being sent south to stop the Allied advance. As soon as he got his uniform, he had a photo taken, which he sent to his sweetheart Bruna, back in Liguria.

As he trained, he followed with fascination the political developments happening a couple of kilometres from his barracks. On 25 July, the Fascist Grand Council passed a resolution that Mussolini should resign as ruler of Italy, and that King Victor Emmanuel III should take on his powers.

Mussolini said this was meaningless, because the council was merely an advisory body, but when he went for his weekly meeting with the king the next day, Victor Emmanuel asked for his resignation and told him he had appointed an old soldier named Pietro Badoglio as prime minister. Outside the king's door, Mussolini realised he no longer enjoyed the support of the army when police bundled him into an ambulance and took him into 'protective custody' – which actually meant imprisonment in a mountain fortress south of Rome.

There were marches in Sarzana, Milan and Genoa that month to celebrate the fall of fascism, but the festivities were premature. Having removed Mussolini, King Victor Emmanuel and Prime Minister Badoglio proved less decisive in the ensuing weeks. Thousands of Italian troops were laying down their arms, but Badoglio announced that 'the war continues'. This was apparently designed to keep the Germans calm while Badoglio secretly negotiated terms of surrender with the Allies. Germany responded by pouring reinforcements into the Italian mainland.

On 8 September 1943, Badoglio announced he had signed an 'armistice', and told Italian soldiers to stop fighting. He gave no advice on what they should do about the Germans. He and the king fled Rome and ended up in Brindisi, on Italy's heel.

Two mornings later, Mauro Galletto and his fellow trainees woke to find their army base strangely quiet. Their officers had disappeared. With nobody in charge, and the war apparently over, Mauro decided to go home. Still in his uniform, he climbed on a train headed north, and eight hours later climbed off at Avenza di Carrara, the nearest stop to Sarzana. He was looking forward to seeing his family and his sweetheart.

But the platform was crowded with German soldiers, who grabbed Mauro and bundled him off to a holding camp at Marinella – the seaport from which Carrara's marble is shipped to the world. Mauro had not realised that his area was now under the control of the Germans. He was classified as a deserter.

This part of Italy was a disputed zone occupied by increasingly desperate German troops, helped by a small number of local Fascists who called themselves Brigate Nere (Black Brigades) or Maimorti. Because some members of the Italian army had joined the Allies in trying to take control of Rome, anyone in an Italian army uniform was now under suspicion. From the holding camp, Mauro would be shipped to a concentration camp in Germany. But an old friend of his father saw him being carted from the station, and bicycled immediately to Ca' Rósa to tell the family. They began to plan.

Security behind the barbed wire fence was lax, to say the least. One day, two ladies with square baskets on their heads came through the gate, bringing food to the prisoners. A short while later, two ladies with square baskets on their heads left the camp. The guards didn't notice that one of the ladies had become taller during her visit. Later, another bunch of ladies arrived for a visit, and left again. The guards didn't notice that one more came out than went in.

The two ladies who entered first were Mauro's aunt Angiolina and his cousin Nella. The two ladies who went out were Nella and Mauro himself, dressed in a long robe and headscarf that had been in the baskets under the food. His uniform was in the basket on his head. The extra lady who came out with the later group was brave Aunt Angiŏ.

Mauro made a quick visit to Bruna, where he got a kiss for good luck, and risked staying one night at Ca' Rósa, where his family gave him a change of clothes and a briefing on the local situation. 'Some of the old socialists are setting up camps up in the hills for escaped soldiers,' his father Giovanni told him. 'The Germans are in retreat. It won't be long before the Americans or the English get here, and then you can come back down.' It turned out to be 17 months.

Mauro found the partisans in a chestnut forest near the town of Fosdinovo. He was surprised at how well they were organised already. They called themselves the Garibaldi Brigade. Their commander, a university student who shared Mauro's surname – Galletto – told him to forget his own name, because from now on he would be known only by a *nome di battaglia* (battle name), which would be Merigo.

The commander was to be called Orti. If any of the group were captured and tortured, they'd only be able to reveal the code names of their comrades, so there couldn't be reprisals against families.

It was a good theory, Mauro thought, except for the fact that he'd been at school with half the guys in this brigade. But he quickly got into the Merigo habit.

Orti told his troops they were now, technically, at war with a country called the Italian Social Republic. The Germans had rescued Mussolini from his mountaintop prison and put him in charge of a puppet regime based in Salò, near Milan. In theory, the Repubblicca Sociale Italiana was the government of everything above Rome (a territory that kept shrinking as

In the summer of 1944, Mauro came down from the hills to meet Bruna at Ca' Rosa

the Allies pushed north). Merigo found himself part of a network of guerrilla fighters that stretched to Florence, Milan and Genoa, increasingly in radio contact with the Allies.

It was a tough winter, as the partisans began their program of sabotage against the Germans. Merigo became all too familiar with the various ways chestnuts could be rendered edible. He was fascinated by the way chestnut flour turned into pasta that was too soft and cakes that were too tough. But the local farmers provided more interesting food for the partisans whenever they could get past the Fascist spies.

One night Orti took his troops to a church where, he said, a partisan with the nome di battaglia of Ciccio was going to cook them a meal. This Ciccio had apparently been able to smuggle a calf up the hill and was going to roast it.

One glance at Ciccio, and Merigo burst out laughing. It was his brother-in-law Gino, whose nome di battaglia – which translates as 'chubby' – had clearly not been chosen at random. Ciccio was still running his gelateria and butchery down in Sarzana. Pedalling around on his carretto was proving to be a handy way of moving food and weapons across the countryside, and of observing troop movements. Once he'd even fitted an escaped prisoner inside it, and carried him past a line of Germans. Fortunately none of them thought to order an icecream that day.

Ciccio's charmed double life ended in May of 1944. On her way to open the shop one morning, Anna ran into a woman who lived near a local Fascist family. 'You better not open the shop today,' the woman whispered. 'They are going to smash it up. They know your husband is helping the partisans.'

Anna turned around and went home, collected her two-year-old daughter Graziella and her one-year-old son Mario, and drove their horse and cart up the hill to the village of Giucano, where she had some distant relatives. She and Ciccio didn't return to Sarzana for a year. Food was harder to come by up there, despite regular parachute drops by the British and Americans, but at least she was closer to her husband and her brother.

As 1944 proceeded and the partisans became more effective, the Germans began a policy of reprisals. The territory of Merigo's detachment was right on what the Germans called The Gothic Line, which was the point at which they had to stop the Allied advance, or give up their control of northern Italy. The Gothic Line started just south of Bocca di Magra and ran for 300 kilometres through the Carrara mountains, defended by 24 machine gun nests and thousands of land mines.

General Albert Kesselring (condemned to death as a war criminal in 1947 but never executed) issued an order that 'the normal rules of war' should not limit the task of controlling the partisan nuisance, and handed the problem to the SS. Anna kept hearing rumours about villages where ten innocent civilians were lined up and shot for every German killed as a result of guerrilla activity.

The Partisan Museum at Fosdinovo has a handwritten report of a meeting of leaders held on 21 August (when there were 100,000 partisans operating in northern Italy, of whom 20,000 were women). The meeting was certainly attended by Orti, and probably by Merigo. This letter, from a leader named Emilio, expressed the continuing dilemma of the guerrilla fighters:

> Elio's group attacked a German jeep, killed two Germans and wounded two. Afterwards the Germans killed eight civilians and burned houses at Castelpoggio.
>
> When we do an action near a village, we have to be ready to defend the women and children afterwards. Comrades, what idea will the population have if we leave them undefended? Every action we do must also have an answer in defending people. Let them leave the village and put themselves under our protection.
>
> It is necessary for the whole brigade to be mobilised when we act against Germans. Because the 50 Germans who participated in the burning of the village could have paid with their lives, instead of innocent civilians.

The museum filmed interviews with people who experienced the German occupation in 1944. These are the kinds of things they said:

- The Germans being the illegal occupiers of the country, they cannot claim the allegiance of the people. If the king had been stronger, the struggle would have been more effective. The Italian army could have been turned against the Germans. But the king did nothing.
- It took until January of 1944 to organise into proper fighting units. We had to start with weapons stolen from the Germans. The partisans had a kind of uniform, with green pants left over from the army and a red *fazzoletto* [scarf] for the communist brigades or a green scarf for the Catholic brigades. We stole boots from the army, or made boots out of raffia sometimes. We carried dried chestnuts for food. Everyone was saved by those chestnuts in the winter. And we put glue in the tree branches to catch the little birds.

Mauro and Bruna combined their wedding with Christmas festivities in 1946. Mauro's parents are on the right, his aunt and uncle on the left.

- One day my mother said, 'I'll put the testo on and you call them to eat'. She made testaroli for all the local partisans. Other houses would give them wine or cheese.
- The partisans kept good contact with the factory workers in La Spezia [the nearest industrial town], arranging for them to interrupt work on German projects. Every factory had a partisan cell to coordinate the disruption. People involved in strikes were deported to concentration camps in Germany, but there were other ways to slow down production.
- When the Fascists and the Germans came to the door, they'd say, 'We think you're feeding the partisans'. I'd say, 'How could I, I don't have enough for myself'.
- My girlfriend was in the barn, milking a cow. The Germans came, put her against the wall, and said, 'We count to ten. If you don't tell us where the partisans are, we will shoot.' She didn't know anything. In the end, they didn't kill anybody, but the entire village was burned down, even the church.
- The liberation was not just a political change, or the arrival of the Americans. It meant the reunification of families. People who had been away from each other for years came down from the mountains, back from the prison camps.

And so we come back to Merigo and Ciccio down the hole, the result of a German final solution to the Garibaldi brigades around Fosdinovo. Three hours went by before Ciccio dared to push up the trapdoor and see that the Germans had gone. Mauro's hand was paralysed around the grenade – he told his sons later that it took him a week to get his thumb working properly again.

But what they did with the grenade must remain a mystery. Although being trapped down the hole became a favourite story in both the Guelfi family and the Galletto family, neither is confident about the conclusion. Mario thinks they managed to find the pin and put it back into the grenade. Lucio assumes Mauro must have thrown the grenade as far as he could while the boys ran in the opposite direction.

In any case, they got away. Realising the detachments to which they belonged had been decimated, Merigo and Ciccio headed for Carrara, to join the Garibaldi brigade that was still operating there. Merigo managed a two-night stay at the home of Bruna's family on the way. While there, he proposed to Bruna. She said yes.

At 5 pm on 25 April 1945, the German SS General Karl Wolff agreed to end hostilities. On 27 April 1945, the 52nd Garibaldi Brigade, guarding a road along Lake Como, stopped and searched a group of departing Germans. Inside one armoured truck, wearing a German uniform, was Benito Mussolini, with his mistress Clara Petacci. On 28 April, Mussolini and Petacci were shot, and on 29 April their bodies were hung upside down in Piazzale Loreto in Milan – the square where 15 partisans had been executed by a Fascist reprisal squad in August 1944.

Just after Bruna's death in 2000, Aulo found a letter she had written for him and Lucio. She expresses her love for them and for Mauro, and says she wants them to know about what happened on 25 April 1945, 'The Day of Liberation':

The Germans were in retreat. As you know, we were living in Via Nerchia [on the outskirts of Sarzana] in the house of my Aunty Ro, sister of my father. At home there were myself, my mother, Aunty Fortuna, Uncle Tunin and their children Adriano and little baby Carla.

The Front was advancing and we were seeing the Germans going by on foot, not on the railway. My mother was saying 'Let's go and hide because when they are pushed out, they are very nasty and they could kill you.' We were locked in the house.

Then luckily when the Front finally arrived, it was your dad, other partisans, Americans and blacks. [The blacks would have been members of the US Army's 92nd infantry division, nicknamed the Buffalo Soldiers, of whom 15,000 had been dropped into Tuscany.]

It was like a circus, camped in front of the house next door. Boys, this is a thing I will never forget. We were engaged – good times! Dad came to see us with two black men, and then he took me back to where they were camped, and they really cheered a lot. And then they offered me some coffee, and guess where: in beer cans that I had never seen before. But I have to tell you that they gave me great respect.

From there the next day they left for Sarzana, where they stopped for a couple of days. Then they continued for Pontremoli, and there, dad finished his wanderings.

He came back home but then he got into the service of the Committee of Liberation for one year. And then he went back to normal life. So boys, I wanted to tell you so you will remember our times.

Before they found that letter, Aulo and Lucio already had a mental image of the day of liberation. Mauro had told them he arrived in Sarzana sitting on the cannon of an American tank, with the crowds cheering and his red scarf flying in the breeze. Then he wrapped the scarf around his partisan revolver, and put it away in a drawer, to show his children one day.

The war was over. Merigo was Mauro again. Ciccio decided he liked his battle name and stuck with it. Mauro and Bruna got married on 26 December 1946 – carefully timed to coincide with Christmas festivities. Ciccio had suggested they run away together, just as he and Anna had done, but they'd thought of a better way to save money.

In a referendum, the people voted to throw out the king. It was a new Italy, and all things were possible.

'SEMBRA CHE LA TRADIZIONE SIA IL FUTURO, QUI IN TOSCANA.'

Into Tuscany

Fausto Guardagni, tall and thin with a scraggly beard, is standing proudly in the middle of a marble-lined room that looks like a children's tomb. He is surrounded by small marble coffins. He lifts the lid of one and urges, in sepulchral tone, 'Put your finger in that – feel the cold'.

Lucio obeys, and encounters a brown slush that tastes very salty when he licks his finger. The 1-centimetre depth of slush, made of garlic, rosemary, oregano, pepper, salt, cloves and cinnamon, is preserving and flavouring Fausto's treasure: a product called *lardo*. Fausto is demonstrating how marble is the best possible material in which to marinate lardo for the nine months that is needed to mature it.

Lardo is fat from the back of a pig. Mario has driven Lucio deep into the mountains behind Carrara, past white quarries that have been making Rome magnificent for 2,000 years, to meet Fausto, who is a local legend. He put the tiny village of Colonnata on the map by fashioning a luxury item out of a substance that used to grease the bottom of the marble blocks so they could slide downhill. In health-conscious New York, they're paying a fortune for pig fat, because, marketed as 'the white prosciutto', it's the latest in 'peasant-chic'.

Fausto is aware of the irony, but he's devoted his life to producing the best possible lardo. The key to his success, he says, is that he's not using just any old pig fat. His raw material comes from a 'superpig' called the Cinta Senese, which eats acorns in the forests near Siena. 'It's a race of pig that had almost died out, but a group of farmers in Tuscany started breeding them again about 20

years ago, and I'm their best customer for the backs. I don't care what they do with the rest of the meat.' This superfat absorbs 'micro-energy' from the marble, which converts it into a more healthy comestible.

'Lardo has less cholesterol than butter and less calories than olive oil and it's no fattier than cheese,' says Fausto. 'The health authorities of the EC were worried that it might get bacteria, make you sick, but they've done all the tests and they find it's totally pure. That's because of the marble and the salt.'

Word is spreading. Recently Fausto won a prize in Sweden for a recipe which combined his lardo with reindeer meat. If the Swedes have discovered it, can Australia be far behind?

'If you want to taste lardo served with its proper relishes, go across the road to my daughter's place, Trattoria Apuana,' he recommends.

Mario and Lucio do that, find the fullness of the white fat is beautifully balanced by the sharpness of relishes made from mustard-soaked figs, juniper berries, apple, ginger, melon, pumpkin and ginger. They pronounce the lardo splendid, but they don't want to fill up because, unbeknownst to Fausto, they are due to lunch at the restaurant of his one-time rival in the lardo business, Venanzio.

Colonnata is a mist-shrouded village of grey three-storey buildings. In the middle is a one-storey grey building with a red awning. That is Venanzio, rumoured to be the best eating place in Carrara, if not the whole of Lunigiana. But the man who created that reputation (as well as starting the craze for lardo which Fausto inherited) is now retired at 67, and his former head waiter, Roberto Ferlini, is running the place, with the kitchen under the control of wife Bruna and a 26-year-old chef.

Lucio is worried that he might be in for another lonely experience alla Paracucchi, but he enters to a cosy buzz of sound and bumps into two Germans preparing to leave.

'Did you have a good time?' he asks in English.

'We had 18 courses – what do you call that?' says the man.

'A degustazione,' says Lucio.

'Yes,' says the German. 'It's the best meal we've had in Italy. We had two bottles of wine and two glasses of grappa each and now I'm going to drive down the hill.'

'Good luck,' says Lucio. 'We'll watch out for your car on our way down.'

Even though he is now the padrone, Roberto still wears the red waistcoat that marked him as a waiter, because he thinks Venanzio is there in spirit. He proudly points to a plaque which says, 'To Venanzio Vannucci, poet and interpreter of a sublime cooking, painter of the thousand colour shades, able to liberate flavours and perfumes symbolic of joy and life. Buon Italia.'

Asked to recommend some dishes that are typical of the area, he says, 'We try to use local ingredients in a refined way. We used to do more crude dishes – tripe, bean soup, pork skin, but the women at the table started to complain. Now we only do them for a couple of weeks in midwinter.'

Misty Colonnata, where Venanzio serves rolled rabbit topped with lardo.
The Colonnata shopkeepers proudly display the new fad in ancient eating.

The meal Roberto constructs combines gutsiness with lightness and tradition with adventure. He even gets it right when Lucio says he wants a dry white wine that is *fresco, giovanissimo* (fresh, very young). Candia dei Colli Apuani is the sort of stuff Michelangelo would have consumed with his sardines 600 years ago.

The meal starts with *carne in salamoia* – beef preserved in a marble *conca* (bath) in the same way as Fausto preserves lardo. It's tender and salty, accompanied by a cheese and vegetable flan, with carrots and zucchini. Then they move to eggplant parmigiana; *testa in cassetta* (a terrine of pig's head); a tartlet with onions, rice and deep green onion leaves; wide pappardelle noodles with sharp borage and porcini mushrooms; slices of beef in soy sauce with cauliflower; and rolls of rabbit wrapped in lardo so finely sliced it's translucent, with spiky herbs – oregano, onion leaves, fennel flowers.

Instead of dessert, they have a sheep's milk cheese called *pecorino di fossa*, which has been wrapped in straw and hessian and buried in the ground for six months to mature. Like Fausto's lardo, Roberto's pecorino has stirred the interest of the EC health authorities. 'They wanted us to bury the cheese in a sealed box,' says Roberto. 'What would be the point of burying it then? The idea is for it to taste of the earth. They don't understand the traditions. But they seem to have stopped bothering us now.'

After lunch, he leads Lucio and Mario out to the main square and introduces them, with slight inaccuracy, as 'chefs from Australia' to a bunch of grizzled *cavatori* (marble miners) who are sitting in the main piazza.

One of the quarrymen jumps up and says, 'I am Australian! Come and have a drink with me.' He tells them he spent ten years, between 1961 and 1971, looking for gold and opals in Australia. He made enough money there to buy his own quarry near Colonnata, which he worked for 20 years until the marble became useless. Now he's on a pension from Australia and a pension from Italy, which enables him to start drinking at 9 am.

Another glass of Candia makes Lucio glad that Mario is the one with the task of driving back down the narrow twisting roads, past trucks loaded with massive white blocks.

The quarries of Carrara

Mick's menu

IN THE EARLY 1500S, MICHELANGELO BUONARROTTI SPENT MANY MONTHS AROUND CARRARA. HE CHOSE BLOCKS OF MARBLE FOR THE TOMB OF POPE JULIUS II, DESIGNED A ROAD SYSTEM TO MAKE THE TRANSPORTATION OF THE BLOCKS SAFER, ARGUED WITH BOATMEN ABOUT THE COST OF SHIPPING THE MARBLE TO ROME AND WITH THE AREA'S DOMINANT MALASPINA FAMILY ABOUT TAXES THEY WANTED TO CHARGE, AND WROTE POETIC LINES SUCH AS 'THE FINEST ARTIST CAN'T CONCEIVE A THOUGHT/ THAT THE MARBLE ITSELF DOES NOT BIND/ WITHIN ITS SHELL, WAITING TO BE BROUGHT/ OUT BY THE HAND THAT SERVES THE ARTIST'S MIND'.

Michelangelo had a love-hate relationship with the place. In 1515, while in Rome, he wrote to his brother Buonarroto that he needed marble but didn't want to go to Carrara because 'whoever's not a cheat is a lunatic or a scoundrel'. Then, in 1518, he wrote to his brother: 'Oh cursed a thousand times are the day and hour when I left Carrara. It is the cause of my undoing, but I will return there soon.'

He also ate in Carrara, though not lavishly, because 'he was very frugal in his lifestyle, eating more out of necessity than enjoyment', according to a biography by his assistant Condivi.

To his friends in Rome and Florence, Michelangelo sent samples of Lunigiana wine, cheese, sausages, chickpeas, beans and chestnuts. He wrote shopping lists on the backs of any pieces of paper he found lying about, including frequent references to spinach, anchovies, salami, bread rolls, fennel, pasta and *minestre di farro* (which must have resembled the farro soup now served in Ciccio's). This was a time in history before the tomato had been brought to Italy from the Americas.

On the back of a letter he received in 1518, he scribbled what appear to be three menus, accompanied by doodles illustrating the items. This is what he wrote, in a mixture of dialect and loose spelling:

pani dua (which may be short for *pane d'uva*, literally 'bread of grape', a kind of fruit bread, or possibly just 'bread rolls two').
un *bochal dvino* (a jug of wine)
una aringa (a herring)
tortegli (a kind of ravioli).

una salata (one salad)
quartro pani (four bread rolls)
un *bochal di tondo* (a jug of wine)
e un *quartuccio di bruscho*
(and a quart of another wine)
un *piatello di spinaci* (a small plate of spinach)
quatro alice (four anchovies)
tortelli (tortellini)

sei pani (six bread rolls)
dua minestre di finochio (two fennel soups)
una aringa (one herring)
un *bochal di tondo.*

Your challenge now is to make an interesting meal using only those ingredients. Plus, of course, olive oil, 'the gold of Lunigiana', which Michelangelo didn't need to mention.

The man who makes the statues

CARRARA IS THE LARGEST PRODUCER OF MARBLE IN THE WORLD, SHIPPING 1.5 MILLION TONNES OF THE STUFF EVERY YEAR. ABOUT ONE PER CENT OF THE STONE PULLED OUT OF CARRARA'S 250 QUARRIES IS USED FOR SCULPTURES. AND IF YOU WANT TO GET A SCULPTURE DONE IN CARRARA, THE MAN TO SEE IS CARLO NICOLI. THIS IS WHAT HE TOLD LUCIO:

I buy 100 tonnes a year of white Carrara marble from the quarries, and I am the most important studio for model sculpture. People come from all over the world to work in marble here. The special white marble called *statuario* is more tender than normal Carrara white, has warmer colour, with crystals in it so it looks like grana cheese. It is ten to 20 times more expensive than normal white. But if the statue is to be installed outside, you use the normal Carrara white, because it is stronger. It can make sculptures as well as slabs for building.

Some sculptors work directly on the marble block, but sometimes the sculptor makes a model called a maquette, sends it to us and then we realise it full size in marble. We use a traditional way of realising sculptures through points, using huge compasses to scale up from the maquette.

Now some people say naively that this means the sculptor hasn't really done the work. The point is that if you are able to invent, to have a new idea, and after 50 years they still endure, it doesn't matter who did the realisation.

And then it is also a matter of how it is realised. You see so often these sculptures that have been made for cemeteries, from a little model. They have made a copy of a Pieta, and you see the head of the Madonna that is like a watermelon. That would not be a realisation from my laboratorio.

My family has been making sculptures in this laboratorio for more than 200 years. My great-grandfather Carlo made a Queen Victoria for the city of Bristol and a Gladstone for Parliament House in London. A brother of my grandfather was working for the Tsars in Moscow.

There is nowadays an environmental argument – the ecologists are saying we should not cut our mountains. But if we do not cut our mountains, we are like beggars. They want us to cut the marble from inside the mountains. But if we went inside the mountains, there is no light, no air and great danger of accidents. Outside quarries are much better.

Carrara has a great connection historically with the anarchists. The anarchists are my old friends, the descendants of the workmen of my grandfather. The quarry people, so far from the authorities, were individualistic. Before the war, there were not even any roads, just trails. The miners up there were ten hours on foot from any police, so they were obliged to do justice by themselves. It was a kind of self-control, self-education, a utopian way of thinking, but wild people.

My first purpose after the war was to keep alive the studio, and in this I succeed. Just after the war the marble was connected a little with fascism, so nobody wanted to use it and there was a problem selling it. Now the Americans, the Arabs, the Japanese love the marble and Carrara is still booming.

The Russians have come to us wanting somebody from Carrara to control all their quarries. The Greeks have reopened the quarries that existed 200 years before Christ. They taught the Romans how to do it and they want us to teach them.

I was born in 1931, but I still work every day. As a management task, it's hard, because I am dealing with anarchists, communists and artists. I love my work. I am like a young boy, going around in my racing car.

I am still designing new sculptures: I want to know why the Madonna has to be so totally unsexy? Caravaggio was making Madonnas sexy, so why not us? I will make a Madonna with nice breasts.

Mario remembers the cavatori coming to Ciccio's when he was a child. 'They'd get drunk and smash plates and glasses, then come back the next day, very apologetic and pay twice as much as the things were worth. So my father looked forward to their visits.'

In the centre of Carrara they visit the laboratorio of Mario's friend Carlo Nicoli, whose family has been carving marble into meaningful shapes on this spot for 200 years. Sculptors come from all over the world to work here, and most of them seem to leave their projects behind when they return home. The place is packed with half-finished vaguely religious statues, tall and short, wide and slim – but none of them achieve Nicoli's dream of one day doing 'a sexy Madonna' (as in the mother of Christ, not the singer).

The quarry where Michelangelo sourced most of his marble

DAY TWO

Lucio drives back to Carrara the next morning to meet Alma-Vittoria Cordiviola, a local historian who specialises in food. Years ago, Lucio bought a book of Lunigiana recipes Mrs Cordiviola had collected, so he's confident she'll have useful background for him. Mario has told him her father was a local communist leader, and the commander of a partisan brigade in Carrara.

Mrs Cordiviola and her husband run a fruit shop in one of Carrara's oldest streets, but she's out when Lucio arrives, so he goes to wait in a tiny wine bar next door.

It's called Da Sainé (dialect for 'if there's any'), and its customers are proof of the proposition advanced by the quarryman in Colonnata that cavatori start drinking at 9 am. Four high-spirited leathery men are sitting at a low table playing cards, with a half-empty flask of pale yellow wine between them. On the wooden wall behind them is an ancient clipping from a magazine, showing Sophia Loren with no shirt on.

Lucio compliments the burly man behind the counter on the delicious smell in the room, who replies, 'Thank you, my wife has just made *baccalà* [marinated salt cod].

Would you like some?' One of the card players says, 'Have it, have it. It's very spicy. We like it because it makes us drink more.'

Lucio hasn't breakfasted yet, so he tries it and agrees it tastes as good as it smells. When he pops back into Mrs Cordiviola's shop, he mentions the hospitality of the people next door, and she says she has written a poem about the place.

It's in Carrara dialect, full of scratchy sounds to Lucio's ear, but with agreeable sentiments:

If you happen by Via al Plebiscito around 6 pm, you'll be hit by the smell of baccalà fritters. It makes your mouth water. It is Giovanna of Sainé who is frying them beautifully hot in the kitchen. You go down two steps and find a typical Carrara cantina. The floor is white slabs, genuine evidence of history.

Here you find also wine of Moneta, rough and good. The people speak the pure dialect because they were born here. And around the tables men play briscola and pour themselves a glass of wine. Then suddenly Alfio, called The Baron, starts singing a folk song.

Every now and then you see certain people who want to dive into the real Carrara – the place of the people and of the workers. And eating tajarin and baccalà they find that atmosphere of simplicity that is so good for the heart.

This is how the Carrara dialect looks when transcribed: '*Ke bele kalde a de a friz'rle'n kuzina T'send do skalin e t'trov la tipika kantina kararina.*'

Mrs Cordiviola views her shop as part of her history studies. She tries to sell mostly produce that is native to Lunigiana. She points out that *fava* (broad beans) and *fagioli dall'occhio* – little beans with a black spot like an eye – originated there.

Lucio says they remind him of his childhood, when fava beans were 'the gift of spring', the first sign that good things were about to rise again. 'Fava beans with pecorino, or just with olive oil, was one of the pleasures of spring that we looked forward to in our house,' he says.

Mrs Cordiviola agrees: 'To have things out of season, as we do these days, takes something out of life. A sense of celebration is gone.

'But I think we're getting it back in Italy now. I go around the schools talking about the history of our food, and I teach the tourist guides. We went mad for this idea of progress and being modern in the 1960s and 1970s, and Italy wanted to copy the Americans. But people are coming to see value in our traditions.'

Lucio remembers his father, in the mid-1960s, installing an 'American kitchen' with formica tabletops in their house. But Bruna made him put the old marble slab over the formica. *She* knew modernisation was a passing fad.

Lucio tells Mrs Cordiviola about his recent conversation at Luni, where the guide Sara referred to the Liguri-Apuani as 'my race'. Mrs Cordiviola turns out to be another Liguri-lover.

'I have *dente avvelenato* [poison fangs] against the Romans because of what they did to those people,' she says. 'They made them slaves in the quarries. The city of Rome was built on their blood.'

The Carrara wine bar called 'If there's any', which displays Sophia Loren's interpretation of Cleopatra

She portrays the Liguri-Apuani as blond, blue-eyed and democratic – the women fought alongside the men and everyone shared the land and had a say in the running of the tribe. She sees their way of life as an early form of communism – in the idealised form, not the corrupted twentieth-century form. She has written a poem about a woman called Apua, who personifies their virtues.

'The Roman historian Livio described the Liguri-Apuani as *durum in armis genus* (hard in arms people), but they were simply protecting their independence,' she says. 'They were shepherds and grain growers. Around every village were plantations of vegetables and cereals. They worshipped forces of nature – springs, rivers, mountains, animals and stars.'

She talks with such passionate eloquence that Lucio thinks, 'If I were 20 years older, I could fall in love with this woman'. He wonders if the people she's discussing were Galli, who came originally from France. He's always assumed his own background was Gallic, because of his name. The word Galli is translated into English as 'Gauls', but it literally means 'chicken people', bestowed by the Romans presumably because of the tribe's eating habits.

'I don't think they were the same as the Galli,' says Mrs Cordiviola. 'We do know they were in the area for at least 200,000 years before the Romans arrived, because they left traces in caves. Liguri-Apuani was the Romans' name for them. We don't know what the tribe called itself because their only writings are inscriptions on the stone statues they left behind.'

Ah, the spooky sandstone statues, known in the area as *stele* (pronounced stell-eh). Some of them are 5,000 years old, but most of them were only discovered in the

Alma Vittoria Cordiviola in her shop; the fish market at Viareggio

twentieth century. They look like something Erich von Daniken, author of *Chariots of the Gods*, would have used to justify his theory of frequent alien visitations.

Mrs Cordiviola urges Lucio to go into the mountains, to Pontremoli, where the stele have been put on display in the old castle. He'll do it.

Mrs Cordiviola adds another layer to the mystery of how Luna got its name. It may not have been derived from the Roman word for moon or the Etruscan word for port, but from the Liguri word for swamp – *lugna*. Could they have been so far-sighted about the ultimate fate of the city by the bay?

DAY THREE

Fausto's lardo stories have made Lucio curious to see the ancient race of superpig that produces fat of such wonderful flavour. He decides to make the journey to Siena to meet one of the farmers who are bringing Italian food back to its origins. He'll coincide that with a visit to the family who will be looking after his teenage daughter Michela later in the year in a student exchange program. They make wine in the Chianti region, so that will be instructive too.

On the way he drives along the Tuscan resort coast called Versilia, which is lined with seedy-looking nightclubs and restaurants catering to the summer sunbakers. He stops for lunch at the grand Ristorante Lorenzo in Forte dei Marmi, which is a shopping resort town for the richest Tuscans. The footpaths are red, and the shops near Lorenzo are full of leather jackets and leopardskin pants.

Lorenzo Viani is a hero of the glossy food magazines, specialising in seafood no other restaurant seems able to source, and quoted as saying, 'Fish have 24 virtues and each hour that passes, they lose one'. As Lucio sits down at 12.30 pm, a tall, dignified man in a tweed jacket is walking around the restaurant clapping his hands. Lucio realises it is Lorenzo Viani himself, and that he is killing mosquitoes.

The service is excessive – three waiters in black hover constantly, with Lorenzo giving a running commentary on their inadequacies. The place is expensive – 18 euros for an appetiser of four slices of lardo (made by Venanzio).

But amongst pretentious dishes such as *soufflé di fagioli di sorana con scampi e fonduta di zucca* (soufflé of beans with scampi and pumpkin cream), the meal includes the best fritto misto Lucio has ever eaten. Feeling as if he's betraying his mother, Lucio must admit that somehow Lorenzo has got the dusting of flour and the temperature of the oil just right. Does this justify a price of 35 euros for a dish called *La Nostra Frittura*? In Forte dei Marmi, it's actually quite reasonable.

Further south, Lucio drops in on Mario's nephew Filippo, who works with a seafood distributor based at the fish markets in Viareggio. The afternoon market is underway. The fishermen have laid out their silver catches, some still wriggling, in polystyrene boxes. Assorted distributors and restaurateurs are giving their bids, in soft, measured tones, to an apronned official with pencil and pad.

Filippo says proudly that he has inherited Registered Buyer Number 2, which was allocated to his grandfather Ciccio when Viareggio markets first opened in the 1950s. Lucio mentions the Lorenzo lunch to Filippo, who responds: 'We supply him! You know he used to be a customer at Ciccio's before he opened his place? He's so fussy, we fight all the time. Lorenzo says he's never going to use us again, then he's on the phone three days later, saying "What have you got?" '

Lucio is playful: 'Ah, so your best seafood goes to Lorenzo, not to Ciccio's?'

Filippo: 'No, no, the first selection always goes to Mario. That's family.'

Lucio steers inland, and hits red-washed Siena about 5 pm. He's been told he needs to see the artworks inside Siena Town Hall, particularly a 900-year-old mural called 'La vita in campagna'. Up many stairs, he finds it: a scene of beautifully dressed noblefolk riding out the castle gates to go hunting while a peasant in grey rags wearily prods a pig up the hill towards them. The pig is black but seems to be wearing a white corset. That is the 'Siena belt' that gives the pig its name. Tomorrow Lucio will see the real thing, along with the peasant who prods it uphill these days.

He steps back out into the main *campo* (square) of Siena and remembers when he brought Sally to see the *palio* (bareback horserace), which is held every 2 July and 16 August. The race lasts about a minute, but for thousands of Sienese the rest of the year is spent in preparation.

Siena is divided into 17 competing districts called *contradas*, symbolised by animal statues in their streets. For the race, each contrada is assigned a horse, which is pampered, protected and trained until race day. Contradas spend a fortune hiring jockeys (and bribing competing jockeys to go slow). The weeks before the races are filled with increasingly frenzied festivities in the streets. The Palio is a banner that is given to the winning horse and displayed in the contrada's clubhouse until the following year's race.

Lucio heads out of town for dinner at the farmhouse of the Sderci family, who will be

Following page: Siena, and its belltower from the courtyard of its town hall.

It's an illustrious neighbourhood: Leonardo painted the Mona Lisa near here, Machiavelli wrote 'The Prince', and Galileo made wine.

The Chianti renaissance

CHIANTI GOT A BAD NAME IN THE 1960S WHEN A CHEAP VERSION WAS EXPORTED AROUND THE WORLD IN LITRE FLASKS WITH BASES MADE OF STRAW (OR FAKE STRAW). IT BECAME SYNONYMOUS WITH THE CLICHÉ TRATTORIA SERVING SOGGY SPAGHETTI, TOUGH VEAL AND FOSSILISED GELATO. (THE ITALIAN WORD FOR FLASK IS *FIASCO*, AND ITS TENDENCY TO FALL OVER BROUGHT IT INTO ENGLISH AS A SYNONYM FOR EMBARRASSING FAILURE.) THE SDERCI FAMILY IS TRYING TO BRING CHIANTI BACK TO ITS GLORY DAYS.

The style was defined in the middle of the nineteenth century by the 'iron baron' Bettino Ricasoli, whose family had been making wine for more than 600 years. His lesser claim to fame was being the second prime minister of newly united Italy (after Cavour, whom we'll meet later). His greater claim comes from specifying the formula for the perfect Italian red.

It must have 70 per cent sangiovese grapes, for body; 15 per cent canaiolo nero grapes for softness; and 15 per cent white malvasia grapes, to lighten the colour. In the 1920s, 33 winemakers in the Chianti area got together and agreed that wines which met that formula should signal their perfection by putting a black rooster symbol on the label and calling themselves 'Chianti Classico'.

The rooster was a significant player in a legend from the thirteenth century, when Florence and Siena were perpetually at war. During a brief period of peace, they agreed on a method for settling the issue of where each city's territory ended. Each town would appoint a rider, who would wait until the first cock-crow on a particular morning and then ride as fast as possible towards the rival city. The spot where the southbound Florentine horseman met the northbound Sienese horseman would mark the borderline.

The Sienese claim that the Florentines cheated by lighting candles to trick their rooster into crowing early, while the Sienese allowed dawn to wake their bird naturally. Thus the black rooster symbolises the honesty of the Sienese winemaker.

Allessandro Sderci doesn't put his wine in fiascos. He uses serious Bordeaux style bottles (with 'shoulders') and a dignified label, with the rooster discreetly visible in a band around the bottle's neck. His brand name is Il Palazzino.

Nowadays the rules for chianti classico have loosened a little. It must be mostly sangiovese and it should have some canaiolo, but there's a 5 per cent latitude which some revolutionary winemakers are filling with the French (and Australian) favourite, cabernet sauvignon, which adds a little bite to the wine. Lucio remarks that the Sderci's medal-winner does have a slightly Australian taste to it. They'll make a red drinker of him yet.

hosts to his daughter. The Sderci parents work for the main bank in Siena, where they have a townhouse, and in their spare time make wine on their farm just north of town. It's an illustrious neighbourhood. Leonardo da Vinci painted the Mona Lisa here; Michelangelo's family came from here; Machiavelli wrote *The Prince* here; and Galileo made wine here.

The Sdercis serve excellent veal cutlets and report modestly that their chianti recently managed to gain the maximum 'three glasses' award from the Gambero Rosso wine guide. They explain that there are strict rules about any wine that calls itself Chianti classico.

The Sdercis ask Lucio about his restaurant, and when he says it displays paintings by Australian artists, Mrs Sderci asks suddenly: 'Do you know a man named Edmund Capon?' Out of context, Lucio has trouble placing the name, and then says, 'The guy who runs the Art Gallery of New South Wales?'

'Yes,' says Andrea Sderci, 'I met him the other day. He wants our Caravaggio.' 'You have a Caravaggio?' asks Lucio, increasingly confused. 'The bank has, and he wants to show it in Sydney. It will be a big insurance problem, but we'll try to help.' It develops that Mrs Sderci runs the bank's art department, which owns many paintings of which the Caravaggio is the most valuable.

Alessandro Sderci takes Lucio outside in the rain to see the grapes he uses for his sweet sherry style wine called Vin Santo. They are tiny and shrivelled and covered with white mould, hanging off wooden pillars in a shed. The mould is what gives the grapes the intensity of flavour that makes the wine worth 100 euros for half a litre. The cold and damp makes Lucio appreciate the flavour all the more when he gets back inside. Unfortunately he can't order it for his restaurant. The Sdercis make so little Vin Santo that their bottles barely travel beyond their home town, which Lucio finds perversely pleasing. He's glad we're not yet in the kind of world where everything is available everywhere. For some things, you must come to Siena.

It's hard to imagine a better life than that of the Sdercis — a thirteenth-century house in Siena, an award-winning vineyard in Chianti, and the opportunity to look at a Caravaggio whenever they feel like it. Lucio muses that not only will he be happy to swap children with the Sderci family, he wouldn't mind swapping lives with them for a while. But he wonders how this refined family would function in Australia.

DAY FOUR

The next morning, Lucio is off to see the superpig. On the phone, farmer Nicola Zanda is frustratingly vague with directions, naming villages which do not appear on Lucio's map, when all Lucio wants to know initially is how to get out of Siena. It's almost as if Nicola hasn't heard of Siena, leaving Lucio with a mental image of a rustic yokel wallowing in campanilismo. But as he comes close to the pigfarming area, Ville di Corsana, and Nicola says just to look out for *la villa gialla* (the yellow mansion), suddenly Lucio realises he has found another aristocrat.

He pulls into the pebbled courtyard of a four-storey mansion surrounded by forested slopes. Nicola Zanda proves to be a tall, handsome Tuscan in his early thirties, with an equally handsome wife who is a doctor at Siena hospital, and two angelic children.

The superpig

NICOLA ZANDA, PRESIDENT OF THE CINTA SENESE FARMER SOCIETY: 'CINTA SENESE WAS THE STANDARD PIG OF THIS AREA 100 YEARS AGO, BUT THE RACE ALMOST DISAPPEARED, BECAUSE IN THE 1960S THE FARMERS ABANDONED THE BREEDING. IT WASN'T COMPETITIVE WITH NORTHERN EUROPEAN PIGS, WHICH WERE MUCH LEANER AND MUCH FASTER GROWING.'

'People in Italy were earning more money, leaving the peasant life, and they wanted more meat, so everything had to go into mass production. The large white pigs can be ready in eight months, while the Cinta Senese needs 15 to 18 months to reach the right size. And the white pigs produce twice as many babies as the Cinta.

'The meat producers wanted to make cheaper, cheaper, cheaper, but the quality was worse, worse, worse.

'I started in 1997, from no knowledge. I read about the disappearance of the race and I thought this was a project I could undertake. I had inherited 100 hectares of forest, which my family had owned since 1939, but forest brings no income. The pigs could walk in the wood and eat acorns. They don't need much care because they are stronger than the mass production ones. They can live outside the whole year, through rain, snow, heat.

'I found one farmer who had nine sows, then I went in search of boars that were not too closely related to them, and I started my whole business from them. Now I have 200. There are about 160 farmers breeding them in all Tuscany and 700 pigs recorded in our local register as having the white belt and white feet, and being able to reproduce.

'I get up at ten to six each day, do some office work, take my two children to kindergarten, feed the animals, go around and check the fences, look for sows who might be giving birth – they have about 15 babies in two years.

'Every second Monday we kill a pig and turn it into lardo, prosciutto, salami and sausages. I like it because it connects me to history. It's a laboratory where I am experimenting. I have invested a lot but it's a lovely way to play. Instead of doing what everyone else does, for money, we are finding our local way to survive.

'Now that New York has discovered this delicacy, our problem is the demand. We have to protect it from people who want to lower the standard. Fausto feels the same way. So our *consorzio* (consortium) will do an exclusive deal with Fausto's lardo-making consorzio. I would say that tradition is the future here in Tuscany.'

Lucio knows he would not want to swap lives with Nicola Zanda. 'I admire what he's doing,' he says, 'but for me, there would be no joy there. It looks like a rather lonely life. It's nice to see the faces of the people who receive your work.'

Above, Nicola Zanda and his Cinta Senese; opposite, the fish soup, risotto, and classic menu at La Mora, near Lucca.

After introducing his family, Nicola says, 'But you're here to see the pig,' and, walking round to the back of the villa, makes a kind of warbling sound in his throat. A plump black and white porker trots up the hill to see why she's being called when it's not feeding time. Lucio is looking at both the past and the future of authenticity in the Italian food supply.

The Italian dream, at least in the 1950s, was to move in two generations from a peasant life to urban wealth. Nicola did the opposite. His grandfather ran an engineering company which built bridges all around the world. His father was a professor of medicine at Siena University. And Nicola raises pigs.

His family had him lined up to go into the diplomatic corps, the classic career of the Tuscan aristocrat, but Nicola decided he'd rather save a race of black-and-white pigs that were about to become extinct.

His curiosity coincided with a social movement towards authenticity and flavour. 'People appreciate that this pig has something new for them – fat which is *gradevolissimo* – very pleasant.'

Lucio asks: 'And also healthy?'

Nicola laughs. 'Well, it's a luxury, like wine. You don't have to eat it every day.'

On the way back to Bocca, Lucio drops into the red-walled town of Lucca, which once controlled the whole of Lunigiana. He checks out the Holy Face statue in the church there, notes that it is more dramatic than the one that washed ashore at Bocca, and visits the highly recommended La Mora restaurant for lunch.

La Mora could best be described as 'modified modern' in style. Lucio finds the *cacciucco* made with freshwater fish to be beautiful but bland, thinks the rare pieces of pigeon with the risotto are a French affectation, and finds the meticulous but aloof service typically Tuscan. He suspects his next destination – the region of Emilia–Romagna – will be more exciting. They're all food fanatics up there.

Lucio finds the cacciucco made with freshwater fish beautiful but bland, and the rare pigeon a French affectation.

CA C'È
STA
Ciccio..

Ciccio Guelfi loved to surprise people, even shock them. His children Mario and Graziella remember coming home from school one afternoon and finding 16 sheep in their apartment, and a teepee pitched in the hallway. Ciccio had borrowed the sheep from a farmer friend so the family could play cowboys and Indians. And when their baby sister Rosi was born, Ciccio smashed one of the panes in a window and told them that was where the stork had come in. Life with Ciccio was constantly hilarious.

But the surprise he pulled on the residents of Bocca di Magra in 1952 came close to ruining him. With the help of Mauro Galletto, he'd added a dance floor to the gelateria they built on the patch of sand where the river entered the sea. For the first few Saturday nights he played records, with Mario acting as disc jockey, but now he'd hired a small band. And when the dressed-up crowd got off the bus from Sarzana, some of them found the piano player disturbingly familiar. It was Galli, once the most enthusiastic Fascist in the neighbourhood – the same Galli who had led the Germans in pursuit of Ciccio and Mauro on the night after the rastrellamento.

This was an outrage.

Graziella: 'It was a strong issue for him to have a Maimorto working there. Many people were angry and they complained. But Ciccio said it was an evolution of the times, you must forgive and forget, you must allow people the opportunity to change themselves.

'In any case, he said, Galli had been all talk. He never killed anybody personally. If he'd been as bad as people say, he would have been taken out in one of the revenge killings that went on through 1946.

'After a while it became accepted, even a point of interest for the place: the Fascist playing the piano, the partisan doing the cooking. Nobody would speak to him, but at least they would dance to his piano.'

One of the fishing families had a vegetable garden they weren't using, right on the river bank. It was the perfect size for a gelato stand.

It was a testament to the reputation Ciccio had built up, both as a cook and as an entertainer, that he got away with it. But we're ahead of ourselves again. We need to explain how the Guelfi family and the Galletto family came to be in Bocca di Magra in the first place.

The war ended. The main square of Sarzana changed its name to Piazza Matteotti, in honour of a murdered socialist hero, and on that square, Anna went back to running a gelateria, increasingly helped by first-born daughter Graziella.

Mauro and Ciccio became travelling salesmen – well, Ciccio did the selling, Mauro did the lifting. They drove their horse and cart all around Lunigiana, buying cheese, sausages, wine, even soap, in one valley, selling them in another. They travelled along the old Via Francigena through the Cisa Pass, as merchants had been doing for a thousand years. The sight of tall, thin Mauro and short, round Ciccio setting up their stall became a pleasantly anticipated break in the monotony of life in many a mountain village.

Mario: 'My father and Lucio's father would go into the mountains and over to Parma to buy cheese. My father was the best in Italy at tapping the cheese with a little hammer called an *orecchio* to see if there were air pockets. Their market stall became famous for the best cheeses.

'I remember the day the horse died, near the town hall of Sarzana. It fell down, and Mauro was crying, trying to get the horse up, saying "Come on, come on". My father took me away so I didn't see, because they had to kill the horse. They changed then to a three-wheeled Vespa with a cart behind, which was not much faster than the horse and cart.

'We had a seven-bedroom apartment overlooking Piazza Matteotti, and it was always crowded. My grandmother lived there with us. She was always crying about how the family used to have money but her brother gambled it away. There was a medical student renting one room, and I would charge my schoolfriends to see the skeleton he had hanging up. One toilet, just a hole in the floor, and we took our baths in the kitchen.

'Ciccio kept bringing people in. He felt sorry for a homeless man called Gaetano, who had fought at the Russian front, and he came to live with us. Gaetano learnt to make gelato and became the best gelato-maker in the area. Fishermen used to come to the door with their catch, and Ciccio would always invite them in for a conversation.

Ciccio's, advertised on the road entering Bocca di Magra, became the favourite spot for wedding receptions. Above, Ciccio's daughter Giovanna, Lucio's mother Bruna, and the maestro serve a midsummer dinner.

'At night it was like a restaurant. Ciccio would cook these huge meals, and they were served on a long table in the hallway, which was about 4 metres wide. My father was selling tripe and horsemeat at the time. After the war they gave it to many boys because it was rich in iron. What he didn't sell, we would eat. I didn't like horsemeat. It tasted too sweet.

'It was a crazy atmosphere. There was always something going on in the piazza. In 1947, the coalminers rioted there because the owners wanted to close the mine. They overturned a police jeep and then ran upstairs to our apartment. The police were firing tear gas to try to get them out. The MSI [neo-Fascists] would try to give speeches, but they had to have 200 police with them because people wanted to stop them.'

They were cheerful times, as Italy slowly turned an economic recovery into an economic boom. But in 1950 two factors combined to push Ciccio and Anna out of Sarzana. The landlord of the gelateria wanted to sell it to some people who were going to set up the Marco Polo travel agency. And seven-year-old Mario had developed a nasty wheeze, which these days would probably be diagnosed as asthma. The doctor's only advice was that he might be helped by sea air.

The village of Bocca di Magra at that time contained about ten houses and a small hotel called Sans Façon, which had started in the nineteenth century as a lodging for French workers digging out sand for use in the expansion of Nice.

Local folklore has it that the hotel got its name in the 1850s after the owner, Luigi Germi, improvised a meal of grilled mullet, over which he squeezed unripe grapes because he didn't have any lemon. Some visiting French sailors admired the way he'd done it *sans façon* (without fuss). A French chef would have made it more complicated. Germi adopted the compliment as the name of his hotel. Some 70 years later Germi's grandson became the ferryman on the Magra, and set up a trattoria named after his job – Il Pilota – across the river from the hotel.

The village had become a summer haven for impoverished writers in search of silence and inspiration from nature.

Anna liked Bocca di Magra because, when she was a teenager, she used to bicycle over there to visit a cousin. Ciccio liked it because his friends the fishermen would unload their catches there. And one of the fishing families had a vegetable garden they weren't using, right on the river bank. It was the perfect size for a gelato stand.

A small problem arose when Ciccio applied for a licence to run a café there. A year earlier he had spent three months in jail for failing to pay his taxes, so he was not allowed to put his name on a new business. Mauro said: 'Why don't you put the place in our name?' So officially, the founder of Capannina Ciccio was Bruna Martini. They opened on 3 May 1951 – the feast day of Santa Croce, calling it initially *La Capanna di Ciccio* (the hut of Chubby) but soon changing that to the diminutive 'capannina', which means 'cute little hut'.

Ciccio became a pillar of the Bocca di Magra community, catering for every festivity, while Mario, Graziella and Giovanna grew up on the beach and on the river.

Even on the nights when there was no music, there was always the theatre of Ciccio, experimenting with new dishes and convincing the customers to try them.

From left, Graziella, Rosi, Aulo, Mario and Giovanna on the river, where, opposite, the fishermen caught the specials of the day for Ciccio.

Mauro built some low brick walls and a roof of canes supported by old telegraph poles. Ciccio and Anna constructed a menu based on the kind of seafood they used to make at home. They stuck hand-painted signs on the telegraph poles saying 'Specialità cacciucco, pesce fritto, spaghetti con frutti di mare.'

The family was surprised at how quickly the place took off that summer.

Mario: 'Three buses a day stopped at Bocca di Magra, bringing tourists to the beach from around Sarzana and Ameglia. When the bus drove away, there'd be 100 people waiting for icecream. Then in the afternoon they'd come back for fish soup. For a lot of that summer we slept in the place. Then in the winter we went back to Sarzana and sold cheese.'

They began by cooking over flames from two gas bottles, but soon expanded into a smooth operation wherein Anna was on pasta and fish soup, Bruna was on frying and *insalatina* (poached seafood salad) and Ciccio was on main course, grilling, and risotto. Two of Mario's aunts would clean all the fish before lunch and wash up after lunch.

Ciccio and Graziella's boyfriend Giuseppe took orders, one course at a time. Service involved simply asking, 'Do you want antipasto [steamed mussels, sea dates, or sea snails, according to what the fishermen produced that morning]? Do you want spaghetti? What fish do you want?' and then telling the kitchen. There was never a docket. Ciccio would estimate a price at the end of the meal and tell the table, then put the cash in a wooden box.

Ciccio decided to add entertainment on Friday and Saturday nights, and after the small hiccup of community reaction to Galli on piano, that was a huge success. Even on the nights when there was no music, there was always the theatre of Ciccio experimenting with new dishes and convincing the customers to try them.

After three years, he had a serious talk with his son.

Mario: 'I wasn't happy at school. I think I had what they would now call dyslexia – trouble reading, but if you told me something, I could remember every detail. My father said, "If you're not going to work at school, you have to come and work with me". So I started doing the bar in the summer and helping at the market stall in the winter. My father bought a beautiful car which the police had confiscated from a cigarette smuggler,

The garlic and parsley was for Ciccio's soffritto, the base of his sauces.
Sometimes he'd wipe a bundle of herbs called 'a mazzetto odoroso' through the oil.

The writers of Bocca di Magra

THE WRITERS CAME TO BOCCA DI MAGRA LONG BEFORE CICCIO GUELFI, BUT HE GAVE THEM A PLACE TO DRINK. THE FIRST TO CELEBRATE ITS PLEASURES WAS THE GENOESE POET AND ESSAYIST EUGENIO MONTALE. WHEN HE WAS THERE IN THE 1940s, IT WAS JUST 'FOUR HOUSES AND A SMALL HOTEL'. TO EAT, YOU HAD TO GET THE BOATMAN TO ROW YOU ACROSS THE RIVER TO A TRATTORIA CALLED IL PILOTA.

Montale wrote about a couple who took a train to Sarzana late in 1943:

> They got there between one air raid alarm and the next, rented a horsecart that took them to Sans Façon, the famous host of Bocca di Magra, on the elbow of the river. In a one-storey house, a pink cube of four rooms, they wanted to celebrate the end of the dictatorship and the start of a new life. The Magra was very meagre that year, the horse was malnourished, the road was terrible, they argued with the driver over money.

Vittorio Sereni, who had a house on Via Fabricotti, wrote in 1951:

> The passage across the river was like making an important decision, a ritual, a spell, almost like passing from one world to another. If you stayed at Sans Façon, you had to row across to go dancing at Il Pilota. A little gossip: [the novelist] Elio Vittorini didn't like the dance music from across the river. It spoiled his concentration. Intellectuals went late to dance when the mob had left.

Sereni's poem 'Un Posto di Vacanza' (A place of holidays) was published the year Ciccio's opened. (Lucio remembers Sereni in later years as 'a tiny smiling gentle man, riding his bicycle to the restaurant, who came mostly for gelato or a slice of prosciutto when it arrived from Parma'.)

The novelist Luciano Bianciardi wrote in 1960:

> This year I had a fine holiday in a place where intellectuals of the Left gather. It's on the mouth of the river that marks the border between two very civilised Italian regions, having taken the best from each of them. It's of a measured beauty – tidy, a bit tart.
>
> At the beginning of the Fascist period they used to go to the beaches further south but then, disgusted by the crowds of butchers and bureaucrats (salumai e federali) that were invading those sites, they migrated north until they found the river and the mountain.

Before then, it was a site where a few fishermen were living, and some contadini had little vegetable gardens. The intellectuals used to camp in a few houses, sleep on a few sacks. Because there was no running water, they used to wash in the public fountain or not at all. Life was tranquil. Sometimes they went fishing or sunbaking naked between the canes along the river.

We got up early and stayed on the balcony to look at clouds and guess how long the sun would take to rise. Then at one o'clock we ate mussels.

The poet Zeno Birolli offered this description of Ciccio's in the late 1950s:

> It has a feeling of festive tranquillity. Regardless of age, name, or wealth, everyone dissolves into this atmosphere, becoming one family. When the television shut down for the night, the writers would come to play chess and talk. Before dawn, the fishermen would come down to their boats, see us there and say 'what are you doing still up? Go home.'

In the early 1960s, the writers formed an activist group called 'Friends of Bocca di Magra' to protect it from property speculation and over-development. They met in Ciccio's and drafted zoning regulations to guarantee green in the landscape. Hundreds of writers and politicians ultimately joined, and they won most of their battles.

They invented a joke marching song, along the lines of the French anthem 'La Marseillaise', which began 'Orsú amici in folta schiera, defendiamo la scogliera':

> Come on friends in tight formation, let us defend the shoreline. Let us loudly oppose the greedy speculator who subdivides and cuts and takes away … Let's defend from every evil the natural habitat, so beautiful and rich and varied. Superior minds and sincere hearts, come on friends it's our duty to defend Bocca.

and we would drive up to Parma to buy prosciutto. He was the first in Bocca di Magra to have a car like that.'

Ciccio liked being the innovator. He started renting out deckchairs and umbrellas to people who wanted to sit on the beach. He installed the first telephone in Bocca di Magra. There was a booth in the bar, where locals could arrange to make or receive calls. If the phone rang for somebody in the village, Mario or Aulo would be sent running to fetch them.

In 1956, the year after television came to Italy, Ciccio installed a set in the bar, and found that every night the locals would bring their own chairs and treat the place as a cinema. Sometimes they'd buy drinks, coffee or icecream, but Ciccio didn't mind if they just sat there. He enjoyed being the entertainment centre.

The arrival of the TV set was a bit offputting for the writers who had come to Bocca for peace and quiet, and who came to Capannina Ciccio for a drink, a conversation and a game of chess. But they were already having to tolerate an increased noise level. The fishermen, who had always operated from little sailing boats, casting their nets gracefully over the slow-running river, started putt-putting up and down in motor boats, and some of them started using dynamite to simplify their task.

Mario: 'One fisherman threw a bomb and instead of going off underwater it hit the rocks and smashed all the windows in the village. The police got involved then and ordered the fishermen to stop using bombs. They would come to check the kitchen in the restaurant to make sure we were not using bombed fish. We never were, because Ciccio wanted to show healthy-looking whole fish to the clients.'

In 1960, Anna and Ciccio finally made the big decision: they would leave the Sarzana apartment, live in Bocca di Magra, stay open all year, and become full-time restaurateurs.

Mario: 'We had very few clients that first winter, but we stayed open because we lived there and we were a big family and we ate in the restaurant anyway. If somebody came, they ate what we ate. The money we made in the summer barely kept us going through winter.'

But the following year, the Ciccio season seemed to start earlier, and by 1963, they were thriving on winter Sundays and crowded from the beginning of April.

One lunchtime in June of 1963, there was a commotion in the kitchen. Anna ran into the dining room and grabbed a doctor friend who was eating his lunch. 'Can you help? Ciccio has collapsed.' Ciccio was unconscious. He'd been cutting bread for the tartina and he just dropped to the floor. They carried him to the doctor's car and drove him to the hospital at Sarzana, where they assumed he'd had a heart attack.

In fact, he had gone into a diabetic coma. Nowadays, he'd have been treated and back at work within 24 hours. But this was a small town in Italy in the early 1960s. Ciccio died a few hours later.

They laid him out on a bed in his brother Camillo's apartment overlooking Piazza Matteotti. Anna sat by the bedside for three days. Camillo, who had experience cooking in factory canteens, went to run Capannina Ciccio. He died two months later.

Mario estimates that 7,000 people came to pay their respects to Ciccio, at Camillo's place or at the church service or at the funeral. The poet Zeno Birolli described him as '*un uomo prodigo e fantasioso*' (a man 'prodigal and fantastical', or 'lavish and imaginative'), with Capannina Ciccio an extension of his personality. How could it go on without him?

'OGGI, QUANDO LA GENTE COMPRA, NON VUOLE SOLO UN PRODOTTO, MA ANCHE UN RACCONTO. QUESTO È QUELLO CHE L'ITALIA FA MEGLIO: NOI FORNIAMO IL SOGNO.'

Into Emilia

As Lucio walks into the Osteria di Rubbiara at 1.30 pm, he happens to be talking on his mobile phone to the manager of his restaurant in Sydney, where it's after midnight and the last guests are just leaving. A young woman standing in the osteria's front room stares at the mobile in alarm, and scurries off through an archway. Then an angry-looking man with grey curly hair emerges, glares at Lucio and holds out his palm. Lucio says goodbye and hands his mobile to the man, who locks it in a small wooden cupboard.

This is the maestro Italo Pedroni. Lucio doesn't want to piss him off, because he's hoping he will explain this afternoon how he makes the finest balsamic vinegar in the Modena area. Unfortunately, it is extremely easy to piss Mr Pedroni off.

Lucio sympathises with his policy of confiscating mobiles so that customers don't talk on them during meals. If there's one thing Italians don't need it's another opportunity to natter. Mario, for example, has two mobiles – one in the left pocket for home matters and one in the right pocket for business matters. He's been seen walking along with a mobile on each ear, transferring information from one caller to the other. Lucio is relieved to escape the *cellulare* for a while. But if he says this, he's sure Italo Pedroni will think he's sucking up.

It's been hard enough finding the place. After driving up and down on the outskirts of Modena for a while, he finally concluded the Osteria di Rubbiara had to be a yellow three-storey building at a crossroads, with a vineyard behind it. Outside were several small signs in incomprehensible local dialect.

Lucio apologises for being later than his booked time, and remarks that he had trouble finding the place. 'I took the sign down last year because too many people were coming,' says the maestro. 'I took us out of the phone book, too.' Lucio realises why Mario was so amused

The liquid begins its journey through the woods, shrinking as it evaporates, first 100-year-old mulberry barrels, then chestnut, then cherry, then juniper, then oak.

yesterday when he gave him Mr Pedroni's phone number.

Mr Pedroni leads him through a series of wood-panelled rooms to a small table next to a larger table where 12 people are settling down to a three-generation Sunday lunch. Then he summarises what he'll be serving. When he concludes with mention of a fruit pie, Lucio says: 'Could I perhaps have some local cheese instead of the pie – I am diabetic'.

Mr Pedroni frowns. 'You don't tell me what you are going to have – I tell you what you are going to have. The last time any customer placed an order in this place was 1971. And don't ask me for bread – I'm not giving you any until after you've eaten your pasta, because you'll fill up on it. The bread is for wiping up sauce. And we don't change the cutlery between plates.' He walks off.

The obstacle course towards understanding balsamic vinegar has begun. Lucio is wondering if it is worth it. Balsamic is not part of his background, nor does it have anything to do with the food culture of the Lunigiana. Historically it was an indulgence of aristocrats, who had servants to nurture it in the cellars of their mansions. No peasant would see the point of making a product that takes 25 years to reach its best.

The only vinegar Lucio knew as a child and as a waiter at Ciccio's was red, and he remains convinced that red vinegar is the only combination with Ligurian olive oil on salads. He first heard of balsamic in Australia, when his rich clients started asking for it as part of the rising tide of enthusiasm for anything that could be perceived as 'Tuscan' (even though balsamic is Emilian).

Since balsamic has become such an international fad, and because he likes the taste of it on steak, Lucio is curious about how it is made, and Italo Pedroni is the best possible person to show him – if he decides to talk.

The meal is solid osteria fare, enlivened by Mr Pedroni's rule that 'you don't get your next course until you've finished the previous one': hand-made tortellini in a chicken broth; noodles with a mild meat sauce; a platter of roast meats accompanied by potatoes over which balsamic has been dripped; pieces of chicken which have turned pink because they've been simmered in the favourite local wine, lambrusco; then a selection of dry pastries and a piece of parmesan. As he plonks down the pastries, Mr Pedroni says, 'You better hurry and eat them if you want to see the *acetaio* (vinegar-making)'. Lucio politely nibbles a macaroon, leaves cash for his bill (no credit cards here), and says, 'I'm ready'. Mr Pedroni says, 'Follow me'.

They arrive in a hot room lined with dark brown polished barrels. Mr Pedroni races through an explanation of the process he learnt from his grandfather. He begins by gently cooking the must (pulp) of Trebbiano di Spagna grapes for 24 hours, then puts it in 100-year-old mulberry barrels. There the liquid begins its journey through the woods, moving through a series of ever smaller barrels, shrinking as it evaporates and becoming more intense as it absorbs the flavours of first mulberry, then chestnut, then cherry, then juniper and so on. It must spend at least six years in the woods, but doesn't become interesting till the twelfth year, and is at its best at 25.

Mr Pedroni says 100 kilos of grapes produce one litre of vinegar, which is why you can pay 200 euros for a 100 millilitre bottle. He makes only 500 litres a year, so you may be forced to buy the work of an inferior acetaio. You need to be sure it is one of the 100

At his osteria, the maestro Italo Pedroni makes balsamic vinegar and serves chicken in lambrusco and tortellini in chicken broth.

members of the consorzio in Modena, who are the only makers allowed to label their product *aceto balsamico tradizionale*. It's not enough to see the word 'Modena' on the label. You must also see the word 'tradizionale'.

He seems to have warmed to Lucio, because he produces a bunch of tiny spoons and a bunch of bottles, and shows how the vinegar changes with the years. The 12-year-old stuff is a pleasant sour-sweet mix, but the 28-year-old is a thick purple syrup that tastes more like honey than vinegar.

Then Mr Pedroni hands back Lucio's mobile, which is just as well, because Mario has been phoning to say he plans to drive up to Modena tonight to check out its nightclubs (in search of ideas for the Latest Project), and could Lucio meet him at 10 pm?

As Lucio drives into Modena that afternoon, he can see the symptoms of balsamic madness. Every second shop has a window full of the liquid at outrageous prices, much of it not tradizionale by the Pedroni definition. The industry seems to have served the citizenry well − the people taking their 5 pm *passeggiata* (stroll) look prosperous and beautiful, as does the redhead in black leather pants who serves him that night in the trendy Zelmira restaurant.

Lucio is particularly impressed with the 'prosciutto' of duck breast served with sautéed pears and goat cheese, with the between-course palate cleanser of strawberries in balsamic, and with the tagliatelle and sauce of rabbit, asparagus and sharp herbs. Despite the fact that most courses come splashed with balsamic in decorative swirls and dots, two young Americans at the next table ask for a bottle of balsamic, and drizzle it on everything.

> **At Zelmira ristorante, everything is improved by a splash of balsamic: duck prosciutto, parmesan, hare and chestnuts and palate cleansing strawberries.**

Lucio meets Mario in a dark disco with neon along its bar and thumping dance music. Mario puts his hand to his head and says, 'Why am I doing this? I'm a restaurateur, not a disc jockey.'

He's wondering what to call his new place. As a kid, Mario was nicknamed *Ciccietto*, which means 'little Ciccio', and that might not be a bad name. 'Or you could call it Cicciolina,' says Lucio, referring to an Italian porn star turned politician. Mario looks tempted.

He wants his new place to have something for everyone. The top floor is going to feature a titanium ceiling which will get all the architects talking. 'It will look like the bridge on a ship,' Mario says. He's asked his designers to create a bar on wheels, 2.5 metres long, which will float around the nightclub section, making drinks for each table. He's wondering if he should install computer terminals for customers. At this rate, the Latest Project is going to leave the cool clubs of Modena for dead.

'Anyway,' says Mario, 'tomorrow we'll go back to what we know. I'll take you to the prosciutto maker and the parmesan maker that I used to visit with my father. And we're invited for lunch at the Barilla factory. They're the biggest pasta maker in Italy.'

DAY TWO

They're driving from Modena to the town of Langhirano, which is the prosciutto capital of the world, because, says Mario, of the 'microenergy' in the air. The town is perfectly

As Lucio drives into Modena that afternoon, he can see the symptoms of balsamic madness. The people taking their 5 pm 'passeggiata' look prosperous and beautiful.

**Giovanni Bianchi,
lawyer-turned-
prosciutto-maker,
displays his
family's heritage.**

placed to get the slightly salty breeze that blows all the way here from the sea and gently dries the pig legs as they hang on racks.

Mario: 'My father would drive me up here in this long American convertible which the government had confiscated from a cigarette smuggler, and as we drove into Langhirano we'd be followed by local boys who couldn't believe such a beautiful machine. Then we'd go back to Bocca with the back seat covered with legs of prosciutto and wheels of parmesan. In the summer we got through a whole leg of prosciutto every day. Because we had the best, people would queue up outside to buy slices for takeaway.'

Ciccio had two favourite suppliers – the Tosoni family and the Barbieri family. The Barbieris bought a house in Bocca di Magra, and spent three months of the year there, eating at Ciccio's every day. So they wouldn't get bored, Ciccio kept trying to invent new dishes for them. But they don't seem to be in business any longer, so it's the company called Pio Tosoni which is receiving today's visit.

It has graduated from a modest family concern to a mass production line, making 100,000 legs a year. The cousins have to don special protective clothing to tour the factory – a kind of white raincoat, rain hat and boots. They're shown around by a grandson of the founder, Giovanni Bianchi, who went off to become a lawyer in Milan but returned because he wanted to be involved with 'something real'. He says that although they now have machines to massage the meat to tenderness, they employ 26 people to trim the legs into shape, rub on the salt and continually check the thousands of legs that hang in long sheds for two years before they can be sold. Checking involves thrusting a needle made of horse bone into the leg, and sniffing it for hints of bacteria.

But only a member of the Tosoni family can decide when to open the windows. Every morning the appointed family member goes outside, sniffs the air, tests the direction of the breezes, and, if conditions are ideal, goes back and presses the button which opens the shutters. Then the air can waft in and add its flavour to the meat.

How to make the perfect parmesan

1. Leave the results of the afternoon milking in a cauldron overnight, to separate.
2. Next day, skim off the cream and add fresh milk from the morning's milking.
3. Add fermenting whey left over from the previous day's cheesemaking, heat and stir.
4. Add rennet from a calf's stomach, so the mixture starts to coagulate.
5. Whisk to break up the curds, heat and stir again.
6. Let the curds settle in a lump at the bottom of the cauldron.
7. Fish out the lump of curds, cut it in half and wrap both halves in cheesecloth. (You can feed most of the remaining liquid – the whey – to your pigs, so their legs will make tasty prosciutto.)
8. Push the curds into round moulds, stamped on the inner side with the insignia of genuine Parmigiano-Reggiano.
9. After letting the cheese drain for three days, put the wheel into salty water for 20 days.
10. Let it dry in the sun, then add it to the stack in your ageing room, turning regularly.
11. After one year, have it inspected and certified by the Parma authorities.
12. Wait another year, and serve.

You will find that 605 litres of milk will turn into one 39-kilogram wheel of parmesan, which will be worth about 1,000 euros.

Above, Giuseppe's parmesan; opposite, Parma by day and night.

Of course, the meat is already full of flavour because the pigs in this area are fed on the whey discarded during the making of parmesan cheese. And that's the next stop for the cousins, in a drive that passes the village of Roncole, massively signposted as the birthplace of Giuseppe Verdi.

As they get out of the car at the farm of parmesan maker Giuseppe Censi, they hear a roaring noise coming from a hangar behind his house. Is there a plane in there? When they ask what it is, Giuseppe at first looks puzzled. Then he realises it's a sound he no longer notices, because it goes on 24 hours a day. It's his robot.

He opens the hangar doors and displays tall metal and wood shelves receding to infinity. Stacked on those shelves are 24,000 wheels of parmesan. Each wheel stays in there for at least two years, and has to be turned once a week. So Giuseppe's robot, called a *voltatrice automatica*, can never stop moving. It inserts its metal arms around the wheel, pulls it off the shelf, rotates it 180 degrees, puts it back, and proceeds up or along the stack to do the same thing to the next wheel.

Mario and Lucio do a quick calculation and work out Giuseppe has 7 million euros worth of cheese in that hangar, with 37 wheels added every day. Mario wants to see if he remembers a skill taught to him by his father. 'Can I check these cheeses?' he asks. Giuseppe knows what he means, and hands him a tiny silver orecchio, which Mario taps gently over several wheels. 'I'm listening for air bubbles,' he says. 'Ciccio was the best in Italy at this. It's just a tiny change in the note, but it reveals that you should not buy this cheese.'

He can't detect any bubbles, which doesn't surprise Giuseppe. 'Making parmesan has been a sickness of my family for 200 years,' he says. 'I work at this from five in the morning till eight at night. It would be longer if I didn't have the robot.'

Every minute of every day, the factory near Parma produces 220 boxes of pasta in 130 different shapes.

This town is obsessed with pig meat. There are hundreds of places doing these traditional things. Why should I do the same?

Now the cousins are ready for lunch, but first they must endure a tour of the Barilla factory, where the executives are keen to impress the prominent local restaurateur and the prominent visiting restaurateur. They learn that Barilla, which started with one family 250 years ago, now employs 7,300 people around the world. Every minute, the factory near Parma produces 220 boxes of pasta in 130 different shapes. They know Lucio will be proud to hear that 20 per cent of the wheat comes from Australia.

But the point of the invitation to lunch at the executive end of the factory canteen is to introduce a new product range called Accademia. Barilla hopes to supply the great restaurants of the world with rare artisan olive oils, balsamic vinegar, prosciutto, parmesan and tomatoes. Barilla won't make these products itself, but will sign exclusive distribution contracts with the best small craftsmen who do make them. One executive observes: 'Nowadays when people buy a product, they want to buy a story with it. That's what Italy is good at: we provide the dream.'

Mario and Lucio nod politely, but agree afterwards that Accademia is not for them. They both choose their own artisan growers, makers and distributors. It would take half the fun out of their lives if Barilla started doing that job for them.

For dinner that night, they visit a restaurant called Al Cavallino Bianco, where chef–owner Massimo Spigaroli is famous for yet another pork product – *culatello*, which, as Lucio tells Mario, Australians would call 'mouldy pig's bum'. It's the most specialised of meats, costing five times as much as the best prosciutto, because it has to be prepared by hand and hang for a year in a damp environment where it develops a mould that sweetens the flesh.

Massimo takes the cousins to the cellar of his house across the road, where hundreds of pink-and-white grenades hang from the ceiling. He complains that he's been having trouble lately with the health inspectors from the EC, who are Germans, and therefore can't understand why Italians would want to risk their lives deliberately making mouldy meat. Eating culatello with dinner, Mario and Lucio have no trouble understanding.

Next day they stroll around Parma, which is painted as yellow as its cheese, and lunch at Parizzi, the finest restaurant in Italy's most food-obsessed town. The meal begins with a little parmesan fonduta on a porcelain spoon, and proceeds via smoked swordfish with crisped eggplant and buffalo mozzarella; cod-flavoured gnocchi with a sauce of tomato, clam and lobster; pappardelle noodles with a sauce of hare, pheasant and pumpkin; guinea fowl with a crust of nuts and fruit; and chestnut semifreddo; to a conclusion of three types of parmesan – one year old, two years old and three years old. The cousins find they agree with the advice of Giuseppe Censi – that a one-year-old is likely to be too moist and waxy, a three-year-old too dry and crumbly, and a two-year-old just right.

The chef, Marco Parizzi, tells them he is constantly criticised in his home town for not doing enough dishes with pork. 'This town is obsessed with pig meat,' he says. 'When this restaurant was started by my grandfather in 1957, it became famous for its meat dishes. But now there are hundreds of places doing those traditional things. Why should I do the same? I want people to come and ask "what will Marco do today?", and always be surprised.

'Some of the older customers complained last year when I didn't do tripe because it's the ritual. But if everyone else is doing it, I don't see why I should be tied down. Italy needs to let its chefs go free.'

Parma's food market supplies the ingredients for Marco Parizzi's restaurant, which offers three ages of parmesan.

Mario

—From the film *Waterloo* (1969), script by H. A. L. Craig.

At the age of 18, Mario Guelfi was going to be Napoleon. There are those in Bocca di Magra now who might say he succeeded in this ambition. But he would say he failed, at least in the sense he'd envisaged – as an actor in London in the early 1960s.

What Mario fantasised about through his teenage years was being a film director, and in pursuit of this dream, he'd gone to London to work with a BBC producer named Harry Craig, who'd been a long-term customer of Ciccio's. Craig was one of the literati who used to pass every summer holiday at Bocca di Magra, renting fishermen's cottages and devoting every day to a strict regimen of swimming in the river and eating, drinking, talking and playing chess at Capannina Ciccio.

Craig had been impressed with the energy and imagination of Ciccio's son, and employed him as an assistant when he turned up in London in 1961. Craig was planning a movie about the life of Napoleon, and decided Mario had the look he needed to represent the little corporal when young. He could dub in the voice later. Mario was intrigued by the idea because of the local myth that Napoleon's father was born in Sarzana, Mario's birthplace, and because he thought this role could be a first step towards a directing career.

Two things stopped his advance: the British actors' union complained about the idea of using an untrained foreigner in a role that could easily be played by a short Englishman; and Mario had to take command of his family's restaurant when his father died suddenly in 1963.

Mario: 'I thought my mother and my sisters could do it, and I would be able to go back to London. But those were times when people believed a man must be head of the business. Now people think about men and women differently, but then, they thought only a man could represent the family. My mother said she was no good for administration, even if she was good at cooking. I said I was no good for administration either. My mother begged me.

'We found that Ciccio's had big debts. Dad had never really paid off the renovations he had done two years earlier. The people he owed money to were happy to let the debts drag on as long as he paid a little occasionally, because they could see how successfully he ran the restaurant. Most of them were customers anyway. But now that a 19-year-old was in charge, they couldn't see the place having much future.

'Every day I would take my mother to the cemetery in Sarzana. She would go inside and "talk to Ciccio" and I would stay outside and stand on the stone bridge and stare at the river. I was trying to see some poetry in all this, thinking to myself that the water keeps going on, and we will keep going on. I was trying to cheer myself up because really I couldn't see how we could keep going on.

'The first time I thought we might be able to get through was Ferragosto [15 August, a public holiday to celebrate the ancient Roman midsummer festival of Augustus] that year. Dad died in June, and a lot of the repayments were due at the end of August. Ferragosto had always been our best day of the year, but the day before, it rained. We thought we'd have nobody. Then on the morning of the fifteenth, the sky was clear, but it was raining people. Everybody was coming down to the beach.

'We served 600 for lunch. Friends of the family couldn't get a table and had to stand up in the kitchen to eat. There were 25 people sleeping on the floor of the restaurant that night because there was no accommodation anywhere around. And when the debt came due, after all, I could pay.

'But I still hated the restaurant because I hated economic things. We made money over the summer, and by the end of the winter, we had spent everything we had saved. I didn't know how to organise what had to be done. Everybody wanted money and the people didn't believe in me because I was so young.

'In my father's time, good food was cheap, and it was a small menu – cacciucco, fried fish, spaghetti alle vongole – and my father was always inventing some new way with fish. So that was not the major cost. Wages were not expensive – there were lots of family members, and on busy days, if we went into the village, we could always find friends to help as waiters or in the kitchen.

'After he died, for three years we served only what Ciccio had been doing. We lost many clients, because they said the food is not as good as it used to be – even though it was still my mother in the kitchen. They needed to see my father.

'So I had to go and talk to them, because people think that if they meet the host, they are eating better. People are eating with their eyes and ears as well as their mouth. If the host is there, they enjoy the atmosphere. But I didn't want to be there. I wanted to make films.

'I was very sad, and a lot of clients asked me why I never smiled. It took me three years to adjust to it, to rearrange my thinking. One day I woke up and thought: it's like theatre, this restaurant. The people are coming and going, doing funny things, and I'm watching the performance. I'm the *regista* [director]. I move the characters around, the waiters, the customers, I seat them, I tell them how to eat the mussels or the *datteri* [sea dates]. I find a new story every day. I finally could see a way to enjoy myself.

'I realised you have to keep changing the scenario, so there will always be something new in the story for the customers, even if they don't register it consciously – change the tablecloths from red checks to green stripes, new waiters' uniforms, extra artworks on the walls. They don't have a chance to become bored. And nor do I.'

Lucio's brother Aulo was there the day Ciccio died, and he watched Mario grow into the role of restaurateur …

Aulo: 'Zia Anna dressed in black for years afterwards and she and Mario were always going outside, where the tablecloths were hanging out to dry, and having these worried conversations.

'Mario was more serious and professional than everyone expected. Before that, he liked to travel, he didn't take much interest in the family business. He was *esterofilo* – mad for foreign things. Bocca seemed very small to him. But because he was the only male in the family, he had to take charge of the situation. He went through a transformation, he got his little briefcase, and he contacted the people he needed to keep the business going.

'He had to concentrate on repaying the debts, and leave the restaurant to run itself. People would lend money to Ciccio because he was a personality, they trusted him. When he died, they got scared, because they didn't know Mario. Some of them made very pressing requests.

'The only food work he did personally during this time was to make the gelato. At least that was satisfying in that if you did it right, it would turn into something good. Money worries are never finished.

'After the debts were brought under control, he turned himself into Ciccio the restaurateur. Slowly he started going into the dining room and he became the figure that his father was. The kitchen loved him, because he could talk a table into having all the same thing. He'd say "We can do for you today antipasto, then spaghetti, then fritto misto," and they'd say "Yeah, great". The customers didn't have to think, and they'd trust him to do it right.

'I became the "official taster", checking the meals before they left the kitchen. I was only 16, but Zia Anna said I had the best palate in the place, and I would know what a dish needs, just as Ciccio had when he was in the kitchen, as well as being good at setting the tables and talking to the customers.

'Zia Anna trusted only me. She would make huge pots of sauce, and give me a taste on a spoon, and I would say "needs more salt, needs more garlic". But she was a good cook, so there wasn't much to retouch.'

**In 1969, Mario opened
a gallery for the artists
who ate at Ciccio's**.

By the late 1960s, Mario was starting to feel comfortable, so he decided to challenge himself.

Mario: 'In my father's time, a lot of writers and poets came to Bocca di Magra. By the 1960s more artists were coming. Some of them gave me paintings to keep the restaurant going. So I opened a gallery and did exhibitions to keep them there, and put on street theatre to keep them entertained.

'But I didn't really know much about art. A friend told me this famous sculptor and painter was staying in the area, so I went to the house to ask if I could display his work. I saw a man sitting in the garden and I said, "Does Martini live here?" He said, "Nobody by that name here." I said, "But is there an artist here?" He said, "Yes, but his name is Marino Marini." "Okay," I said, "Can I speak to him?" He said, "You already are." I said, "Maestro, I'm so sorry, I'll go away now." But he insisted I come in for coffee, and he helped me find other artists to hang on my walls.'

Mario also found time to develop a passion and a talent for chess. And it was chess that led him to a goddess from a distant land.

Wendy Stanford: 'I was travelling in Europe with a girl I knew from school in Australia. She had a cousin who married a fellow from Scotland, and they had taken a villa at Bocca di Magra for the winter, which only a mad person from Scotland would do. We came over to stay with them for three weeks and one night Mario arrived to play chess, looking very smart in his cashmere polo-neck jumper and his corduroy trousers.

'We found out he owned an art gallery and a restaurant. He took us to Rome and showed us this villa which we were supposed to think was his. In fact it belonged to Dino de Laurentiis.

'I was fascinated – he was much better than the sort of fellow I was meeting in pubs in London. Then we went back to London, and I phoned Mario to see if he could find me a job in Italy. I was hoping it would be near him, but it was in Rome, as an au pair with a family. But they had a villa in Bocca for the summer, so we met up again, and he offered me the job of running his art gallery.

'After a while, he asked me to marry him, but I said, "I want to see you in Australia, in my territory, because it's so easy to lose a sense of reality here." He said okay.'

Ciccio's shack kept expanding onto the beach, and Bocca di Magra kept growing around it.

Mario: 'I didn't know much about Australia. I had an uncle who was a prisoner in Australia during the war. He was working on a ship, and it docked in Sydney after Mussolini joined Hitler's side. My uncle was taken off the ship to work on a farm. But he didn't speak about it much.

'And then I had seen a film called, I think, *The Last Beach* [*On the Beach*], about how the world ended everywhere except in Australia. Europe was finished, America was finished, but Australia was fine. It made Australia seem very safe.'

Wendy: 'My parents didn't know much about what I was thinking, because I never wrote letters. So I needed to prepare them. I went home and Mario went to New Guinea. He was having a great time, but after two weeks I was missing him, and Mum and Dad were wanting to see what he was like.

'He eventually rang me and I told him to come over right away. He made his own way to Mudgee. I suppose Mum and Dad would have preferred me to marry an Australian, but they were impressed with Mario's enthusiasm. He loved exploring Australia. He bought a second-hand car and drove up to Lightning Ridge to look for opals, and up to Hill End to look for gold. My parents thought that was enterprising.'

Mario: 'New Guinea was very interesting. They used fishing nets there the same way the fishermen used to throw them in the river at Bocca di Magra. But Wendy told me to come to Mudgee. I talked to the pilot of the plane from New Guinea to Australia, and he showed me how to catch a train to see Wendy in Mudgee. I had to change trains at Lithgow, and that was where I had my first Australian meal – a tinned spaghetti sandwich at the railway station.

'I suppose Wendy's father was testing me by giving me jobs to do on his farm. I had to put the elastic band around the bull's balls to make the balls fall off a week later. I had to cut the horns off the sheep. The blood went everywhere.

'When I go somewhere, I adapt to whatever I have to do. I loved the farm. It reminded me of going to my mother's farm, Ca' Rósa, when I was a kid. There was one big table in the kitchen. On the table were all the time cheeses and salami and bread because the brothers and sons would come home, eat something, and go back to work. One day I took the cow to drink at the well, I pulled the bucket up to give it water. I was incredibly happy.

'That was the sensation I had later when I looked after the cows when I was first visiting Australia. It is natural for me, I decided I am a cowboy. In my mother's area, if they had ten cows they thought they were rich. My father-in-law had hundreds of cows. It seemed like the Wild West.'

Judy Stanford, Wendy's mother: 'I grew up in Melbourne, I was a city girl. Jim Stanford came from a sheep farming family in Orange. I met him in 1943, when he was in the airforce, and I went to a dance at the Australia Hotel where eligible young ladies could meet officers. I suppose I met him the same way Anna met Ciccio. We got married in 1945, and eventually we moved to a sheep and cattle property near Mudgee.

'Our oldest girl, Wendy, set off travelling when she was in her early twenties and wrote from Italy to say she had met this fascinating man, but not much else. Then she came back to make up her mind if she wanted to marry him and then live in Italy. She had lost so much weight worrying about it. So we said he had to come and stay with us.

'What impressed me about Mario was how much he adored working with the cattle. He was having a ball on the property – he went out shooting ducks, got one on his first day. He got himself a whip and an R. M. Williams hat. Mario loves any new experience.

'He even seemed to enjoy our food, which at that time was terribly British. Jim was brought up on a property where they had immense breakfasts, chops, meat three times a day, tea all the time. The only spaghetti we knew came in tins. Nobody knew about pasta or coffee.

'I'd never been overseas, and Jim had been overseas once when he was 13, on a world trip with his parents, which he found boring. One day Wendy said, "We're going to surprise you, Mum" and they spent the whole afternoon making pasta. They cooked the spinach, put it into the flour, made green tagliatelle. It was the first time I'd had good pasta.

'When we got to know Mario, we felt he was the right person for Wendy. He was always able to calm her down. I thought he'd been around a bit, knew what was what, and it was obvious he was madly in love with Wendy.'

Wendy: 'And so we got married, and came back to Italy. Mario's family was very welcoming to me, but I was not keen to get involved in the restaurant because it was that family's whole life. They had it all under control. I didn't want to lose my identity. So I did my own thing, which soon included having two daughters.'

Wendy may have spent more time at home than at Ciccio's, but she inspired Mario to take the place to the next level, to move from trattoria to ristorante. And he was getting useful financial advice from his regular customers. The author Mary McCarthy, whose husband was American ambassador to France, urged him to get involved with a new form of payment called 'the credit card'. Ciccio's became the first eatery in Liguria to take American Express and Diner's Club. Italians were slow to take it up, because pulling wads of cash out of a pocket was part of their sense of *bella figura* [making a good impression], but it appealed to the visitors.

Stage one of the move upmarket was installing a huge fish tank in the middle of the main room, to give the customers, particularly the families, something to look at and talk about. Mario had to go back into debt to build it, but he thought it might have something of the impact that Ciccio achieved when he installed the town's first television set in the bar, back in 1956.

Mario: 'The clients enjoyed the fish tank, especially looking at the lobsters. They were not fashionable when my father was here, because people thought they were "too French" for a place like ours. The fishermen used to throw them back. But around 1970 the story went around that they were an aphrodisiac, so people became curious.

Wendy, left, ran the art gallery and sometimes joined Mario's sisters Graziella and Ornella in the kitchen at Ciccio's.

'We also had a huge sea bass in there, more than 3 kilograms. One time a sheik came for lunch and said he wanted it for his whole party. It took two people to get it out of the tank and carry it to the kitchen, water everywhere, and then my mother had to fight it for half an hour to kill it. She said "never again".

'Then family members kept making pets out of the fish and giving them names and then crying when a customer wanted to eat them. I often wished I'd never got that tank.'

But the tank was pulling in lots more customers. The next task was to get them properly served. And Mario realised he needed professional help.

Aulo: 'The smartest thing Mario ever did was hiring Giuseppe Nucera to run the place. In the old days, all the waiters did everything, but nothing was ever really finished. There was no organisation. We'd sweep and mop the floor, set the tables, wash the glasses, bottle the wine and put it in the fridge, then set every table for lunch with a bottle of wine and a bottle of mineral water. We'd also rake the beach and rent out deckchairs and umbrellas to the visitors.

'Often we'd sleep in the restaurant, get up at 7 am and swim at Punta Bianca, taking a little boat around, or go fishing in the river with some of the holidaymakers. I'd start work at 10 am, set up for lunch, serve lunch, then grab half an hour's sleep in the umbrella storage shed, wake up, serve gelati for people coming back from the beach, then set up for dinner, serve, finish at midnight. Then we would eat our own dinner, and go to bed at 2 am.

'I was sleepy all the time. Once I brought salt shakers four times to the table of Salvatore Pintori, a designer with Olivetti. Eventually he said, "I think I have enough salt now, thank you, Aulo".

'The wine would come in huge demijohns, and half the morning was taken up with bottling, inserting the cork, sticking on the Ciccio label. So in the summer, when everyone is rushed off their feet, it was virtually a daily occurrence that a customer would find a fly in his wine.

'Giuseppe arrived in 1972 and started a system where the waiters would eat before the lunch service, so we wouldn't be falling asleep on the job. He'd just come from Milan, and he had seen how restaurants worked in the big cities. He started buying wine in bottles, so there was no need to do the bottling any more, and he persuaded the family to get a glass-washing machine, and assigned one waiter to be responsible for stacking it. Cleaning the floors became part of the job of the dishwasher, instead of any waiter who happened to get around to it.

'When Giuseppe started, the dining room had three waiters looking after 150 people. Service was haphazard. Giuseppe hired two more waiters, so there were five, which cost more but actually increased the number of customers we could serve.

'The welcoming had always been a problem, because Ciccio's had so many entrances. People would wander in from all sides, from the river or from the road, and stand there till somebody noticed. Now there was a waiter there to greet them and seat them.'

Giuseppe Nucera: 'I was 20 when I came to Bocca di Magra, just out of national service. My family was originally from Calabria but I'd been working as a waiter in Milan and I was looking for a job near the beach, for the summer season.

'I got interviewed by Mario, who told me to start the next day. They asked me to stay on when the season finished, and that was when I found that Ciccio's had no structure, not even official opening hours. It was just various family members coming and going. They would open in the morning when they felt like it, wouldn't set a table until somebody arrived, then close at 9 pm if there were no customers.

'Anna ran the kitchen, and she did the pasta. It was always *alla macchia*, with the sauce put on the top almost as an afterthought. Mario was the manager, but he always consulted his mother. When she started having some health problems, they hired a qualified chef, and that was the beginning of Capannina Ciccio as a professional restaurant, about 1975.

'The food was always very good, but home cooking standard, and the kitchen had trouble coping with big numbers. And the wine was ordinary. It took me ten years to convince Mario of the value of having a wine list. Mario is very passionate, very imaginative, but he's not a professional restaurateur. He's an entertainer who found himself by accident in this kind of life.

Many artists, including Belgian Jean-Michel Folon and Italian Marino Marini, left their doodles in Ciccio's reservations book.

'They were keen to expand, and I thought I could make it work a bit better. I saw a lot of potential in the place, with the position, the united family, and the growth of tourism in this area. I love being a waiter. I like the relationship with people. Perhaps it's because I'm from the south of Italy. We are more communicative than the northerners. We have a certain charm which can sometimes cover up mistakes.

'In the summer, a lot of people had the *pensione* – they paid a set price for a set lunch every day (spaghetti with tomato sauce, fritto misto or *cotoletta* [veal schnitzel], salad or potatoes, fruit and coffee). Wine and mineral water was extra, and we'd write their name on their bottle of wine or *minerale* so they could finish it the next day. Some families ate here every day for nine weeks.

'The problem was to attract customers during the winter, so I started going around to local businesses offering special deals for parties. Four years after I got here, they had gone from one full-time employee (me) to four full-time employees, and after eight years, they had 18 employees.

'Then we had to improve the desserts. We used to buy in semifreddo and St Honoré cake from a pasticceria nearby, but it became very industrial, so with the help of my wife, I started making the desserts myself. The first ones we did were tiramisu and *crostata di mele* (thin pastry with apple and custard). They went well so I made myself the dessert chef.

'In Italy people don't like waiting to eat, so we have to be fast. I decided to hand out menus as soon as they sat down. Mario didn't like using a menu. He thought if they saw the prices, they would not order much. He preferred just to tell them what they could have. But that slows everything down on busy nights. With regulars, I would say "Do you want to see the menu or just have the *menù parlante* [spoken list]?"

'I was promoted to "director-general", and Mario gave me *carta bianca* [a free hand] in every aspect of the business except the money.'

Aulo: 'Giuseppe transformed everything. He was ambitious for the business, which no waiter had been before. The family had no tradition of competitiveness. The restaurant was just like a big kitchen at home, and customers were just like extra members of the family dropping in. They were surprised by what Giuseppe wanted to do, but Mario could see it was making things work better.

'And Giuseppe being there meant I didn't feel so bad when I decided to leave. I told Mario and Anna I couldn't work there any more – they were sad but they understood.'

Aulo enjoyed the new professionalism about the place, but he was on his way to a different career. With a young wife and two small children, he didn't want to work the long hours that are an essential part of being the perfect waiter. His part-time winter job delivering clothes for a fashion store had turned into an offer of a full-time sales position.

He hoped he could pass the torch to his younger brother, who, like him, had grown up between the tables at Ciccio's. But Lucio the dreamer didn't seem all that interested in the restaurant business. Could he ever get his mind out of the clouds and into the dining room?

'The pilgrim quickly learned to choose safer routes that would avoid natural disasters, assault by brigands and paying too many tolls. Where the rich merchants went teemed with cutthroats. The good pilgrim felt obliged to divert from the main road in order to find in himself the spirituality of the journey.'

—Tiziana Neri, *La Vita Lungo La Via Francigena* (Life along the Via Francigena), 1997

IL PELLEGRINO IMPARAVA BEN PRESTO A SCEGLIERE GLI ITINERARI PIÙ SICURI, PER METTERSI AL RIPARO DALLE CATASTROFI NATURALI, PER EVITARE L'ASSALTO DEI BRIGANTI E PER NON DOVER PAGARE TROPPE GABELLE. LADDOVE, INFATTI, TRANSITIVANO I RICCHI MERCANTI ... PULLULAVANO I TAGLIAGOLE. IL BUON PELLEGRINO SPESSO DEVIAVA DAL PROPRIO CAMMINO PER POTER RITROVARE IN SE STESSO LA SPIRITUALITA DEL VIAGGIO.'

Into the mountains

The brothers are on the road north towards the Cisa Pass, retracing the way their father and uncle used to journey by horse and cart to buy cheeses in the mountains. Aulo has convinced Lucio that he needs to walk on the Via Francigena, which was used 1,000 years ago by pilgrims and merchants travelling between France and Rome.

Back then, the way was dotted with little shelters called *ospitali*, from which the English language gets both the word 'hospital' (because travellers could get first aid if they'd fallen victim to thieves or natural hazards) and 'hospitality' (because travellers could sometimes buy a meal). So, as Aulo points out, they were the beginning of Lucio's industry.

The autostrada follows the course of the Magra River, but Aulo pulls onto a tiny side road near the town of Aulla and points to a red-and-white wooden sign on a post that reads, '*VF Madonna degli Angeli*'. As a dutiful older brother, Aulo tucks a bottle of water for Lucio into his backpack and, as they start up a steep track into the forest, breaks off a branch to serve as a staff.

'These twigs you're crunching on are the kind our grandparents would have used to make brooms,' Aulo points out. 'Originally this would have been a dirt road about 3 metres wide, and the richer pilgrims would come along on donkeys or in small carts. But it has

crumbled away. People mainly come here now to pick the red-headed porcini. In November I get masses of them under these trees. Probably the pilgrims used to pick them and take them to the ospitali to cook.'

Lucio ponders: 'How would it go if you sliced the raw porcini thinly and serve them with prawns and parmesan?' Aulo thinks it's not a dish their mother would ever have attempted, because the local tradition is to keep surf strictly separated from turf. Lucio is excited by the idea of blending the contadini style with the pescatori style. Then the 1,000-year-old path disappears, and he finds himself unable to talk as he clambers up a steep bank.

'If we were walking here 700 years ago, we'd have had to pay a toll to the Malaspina family,' says Aulo. 'They controlled all along the road from the Cisa Pass. They fought with the Bishops of Luni. They were supposed to protect the pilgrims but half the time the Malaspinas employed the thieves who would rob the merchants coming along here, so you'd end up paying them two ways. They were the early Mafia.'

After 90 minutes of scrambling through magnificent trees, which leaves Lucio puffing and sweaty and Aulo still in full voice, they reach a white chapel which is on the site of an ancient ospitale. A sign outside says it was 'rebuilt in 1664 by an influential traveller who was saved by the Virgin from brigands'.

Lucio thinks he has experienced enough of the hardships of the pilgrims, and suggests they climb back down to the road and circle back along the highway to their car. But the highway has no footpath. At one point a semi-trailer is barrelling along towards them, and Lucio yells, '*Camion, ragazzi*' (truck, boys). It veers towards the centre of the road at the last second. If there had been a car going the other way, the boys would have had to leap a stone wall and drop 50 metres into the Magra.

Both are shaking as they climb back into the car and head for the town of Pontremoli. Lunch and a glass of local white will be most welcome. For that, they've chosen a little

Opposite, a chapel dedicated to the Madonna, which once sheltered pilgrims walking the Via Francigena – like Aulo and Lucio

place called Trattoria da Bussé, which has been run by the Bertocchi family since the 1930s.

There's a crudely printed sign taped to the glass door of da Bussé: '*Non si cucinano funghi*' (We don't cook mushrooms here). This is not to suggest that you'll never find mushrooms on da Bussé's menu. It means: 'Don't try bringing mushrooms you've picked yourself in the forest this morning, because we're sick of it. We'll decide our menu, not you.' The sisters Bertocchi (chef Antonietta, waitress Maria Luisa) are determined women.

When they sit down, Lucio asks Maria Luisa, whom he guesses to be about 60, '*Cosa consiglia?*' ('What do you suggest?'). It's his standard question in restaurants. In Australia he mostly encounters waiters who have no idea what's on the menu and reply, 'everything's good'. In most Italian restaurants, he gets a discussion – and especially at Bussé, where Maria Luisa describes several dishes as '*molto sexy*'.

Lucio is wondering if Mauro might have bantered with Luisa's mother in this place in the same way. More likely it would have been Ciccio who did the bantering. Aulo thinks the brothers-in-law would not have had time or money to eat in restaurants, and would have stuck with salami and cheese on the cart as they passed through Pontremoli.

Lucio finds the carafe wine disgusting, and asks if he can have a white in a bottle. Maria Luisa says the carafe wine is '*particolare*' ('an individual taste') and brings the old reliable vermentino.

She delivers half-moon-shaped ravioli stuffed with spinach and ricotta, tossed with butter and sage, and a platter of mixed meats that includes cotechino sausage, boiled veal muscle, and thinly sliced veal involtini rolled around spinach and pine nuts, which she describes as '*una favola*' – a fairytale.

Aulo is puzzled at the absence of potato dishes, and reminds Lucio that Pontremoli is famous as the town which first embraced the spud, when the rest of Italy was suspicious of this import from South America. A visionary mayor ordered mass plantings during a famine in 1771 and in the 1790s the church put out a pamphlet explaining how to cook with potatoes. Perhaps they should reprint it.

The highlight of the meal are the testaroli pancakes, which are the kind that are baked in a pot so they get pockmarks on the top, cut into diamond shapes, then boiled like pasta. They are hearty and filling, and Lucio can imagine that for many a shepherd, they would make a meal in themselves.

A man at the next table, unprompted, tells Lucio he is visiting for the day from Tuscany, and that he is '*Fiorentino DOC*' ('certified Florentine'), but he likes to experience the country way of doing things. The food he gets in Florence is too modern.

Clearly one of the sisters has noticed Lucio's interest in their food, because suddenly a plump gentleman in a bright tie comes rushing through the door. 'I'm only the brother of all the sisters,' he says, 'but I make the best *miele di Lunigiana*' (honey of the area).

He offers them a taste and they make complimentary remarks. He seems to be overcome with an attack of shyness, because he rushes out the door again. Maria Luisa drops the bill on the table and announces, 'We don't make coffee here – you'll have to go to a bar. I'm going for my sleep now.'

Lucio and Aulo walk up through the middle of the grey medieval town past narrow

Don't try bringing mushrooms you've picked in the forest this morning ... the sisters Bertocchi are determined women.

Testaroli the Pontremoli way

Pontremoli was a town of poor food, because the local economy was based on agriculture and very small farms. The food symbol of this town is the *testarolo*, which is named from the *testo*, the utensil which is used to make it – a baking dish originally made of terracotta, now made of metal. The bottom of the testa is called the *sottano*, the top is called the *soprano*.

It was a kind of miniature portable oven, and you could put it in hot coals. It was ideal for shepherds who had to travel over long distances. It could prepare focaccia of wheat or chestnut flour, *torta d'erbi* (greens pie), or even meats – lamb or goat cooked in their own juices. They were simple foods not needing elaborate preparation.

To make testaroli, make a runny mixture of water, flour and salt and pour it onto the sottano. Sit the pot on the embers for a few minutes and the mixture cooks by contact with the base. The bottom is brown and the top is pale in colour with little holes that are the result of violent bubbling.

Take the testaroli out, cut them into 'rombi' (diamonds of about 6 centimetres per side) and keep them till you are ready for the second phase, which is boiling for not more than a minute to make them soft and ready to accept sauce. If there is too much contact with water, you will compromise the consistency and they will dissolve and break up. Drain them, transfer them to a plate and serve them layered, with sauce between.

As the saying goes about the testarolo: *La sua morte e il pesto* (its conclusion is pesto). The testaroli are coupled with rough pesto, of Ligurian inspiration but more simple – basil, crushed by pestle and mortar, not too fine, garlic and pecorino, and, if you have any, grated parmesan. Add oil in abundance.

Their purpose is a mystery. Perhaps they were composed around fields or villages to scare off invaders. If so, they didn't work on the Romans.

winding alleys with buttresses to keep the houses apart. There's a pleasant sound of water running over pebbles, and when they go down one of the alleys, they discover they are just metres from the mighty Magra and the tremulous stone bridge from which the town gets its name.

They are discussing some of the people who used Pontremoli as a lunch stop before them. An archbishop of Canterbury called Sigeric went to Rome in the year 990 and stopped in 'Puntremel' on the way back. His diary is in the British Museum. An abbot called Nicolas left a record of his pilgrimage from Iceland to Rome in the 1150s, and described crossing the Cisa mountain: 'Then Pontremoli comes, then Luni. You can walk 10 miles in this Lunigiana and there are cities in every direction and a very ample view.'

King Phillip Augusto of France, who was on the way back from a crusade in 1181, wrote of passing through 'Luni, the cursed town of the bishop', then 'on the 14th day we had lunch in Punt-tremble'.

Apart from filling their bellies, the pilgrims who stopped in Pontremoli would always go to see 'the labyrinth' – a maze carved into the wall of San Pietro church. It was the custom to trace the route to the centre of the maze with your finger, to symbolise the pilgrimage to Christ that is 'complex and uncertain but ultimately reachable'.

Nowadays every visitor climbs to Piagnaro castle on the hill, and goes upstairs to the long room where the grey sandstone figures called *stele* are on display. They are the only surviving artwork of the Liguri people.

So far 59 of them have been discovered in Lunigiana (the first in 1910, the latest in 1969), usually by farmers clearing ground in what used to be remote forests. They are about half Lucio's height, but since they have no legs, they were probably intended to be life size. The archeologists have divided them into three groups, from 5,000, 4,000 and 3,000 years ago.

In the oldest group, the men hold knives or possibly spades with a half-moon handle and a triangular blade, and the women have small, pointy breasts. The figures in the middle group look like hammerhead sharks with smiley faces; they could be representations of people wearing space helmets. There are no women in the youngest group of warriors with spears, and they have writing on them, possibly Etruscan graffiti.

Their purpose is a mystery. Perhaps they were composed around fields or villages to scare off invaders. If so, they didn't work on the Romans.

That night, the brothers try Pontremoli's poshest restaurant, Il Caveau del Teatro, where another architect-turned-chef, Amedeo Poletti, originally from gourmet-central, Parma, is trying to modernise Lunigiana traditions. He specialises in the flavourful lamb from nearby Zeri, where the sheep eat wild mountain herbs. He serves it as both a crumbed cutlet and a barbecued chop, on a chestnut leaf. There's also a potato and leek pie, and a dessert of strawberry and ricotta tart.

'I try to do both typical food from here and original food inspired from all over Italy,' says Amedeo. 'The visitors like the new dishes, the locals don't touch them. I like to be creative, but with testaroli, which is such an important tradition, you have to leave them as they are – thick, cooked in a pot first, then refreshed by boiling for a few seconds. I can't even imagine how you might modernise testaroli.'

The *stele* statues in Piagnaro castle; the 'tremulous' bridge that gives the town its name; and Amedeo and Fernanda Poletti, who serve the lamb of Zeri at Il Caveau del Teatro.

Shepherd Leandro Boschetti milks his little black sheep twice a day.

The brothers politely refrain from observing that the testaroli (or perhaps the pesto dressing on them) were tastier at Trattoria da Bussé. They stay the night at the comfortable hotel Amedeo and his sister Fernanda have created in a seventeenth-century tower above the restaurant.

In the morning, so they can say they've been to the northern border of Lunigiana, they drive over the Cisa Pass, passing a sign that says, '*Inizio zona d'origine parmigiano reggiano*' (beginning of parmesan zone). 'We're in Emilia — ah, prosciutti, tortellini,' says Lucio. 'No,' says Aulo, 'we're in Lunigiana. Those belong to us.'

They discover references everywhere to the Via Francigena. Clearly it's become the latest thing in scholarly tourism. In the town of Berceto, the local bookstore is selling pilgrim plates. Lucio buys one as a souvenir of yesterday's heroic walk, imagining the illustration looks like him. Just out of Berceto is a coffee outlet called Bar Via Francigena. Lucio wonders, 'Is it getting too commercial?'

They escape into the deep mountains for an appointment with a maestro of pecorino. Near the village of Tavernelle, Leandro Boschetti, stiff-backed and white-moustachioed, is leaning on his gate waiting for them. He leads them into green pastures to meet his 200 little black sheep, and whistles piercingly so his dog will round them up.

He has an umbrella slung over his shoulder where his ancestors might have carried a rifle or a bow, but otherwise he could be a shepherd of any time in the past millennium. Every day he walks his flock 20 kilometres over grassy hills in search of grasses and herbs that will improve the flavour of the cheeses made by his wife and daughter-in-law, and of the meat from the sheep.

Leandro is amazed to hear that in Australia, sheep are used for wool, not cheese. He shears his sheep in the summer to make them more comfortable, but throws the wool away.

He milks the sheep at 6 am and 6 pm every day. He assembles them in a barn, ties a little stool to his bottom with a kind of safety belt, and hops round with a small bucket.

Above, Leandro's ricotta cheeses drip dry; opposite, how they make *panigacci* at La Gavarina d'Oro.

The sheep are cooperative, and it doesn't take long. They sleep in the barn overnight, so wolves won't get them.

Leandro: 'We average six cheeses a day from their milk. You get a 2-kilogram cheese from 10 litres, and I can sell that for 16 euros. You should mature the cheese for 60 days, but pecorino is a personal taste. Some people prefer it fresh.

'I've been doing this every day since I was 13 and I'm 69 now. My father showed me and I showed my son, who works with me. I've told him he should get off the land and go and work in the city, like all the other young people around here. It's too hard. We barely make enough to support four people. But he loves it more than me. He won't go.'

For lunch they try one of Aulo's favourite mountain places, Gavarina d'Oro, near the village of Podenzana, which specialises in yet another form of testaroli, called, in local dialect, *panigacci* (which Lucio suspects must come from the same root word as the English 'pancake').

It's a vast space, filled with large families at large tables. There's a roaring wood fire in one corner, and, resting on a grate over it, ten terracotta plates. Every so often a sweaty man with long tongs lifts one of the plates off the grate and puts it on a marble table. Then he ladles white batter onto the plate, puts another terracotta plate on top of the batter, then more batter, then another plate, until he has a stack about half a metre tall.

In one minute the hot plates have turned the batter into what the Mexicans would call tortillas, which are then deftly flipped into a basket by a second sweaty man while the

Chestnuts became unfashionable in the three decades after World War II because they were associated with poverty and desperation. Now there's a revival of interest in traditional foodstuffs.

A citizen of Montereggio makes chestnut pancakes in the piazza,
and at his mill, Giancarlo Moscatelli sells chestnut flour at 4 euros a bag.

first man returns the plates to the fire. The panigacci are delivered to a table, along with a tray of sliced meats and cheeses. The family at the table proceed to wrap the panigacci around the meat and cheese, and munch on the chewy, smoky snacks they've created.

Aulo discoved this place after he stopped working weekends at Ciccio's and started bushwalking. Lucio is delighted with this vision of a cooking process that probably hasn't changed in two millennia.

He wants to try panigacci with fish. Aulo says that makes no sense. The floury texture would clash with seafood. Even if you can sometimes mix contadini ingredients with pescatori ingredients, you certainly can't mix pastori and pescatori. Everybody knows that.

Aulo has heard that they're holding a chestnut festival in the nearby town of Montereggio, so the brothers drop in. Montereggio is famous as a town which produced two generations of young men who worked as travelling booksellers, and it's now the place where publishers take their summer holidays. In August its population swells from 60 to 200. But this isn't August. The festival consists of one 80-year-old lady frying chestnut pancakes in the town square, while six men sit at a table drinking wine.

But this does remind Aulo that it's chestnut season, and he decides to go down into the valley in search of one of Lunigiana's last remaining chestnut mills.

If it exists, it will have to be on the Magra River, so they follow the flow until they reach the town of Fillatieria. In the local bar, some old-timers dredge up the knowledge that yes, there is a water mill nearby, but it's not on the river, it's on a canal. The sun has set by the time Aulo finds it, but Giancarlo Moscatelli is still behind the counter, working under a single lightbulb in a 600-year-old stone tower, waiting to sell bags of chestnut flour to passing nostalgists.

He says chestnuts became deeply unfashionable in the three decades after World War II because they were associated with poverty and desperation. 'There were 1,440 water mills in Lunigiana a hundred years ago, and now there are six,' he says.

Four generations of his family had run this mill – 'I was born in this building' – but to keep it going, he had to get a job on the railways.

It's a time-consuming business. The chestnuts have to be dried over a low fire for 22 days, then peeled, before they can pass through the sandstone grinding wheels turned by the rush of water under the house. And after all that, a 1-kilo bag sells for 4 euros.

Giancarlo's retirement from the railways on a pension five years ago coincided with a revival of interest in traditional foodstuffs, and now he has turned his place into an *agriturismo* (a rural bed-and-breakfast), with a government grant to let people stay overnight and watch him practise his ancient craft. It might just survive to be continued by his daughter's family.

On the way back to Bocca di Magra, Aulo and Lucio debate whether 'the real Lunigiana' is disappearing, reviving, or in the process of reinvention as a nostalgic fantasy.

'Her hands, fluttering butterflies amongst the clouds of flour, brought a creature into the world … You had to think something was being born there, that those hands had an intelligence of their own.'

—Maurizio Maggiani, describing his mother making ravioli, in the novel *Mauri Mauri*, 1996

'LE SUE MANI, FARFALLINE PALPITANTI TRA LE FOLATE DELLA FARINA, FACEVANO AL MONDO

Lucio looks back on his childhood as a perpetual holiday, but he realises that's because he's only remembering the summers, when the family spent every day at Bocca di Magra – his mother ironing tablecloths and frying fish in Capannina Ciccio, his father doing construction jobs in the neighbourhood, his brother Aulo bottling wine and waiting tables, and Lucio chopping up garlic and parsley, eating spaghetti, and swimming in the river with the children of Ciccio's customers.

The other nine months of the year his parents worked every Sunday at Ciccio's, and Bruna worked as a tailor the rest of the week, making and repairing clothes for everyone around.

Mauro loved farming, and would have gone back onto the land full-time if Bruna had let him. But she found nothing romantic in the peasant life. When she was small, her father had fallen into a well and drowned. Her mother persuaded the landlord to let her keep running the farm, in order to feed her four children. But it was very hard for a single parent, especially when her sister committed suicide by jumping into the well after learning she had cancer.

So Mauro did most of the heavy work on the rented farmland near their cottage. Bruna's contribution was tending the vegetable patch, feeding the chickens and rabbits and making interesting meals from what the farm produced. And trying to get some knowledge into the head of her younger son, who was constantly in trouble for 'dreaming' at school.

For Lucio, the sign that the holidays were over each year was when he was called to help his uncle Gugliemo clean the wine barrels, in early September.

Lucio: 'My job was to go inside with a scrubbing brush and hose to get rid of *il gromo* (the crust). My father would take me over there on the back of the Lambretta. Everyone was waiting for me to do my bit so they could get started. The grape crushing machines were in his courtyard.

'I felt very important because I was the only one who was the right size for the job. But once I got inside, I felt sick and kind of dizzy.

'My uncle would shout "*Tira via'r gromo!*" (pull away the crust). I'd yell back, "*I n ven!*" (it doesn't come). He'd yell, "*Pista pu forte*" (push harder). We had the same conversation every year. I'd come out covered in red specks. It left me with an aversion to wine that I didn't get over till I was 44.

'After the summer, every month had its seasonal requirement. In October was the vendemmia, where every family helped every other family to harvest the grapes, crush them, put them in barrels and drink the wine.

'In November, it was time to harvest the olives and take them to the mill. The big day was 2 November, the day of the dead, when we'd meet our relatives at the cemetery, pay our respects to everyone in their graves, and then go and have a picnic.

'And December was when we could look forward to Christmas. We'd know it was close when we heard the sound of the Zampognari in the streets. They were shepherds from the Abruzzi region who travelled around Italy playing Christmas tunes on instruments that looked like bagpipes, made from the insides of sheep.

'The Zampognari were busking for coins and the occasional drink, and the children would follow them around as if they were Pied Pipers. Their arrival was the sign that it was time to get your little figurines out of their box and set up the *presepe* − the nativity scene, laid out in the living room on moss we picked from near the local creeks.

'On Christmas Eve, we'd kill and pluck the rooster we'd been fattening up for the past few weeks, and have a dinner of *cotechino* (pork sausage) with big white beans, cavolo nero and newly pressed olive oil − but not too much, so as to leave room for the feast the next day. There's a saying in the neighbourhood that when everything is done right, down to the last detail, it's like raining olive oil on cavolo nero.

'Doing everything right on Christmas Eve meant putting out one more serving of dinner than the number of people at the table, and leaving the plate untouched while we were eating. When we'd finished, Dad would do the ritual of "feeding the fire". The extra dinner went into the flames to be delivered to the Devil, so he would not bother us in the year to come.

'Next morning, we'd look in the socks we'd left out overnight, to see if Babbo Natale (Father Christmas) had left us some sweets (if we'd been good) or a lump of coal (if we'd been bad).

'In Italy, kids didn't get their big presents on 25 December. That happens on 6 January, supposedly the day when the three wise men delivered their gifts to Jesus, and the giver is not Santa but a good witch called La Befana, with a long nose and a headscarf. How she gets around the whole of Italy I do not know, since she has no sleigh and walks with a stick.

'Giving presents on 25 December would be a distraction from the essential task − feasting with the family. Our aunty, who lived next door, would come in with her children to eat with us. In the morning, Mum would put the rooster on to boil with carrots, bay leaves, celery and onions. The stock produced from that rooster was precious. Some of our neighbours would put tortellini in their broth, and serve it as the first course of the banquet, but our family drank it as a consommé.

'The pasta we liked on feast days was ravioli, stuffed with meat and covered with a rich ragú and parmesan. Usually we'd start with antipasto – bread, slices of prosciutto and lardo, pecorino cheese, and roast capsicums with capers and anchovies, which were one of Mum's specialties. Then we'd have the consommé and the ravioli and sometimes pieces of roast rabbit, which Mum served with a kind of radish called *scorza nera*, boiled then sauteed in butter. With it, the adults drank Dad's home-made red wine.

'The main course was the rooster, served with salsa verde and *mostarda* – fruits such as pears, apricots and quinces marinated in mustard oil and sugar, plus a salad made with green radicchio that was more bitter than the version grown in the Veneto.

'Dessert would be *pandolce genovese* – a dome-shaped form of panettone flavoured with orange water, pine nuts, fennel seeds, sultanas and candied oranges. Usually we'd have nuts with that, and since there was only one nutcracker, which people never passed on quickly enough, we'd have fun smashing the shells on the tabletop.

'By now it was evening, and time for a little supper of leftovers. With any luck, the rooster would keep providing snacks for the family until the day of La Befana's visit.

'December and early January were great eating times, but then supplies got a bit sparse. Sometimes my parents would send me to buy four *fettine* (thin slices) of veal or beef. "Tell the butcher to cut them really thin," my father would say. We would serve them with lots of vegetables or polenta.

'There were always *ambulanti* (hawkers) wandering down from the mountains offering pecorino, onions, clothing they'd made, or animals they'd hunted. Sometimes we'd pay them with eggs.

'The next big eating event was Carnevale, when we'd have *Martedì Grasso* [Fat Tuesday], with lasagne and *fritelle* – fried egg batter, either savoury with baccalà or sweet with pine nuts and sultanas.

'We always had Easter lunch at Ciccio's, because that was one of the busiest times for them. My mother and Zia Anna would go in early and prepare everything for the family feast, then do the lunch for the customers, then tell us all to sit down about 4 pm for a vegetable tart called *torta pasqualina*, which was supposed to have 33 layers of pastry to symbolise Christ's age, and *pappardelle alla lepre* – wide pasta with hare sauce and fried lamb with fried artichokes.

'The next big event was the wheat harvesting (*mietitura*) in June, when these huge red machines, taller than the houses, would rumble through the village carrying red-faced young men who were always shouting and and making everybody laugh.

'That was followed by the corn harvesting, when everybody gathered in the courtyard between our house and my aunty's house to twist the pieces of corn off the cobs and put them in bags to go to the mill. We always did that at night, and my mother handed around *ravioli dolci* – fried pasta stuffed with sweet rice. And then we were ready to go back to Ciccio's.'

Just after Lucio's fourteenth birthday, the perpetual holiday ended abruptly, when Mario told Lucio to put on the black trousers, white jacket and tie and start serving the customers.

He didn't mind the idea of delivering food and wine. He'd cleared plenty of tables. He'd been making coffee in the bar since he was tall enough to reach the handle of the machine, at the age of nine. But now he had to talk to the people. The idea paralysed him.

'I had been swimming and playing with the children of these people as an equal, and now it seemed to me that I had become their servant. I feared I was going to be hooked for life. Not just as a waiter, but in a job. Once you put on a uniform, you were a grownup. I didn't want to be a grownup.

Lucio: 'I locked myself in the toilet. It took an hour to get me out. Mario is saying "You're stupid, we need you, it's busy" and I'm saying, "I'm not coming out, mi *vergogno* – I feel embarrassed". Then Aulo came and tried to persuade me and then my mother came. And I finally came out.

'Once I was in the dining room I was helping everybody, they were helping me, I felt part of the team and I realised there was nothing to be ashamed of.'

And just as well. If he hadn't relaxed into the waiter's uniform, he would never have met his future wife. Lucio continued working as a waiter every summer while studying to be a *geometra*, which is a designer qualified to work on buildings not taller than three storeys. It's the first step to getting a university degree as an architect. The second step never happened.

Lucio: 'During the 1970s Ciccio's started growing. In the '50s, it got the writers, in the '60s the artists, but by the '70s we were starting to see The Beautiful People – actors, directors, TV types. One day Franco Nero and Vanessa Redgrave were walking in Via Fabbricotti. They met while making *Camelot*.

'On the river outside Ciccio's, a yacht would pull up and a beautiful couple would walk down the dock, all in white, white, white, with amazing tans. Some of them seemed to have this speech impediment where they couldn't sound the "r". They'd talk about "cwostino". They'd ask "C'è Mawio?" (Is Mario here?).

'But still the main customers were families on holiday. Nowadays we think nothing of going overseas for a week. In those days, you went to the seaside for a month, that was your annual break.

'There weren't many bookings. People just walk in, get shown to a table, which is already prepared with the local white wine and mineral water open (if you had some left from one table, you'd fill it up and give it to another table). You'd keep replacing the wine, and they'd pay *al consumo* – if they have one and a quarter bottles, they pay for that.

'Nobody ever has red. There's a bit of chianti out the back in case somebody asks for it. Then we give the bread, and ask if they want mixed antipasto. Usually they say yes. Insalata di mare, white anchovies marinated, mussels, tartina. About five little things in individual plates.

'Now you can leave them alone for ten minutes. Towards the end of them eating the antipasto you go and ask if they want pasta, risotto, un po' di pesce [a little fish], un pò di datteri [a few clams] … listing the specialities. You never list the *bistecca* [steak] or the *pizzaiola* or *spaghetti al ragú* [meat sauce] or *spaghetti al pomodoro* [tomato sauce]. They could ask for those.

From Bruna's kitchen: baccalà (cod); scarpazza (greens pie); lardo (pork); pancetta, salami and fava beans; torta di riso (rice cake); and fried porcini mushrooms.

'You go to the kitchen and scream out what they want. You don't even say the table number. The kitchen knows that plate's for Lucio, that's for Aulo, that's for Giuseppe. Anna was the central command point – she would tell my mother to do tartina, other people when to put on the pasta.

'By this time you are relaxed a bit, and you'd say, "*Cosa facciamo per secondo*" what do we do for main – pesce fritto, *branzino*, *dentice*, *mormora* [fried fish, sea bass, snapper, bream]? Whatever the fisherman had brought that morning.

'The main course was easiest to order because there was usually just one dish for the whole group. Fish was roasted in the oven, or *al cartoccio* [in baking paper].

'It was served whole, and we'd fillet it at the table. I learnt by watching Aulo and the other waiters: always use a spoon and a fork, never a knife. You follow the back with a spoon, take the spine and big bones away. Then you take the skin off, unless they want the skin. Then you take the bones from the tummy.

'You never turn the fish over. It's not only bad luck, but you don't need to. You pick up the bone and put it away. Put a slice of lemon on the plate, and a bottle of oil on the table.

'Then as we cleared the table we'd ask, "*Frutta, formaggio, dolce* (fruit, cheese, sweets?). Normally they say, "frutta". Sometimes gelato. There was no dessert trolley then, but we always had St Honoré cake – a long slab with cream in the middle and pastries along on the side, so it was easy to cut – and a log of chocolate-coated semifreddo with candied fruit from a pasticceria in La Spezia.

'Cheese was just pecorino or parmesan. But most of that was eaten by our family. Customers didn't really eat cheese after fish.

'Then they just had *caffè* and that's the beauty about it, they'd ask for "caffè," not decaf cappuccino, flat white, macchiato, all this and that you get now in Australia.'

The wedding feast of Lucio and Sally at Vallechia ristorante in the nearby hills; Lucio and other waiters kill time between the frenzy of lunch and dinner.

Early one summer in 1975, Lucio came to work one morning and saw two stunning blondes having coffee in the garden. One of them he knew – it was Mario's wife Wendy. He got introduced to the other – Wendy's sister Sally.

Sally Stanford was a meat-and-potatoes girl who grew up on a cattle property. She may have had the occasional spaghetti during her two years working as a media buyer for an ad agency in Sydney, but she had no particular interest in Italian food when she set off to see the world – and her sister Wendy – in 1975. But then came the tartina at Ciccio, which changed her life – along with the life of Lucio Galletto.

Sally: 'I was 17 when Mario came to Mudgee and married Wendy. Six years later I set off. Everybody my age was going on a European holiday, so I saved up my pennies and bought a one-way ticket, planning to stay away for two or three years, much to my parents' horror.

'I was travelling with friends, driving in a Kombi van around England and Norway. I got sick of the people I was with, so I decided to go straight to Italy. I arrived at Sarzana station in the middle of summer, filthy dirty from travelling for abut 30 hours.

'Not speaking a word of Italian, I phoned Ciccio's and said, 'Wendy Sally station Sarzana'. I waited about an hour and a half and Wendy turned up. She took me back to Ciccio's and we were sitting outside in the bar, and I was fed and watered and introduced to 6,000 family members.

We started a secret relationship and Lucio would sneak into my room at night ...
We pacified everybody by saying 'It's alright, we're going to get married'.

'I remember thinking when I got there that it looked fabulous by the river. The first thing they gave me was the tartina. I loved it, still do. I met Lucio the very first day, when I arrived off the train. I was sitting on the outside, I was so thirsty and Wendy made me drink an espresso coffee. He was introduced as one of many, and I thought, "Mmm, cute". And then I'd see him go past every day, but there was not much communication.

'Wendy spent a lot of time at Ciccio's – not in the kitchen but working in a kind of public relations role. I remember many times seeing these long tables with Wendy at the head hosting a spectacular meal for visiting artists, writers, journalists, wealthy Milanesi business people.

'Whenever anyone important arrived, especially if they spoke English, Mario would call Wendy to come down and she would meet them, and have a chat or a drink or a meal with them. Her social skills were a huge asset for the restaurant.

'I was going to stay a couple of months, and move on. Mario and Wendy helped me get a job as an au pair with a wealthy family in Milan. I sat at table and was waited on, loved the food. I don't think I'd ever eaten a fig before.

'Wendy got pregnant and the doctor said she had to stay in bed, so Mario asked if I'd like her job in the art gallery he was running then. If someone came in and didn't speak English, I could just send them down to the restaurant.

'I didn't have to sell much because there'd be an opening every month or so and most of the work would sell on the opening night. A major part of my work was serving drinks.

'So I was just in there learning my Italian and reading magazines. Mario spent a lot of time talking to the artists, visiting their houses and looking at their studios. I was staying in a room on the ground floor of Rosi's place, which was a three-storey apartment. I had all my meals at the restaurant.

'Ciccio's was a fabulous meeting place. A lot of customers didn't spend much money, apart from the odd drink, and they'd spend the afternoon there playing backgammon. That's where I learnt to play backgammon.

'I remember all the food being wonderful, from the simplest spaghetti al pomodoro, which was so exquisite it's still my favourite dish. I so looked forward to staff lunch on Sunday, about four o'clock. You'd work hard and then have this huge meal at a table full of family.

'Lucio's parents were there. His father worked in a factory during the week, but came down on Sunday. My recollection of him was with his apron on, slicing lemons all Sunday morning.

'Mario was there every lunchtime, and everyone went to him with their problems. Anna was always in black, she hardly sat at table – she was always working. Giuseppe was there all the time, very devoted, and starting a relationship with Simonetta, who lived across the road.

'I never cooked on the stove. I made salad and I did aglio prezzemolo with the mezzaluna. The kids who used to do it had grown up, and the next generation was not old enough.

'I ran the bar for a while. It was a great bar with cocktails and icecreams and coffees but fairly disorganised. They served a lot of people outside, but they didn't always stock the fridge the night before. I had no experience, but it was a matter of common sense. I added Pimms in a tall glass with fruit – Italians loved it.

'I remember Lucio had just come back from a holiday at Stromboli and he had a lovely tan and blue eyes and he looked gorgeous. We started a secret relationship and Lucio would sneak into my room at night, but Rosi's mother-in-law found out and got very upset. Mario took Lucio down to the storeroom and said: "What are you doing with my sister-in-law?"

'We pacified everybody by saying, "It's all right, we're going to get married". We went to dinner at Lucio's parents' place at Molicciara, with various neighbours and relatives all sitting around the kitchen. We ate rabbit from the oven with potatoes and baby parsnips roasted with rosemary.

'They used to eat the comb when they killed the rooster once a year. I didn't like it but I realised it was a great compliment for it to be offered to me. We had *torta di riso*, rice cake for dessert, which to me seemed like boarding-school stodge.

'Lucio said, "Is anybody going to say anything?" And his mother said, "Are you pregnant?" And his aunt Fortuna said, "Hasn't she got lovely teeth". His father teased him with the rhyme *Donne e buoi dei paesi tuoi* (only get involved with women and oxen from your own land – because you know their history).

'We didn't tell my parents till we decided we would come and live in Australia. We sent them a postcard from Paris signed Sally and Lucio and they got straight on the phone to Wendy asking, "Who is this Luckio guy?"

'So we were married in Castelnuovo by a communist mayor who gave a long speech about how young people should not get married. We don't know if he meant us or not – we were 23. We drove off to Florence in the rain.

'We'd already decided to go to Australia to live, because getting work in Italy for me would have been too hard. Working the bar in Ciccio in the summer is not a career. Lucio had never worked a proper job, so he could start fresh anywhere.'

And so Lucio and Sally were off on the big adventure. What would Australia do with a reluctant waiter qualified to design buildings up to three storeys?

While Lucio practised with his band, Mamma Bruna perfected her skills at the fryer.

'In the middle of life's journey, I found myself in a dark wood, for the straight road was lost. It is so hard to say how rough and savage was the forest. Even the thought of it brings back the fear!'

Dante Alighieri, Canto 1, *The Divine Comedy*

'NEL MEZZO DEL CAMMIN DI

Into the hills

When Vincenzo Guastafierro scored his first crop of olives back in the mid 1990s, Aulo Galletto and some other friends played a practical joke on him. They told him he should harvest the olives when they were green, because that gave the best oil.

Vincenzo had just bought the olive grove after retiring from a management job at the naval dockyard at La Spezia, so he didn't realise that the best oil comes from olives that have absorbed enough sun to turn purple or black. He dragged a few hundred hard green fruits off his trees, put them in a box, and took them to the local *frantoio* (mill), where he learnt that they would produce watery acidic oil. 'Come back in a month with some riper ones,' they said.

Why would Aulo, the kindest of men, play a mean trick like that? 'Well,' reflects Lucio, 'Aulo didn't think Vincenzo would actually follow his advice. Vincenzo is from Naples.' In the view of north Italians, Neapolitans are cunning tricksters, who fool others and are never fooled themselves.

Vincenzo isn't really from the Gotham of the south. He's from the countryside near Pompeii, where his parents grew hazelnuts. He's another example of an upwardly mobile farm boy who found success in urban life but wanted to return to the soil.

He could do this while still in his forties, because Italian public servants enjoy a generous pension scheme. He bought an old olive grove on 5,000 square metres of steep land near the village of Vallecchia, in the hills behind Sarzana. Ten years later, he clearly has no hard feelings over Aulo's joke. Vincenzo and Aulo are clambering along branches unfurling the bright orange nets into which the olives are almost ready to drop. Vincenzo, thin and short with tanned skin and a bushy grey moustache, is wearing pink track pants, a khaki shirt and a green cap, which is almost a uniform for farmers in this area.

The brothers have driven into the hills behind Sarzana in search of the mills where their father used to go to buy olive oil for Ciccio's. With Lucio perched on the back of the Lambretta, Mauro would arrive at the frantoio, ask for a little of their best oil to be dropped onto his palms, rub his big hands together, cup them around his nose and breathe deeply. That was the only test he needed to order it for the restaurant.

For Lucio's family, the new olive oil had religious significance. Once when 11 year old Lucio had trouble sleeping for five nights in a row, his mother consulted a local wise woman, who advised her to make the sign of the cross on his forehead with first-pressed olive oil every night before he went to bed. Bruna paid the nurse-witch for this advice with a live chicken. It seemed to work.

Vincenzo hops down every so often to show Lucio the different sizes of *rastrellino* (little rake) with which he helps the olives off the branches ('I don't use machines and I would never shake the trees or hit the branches like some people do'). From a condition of almost total ignorance when he bought the place, he now knows each of his 300 trees personally.

Olive trees are not native to Liguria – they were probably first planted by Greek travellers 3,000 years ago and cultivated by the Romans and then the monks in the Dark Ages. They are the base of Ligurian eating – perhaps the defining characteristic.

Ligurian oil is expensive (twice as much as Tuscan) because of low yields from the rocky steep hillsides, but worth it, at least to Lucio – a bit lighter than Tuscan, therefore useful in cooking, but best drizzled over soup.

In Lunigiana, oil is mostly made from a type of olive called the lavagnina, but Vincenzo's trees are rarer. His favourite is a 200-year-old called Olivastra, which produces a long purple olive and a sweet golden oil that he reserves for his own family. He bottles it in November and keeps it in the dark to mature till the following March. It gets a special flavour, he says, from growing near bay trees.

He sells the rest at the mill to bottling companies, who blend it with produce from other farmers. They'll be able to label it 'cold pressed extra virgin Ligurian olive oil' (meaning the olives were not heated to extract more oil and the acidity is below 1 per cent), but they may not be able to claim the 'DOP' (Denomination of Origin Protected) for the Rivieria Levante, which was granted by the European Union in 1997, and is designed to guarantee quality and let producers charge a high price.

Selling 450 litres a year at around 12 euros a litre is not going to make Vincenzo rich – but he's not in it for the money. He has his pension.

He doesn't live on the farm – his family home is down in Sarzana, but he has built himself a hut where he sleeps most nights between September and December. There's a toilet, and a barbecue area where he often has family lunches at weekends. Does his family

Vincenzo picks his olives and takes them to the mill where they are crushed into a paste, spread on mats and squashed into oil.

The first pressing was called *Paradiso*, to be used as dressing on soups and salads; the second was *Purgatorio*, for cooking; and the thin pale stuff from the third pressing was called *Inferno*, to be used in lamps.

At Vallecchia, where Lucio and Sally had their wedding reception, the food remains unchanged after 30 years, much to Lucio's delight.

help with the olive growing? 'No, they're not completely stupid,' he replies.

He also spends a lot of time here in April, when the trees produce tiny white flowers. As soon as the flowers drop, Vincenzo sprays the trees with sulphur mixture to kill fungus. He doesn't have to use a lot of other chemicals because the Vallecchia area is high enough (and thus cold enough) to deter the fly called dacus oleae which can ruin oils grown in lower areas.

Does he get lonely up here? 'No, I talk to the trees,' he says. 'When I'm here I feel *bene, bene rinasco*' (well, well refreshed). He isn't pressing his olives yet (there's still some green in them) but when he directs the brothers to the nearest frantoio, they find many other growers are queuing to put their creations through the crushers.

Trucks dump their plastic crates into a tank, a conveyor belt lifts a few olives at a time into another tank, separating the leaves. Then they go into a kind of mincing machine, where revolving metal blades chop them up. Huge discs of sandstone attached to pistons go around and around, crushing the olives, pips and all (in earlier centuries the stones would have been pulled around by mules or pushed around by water, but now electricity moves them).

The pulp is squirted onto mats (nylon these days) which are stacked and then pressed, so the oil dribbles out the sides of the press and falls into a metal basin beneath. From this it spins in a centrifuge so the oil and water will separate.

The frantoio sells its own oil and other products such as soap. There's a mound of brown powder outside – waiting to be collected by less authentic oil producers who will chemically extract commercial cooking oils. (In the nineteenth century, oil in this area was classified into three types: the first pressing was called Paradiso, to be used as dressing on soups and salads; the second pressing was called Purgatorio, to be used in cooking; and the thin pale stuff that came from the third pressing was called Inferno, to be used in lamps.)

Back in Mauro's day, the mills were mostly on rivers, and were powered by water. The one Lucio remembers best was the Mulino del Piano (mill of the flat) which at pressing time was the site of an annual fair where the kids could play on roundabouts while the adults looked at agricultural displays. The last time Lucio went to the fair, at the age of 18, his band performed onstage.

The cook emerges from the kitchen and offers (clockwise) barbecued lamb; sgabei; ravioli; vegetable antipasti; raw baby artichokes and braised fennel; and mixed crostini.

Lucio: 'It was a Sunday and I had to ask Zia Anna for permission to take time off work at Ciccio. We had bongo drums, three acoustic guitars and an old organ that worked when you pumped the air in with your foot. It made a terrible noise. I'd written a song that went for 20 minutes, "E Com'eri Bella" (How beautiful you were) about a girl who gets married and goes from the control of her father to the control of her husband without ever being free. In the end she leaves her husband and then she can fly. In Italian, *volare* not only means to fly but also to reach the heights of sexual passion.

'I was protesting about the old idea of marriage, women as possessions. When you're 18 you can see the injustices of the world. People liked it, but it went on too long. One of my friends kept holding up a sign that said, "Is it over yet?"'

The brothers go for lunch to Vallecchia, the restaurant where Lucio and Sally had their wedding reception. The food is unchanged, much to Lucio's delight. There are *sgabei* (balls of fried bread dough) which you slice open and fill with prosciutto and stracchino

cheese; fried artichokes; crostini smeared with mushroom paste; heavy ravioli in a meat sauce; a rabbit and olive stew; and barbecued lamb chops; with rough carafe white that needs dilution with mineral water.

From his room in Fosdinovo Castle (opposite) Dante looked out the window (above left) and saw the layers of Inferno (above right).

When Lucio attempts to start a conversation with the lady who delivers these dishes, a man emerges from the kitchen and tells her to stop talking to the customers.

After lunch, they visit the Malaspina castle at Fosdinovo, where Dante stayed and supposedly got the vision of the descending circles of Hell that inspired the 'Inferno' part of *The Divine Comedy*. The legend has it that from this room Dante saw 'the great funnel-shaped cave lying below, surrounded by a series of ledges with the slopes converging to the stream Isolone' (where Lucifer lives).

The guide takes Lucio and Aulo to the room where Dante allegedly slept, now marked with a bust of the poet. The view is perfectly pleasant, though it may have been a little wilder in 1306.

The guide is sceptical. He thinks the 'seeing Hell' story was the fantasy of an eighteenth century poet which was then embroidered by the twentieth-century poet Gabriele d'Annunzio, who came and stayed in the room to absorb the Dante vibe. But the nineteenth-century owners of the castle knew a good myth when they heard it, and commissioned a series of frescoes showing Dante praying in the room where he allegedly slept.

The guide is more enthusiastic about the torture chamber, with metal boots designed to slowly crush feet, and an iron maiden to spike the whole body. This was where the Malaspinas punished recalcitrant employees and rebellious peasants.

There's a round cage on display which looks like another instrument of torture but turns out to be a lockable cradle in which each male Malaspina heir was displayed to the local citizenry. The lock is not to keep the baby in, but to keep potential kidnappers out.

When you're hated as much as the Malaspinas were, security is an issue. The castle had a secret passageway through which they escaped during riots connected with the French revolution in the eighteenth century.

Dante in Lunigiana

FOR THE ITALIANS, DANTE ALIGHIERI IS WHAT A COMBINATION OF SHAKESPEARE, DICKENS AND AUSTEN WOULD BE FOR THE ENGLISH. EVERY ITALIAN SCHOOLCHILD SPENDS YEARS STUDYING HIS EPIC POEM, *THE DIVINE COMEDY*, AND GROWS UP CAPABLE OF QUOTING TRACTS FROM IT.

The people of Lunigiana see Dante as their special guest star, because he spent a year of his life working as a lobbyist for the local warlords, the Malaspina family, and negotiating on their behalf with the Bishop of Luni. That year was 1305. The Lunigianese will tell you that the wild forest in which Dante found himself halfway through his life, as described in the opening canto of the 'Inferno' part of *The Divine Comedy*, is somewhere near Castelnuovo.

One of the people Dante sees in Hell is the fortune-teller Aronta, who interpreted the lightning, the flight of birds, and the insides of animals to predict the future. He warned Pompey of his defeat by Caesar by interpreting the intestine of a bull: 'Aronta was the one who lives there, on the Luni mountains, where Carrara is situated. He had his little house between white marbles from which to see the stars and the sea. There was no obstacle to the view.'

Because he had dared to claim powers which are the province of God, Aronta was allocated an ironic punishment – condemned always to look backwards. Lucio reflects with a smile that this is what he is doing in Bocca di Magra.

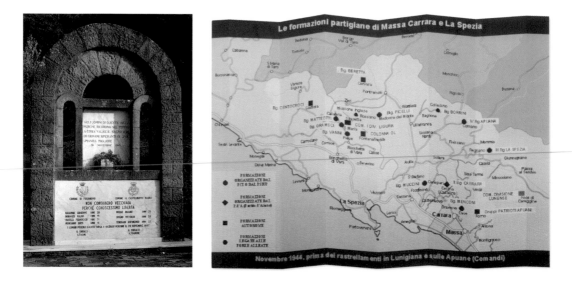

Passing the kitchen where cooks are preparing lunch for the family which now inhabits the castle, Lucio asks, 'Are they making testaroli?' The guide replies: 'They're from Rumania. They wouldn't know what testaroli are.'

A family tree framed on the wall has one branch named Galletto, which intrigues Lucio so much he buys a jug and a vase with the Malaspina 'bad thorn' coat of arms.

DAY TWO

Today Lucio and Mario are on the partisan trail. Mario thinks he can find the bolthole where their fathers hid from the Germans and pulled the pin on the hand grenade. They're also going to visit the Museum of the Resistance and see the filmed interviews with people who would have been comrades of their fathers.

The hills through which they are driving are where Mauro's Garibaldi Brigade wandered for 18 months as guerrillas, living off chestnuts whenever Ciccio was unable to bring them food supplies, and sabotaging the Germans as they retreated from the advancing Americans through the north of Italy.

Every few kilometres they pass monuments, memorials and plaques: '*Agli uomini di queste valli perché ricordino nel tempo a cosa valse il sacrificio di giovani speranti di una umanità migliore. 30 novembre 1945. Non conobbero vecchiaia perché conoscessimo libertà.*' (To the people of this valley, so that they remember in times to come what the sacrifice of these young people meant – hoping for a better humanity. They never knew old age so that we would know freedom.)

'On 29 November 1944, to stop the nazifascisti hordes in the name of freedom, here fell Cervia, Gino, Piola, Giuseppe. The people of Ortonovo remember.'

Every 29 November, Mauro used to take the family to partisan remembrance events, and they would join in singing a song that began, '*E se io muoio da partigiano, Tu mi devi sepellir* …' 'And if I die as a partisan, you must bury me. You will bury me there in the mountains, under the shadow of a flowering tree. And the people who pass by will say, "Oh what a beautiful flower". And you'll say that's the flower of the partisan, who died for liberty.'

Mauro taught the words to the boys as they were working in the vegetable garden together. The women at the remembrance events would sing, 'I woke up one morning, goodbye love. And I found the invader. Partisan, take me away with you, because I am prepared to die.' Some were in tears because they'd lost a husband or son in the Resistance.

They reach the grey stone village of Giucano, where Anna and Ciccio (with baby Mario) moved in 1944 when Sarzana became too dangerous for them. They locate the house where Mario thinks they lived. Some of its stones are blackened, suggesting it was torched by the Germans. But the backyard, where Mario assumes the bolthole must have been, seems to have undergone a makeover. There's no sign of where a manure storage space might have been.

'We'll go and ask Gabriella,' says Mario, referring to his cousin. She is the daughter of Ciccio's brother Camillo, who tried to take over Capannina Ciccio after Ciccio died, but who died two months later.

Gabriella lives with her husband, Francesco, in a modern two-storey house with a walk-in fireplace that has clearly been salvaged from an older building. Her daughter's family lives in an identical house next door. Gabriella hasn't got a clue about the bolthole, has never heard the hand grenade story, but insists the boys stay for lunch. Her daughter's husband is a pilot with the helicopter rescue service, and has the day off today, so the families were planning to make a big lunch together. Two more mouths won't make a bit of difference.

Everybody sets to work, moving between the two kitchens and exchanging family gossip. Armando the helicopter pilot starts making a pasta sauce of tomato, chilli and tinned tuna. 'My brother kills pigs and makes sausages from raw dried pork, and he preserves them in chilli oil. He keeps sending jars up to me, so we'll have some today. I hope you guys don't object to southern food.'

They say they'll love it, and Armando says he's used to being looked down on in this neighbourhood because he's from Naples. 'We are all brothers,' he says. 'Let's not have separation of north and south.'

Gabriella interrupts: 'But we've also been the victim of prejudice in this village, because I come from Sarzana. That's only 5 kilometres away and we got here 20 years ago and Francesco grew up here. It's just a small-town mentality.'

Gabriella has baked rice cake (which she calls *torta scema*, literally 'stupid pie') and *farinata*, which is a kind of flatbread made from ground chickpeas and water. There is white wine in carafes, followed by home-made *limoncello digestivo* (lemon liqueur).

Lucio explains their search this morning for their fathers' bolthole, and Gabriella's husband Francesco suddenly says: 'I was there.'

'Where?' says Lucio.

'At the *rastrellamento*. I was eight years old.'

Francesco: 'My father, who was friends with the partisans, had been beaten up by the

Fascists, and he couldn't run. He had a walking stick. On that night we were woken up about 2 am when the partisans came banging on the door and said, "*Ragazzi, andé via dé chi*" (Guys, get out of here). They said the Germans were coming up the hills and they were burning villages.

'We went outside and I heard the sound of people crunching on leaves in the forest, and I saw fires further down the hill. We ran away, but my father fell over so many times. I was helping him up. There were shells flying overhead. I remember being so scared I wet my pants.

'It was raining. I had a little cloth bag, held together by a metal ring. I wrapped the most precious thing I had in it – a metal box containing some sugar. Every time my father fell, the bag dropped too, and I kept hearing the noise of the metal hitting the ground. I close my eyes, I still hear this bag falling to the ground.

'My mother was in Sarzana, we were trying to get down to see her.

'We finally got there a day later. After two days, they made us all go into Piazza Vittorio Veneto to watch the execution of five partisans. I saw that. My mother put her hand over my eyes at the last minute, but I heard the sound of the shots and the puff of breath from the people when they were hit.'

Lucio and Mario are both thinking, That could have been my father.

DAY THREE

Now Lucio drives past artichoke plantations to meet Salvatore Marchese in Castelnuovo: where the Bishops of Luni had their official seat after they'd finished in Sarzana; where Dante worked as a peacemaker between the bishop and the Malaspina family; where Lucio went to primary school; where he had his first kiss (behind the castle); where he married Sally; and where, according to Salvatore, Armanda's snack bar has been transformed by her son into the hottest restaurant of the area.

The town, with its two medieval towers, is looking splendid. Salvatore explains that every Wednesday's takings for the government-run Lotto game go towards restoration of historic buildings, and Castelnuovo, with its Dante connection, is high on the heritage list.

Lucio tells Salvatore he has been reading a novel in which the local author Maurizio Maggiani describes the people of Castelnuovo as *strampalati* (wild, erratic, irresponsible). Salvatore is not amused. 'The population of the town nowadays is 450, of whom three or four are anarchists,' he says. 'They used to be more angry a century ago because the only work was in the quarries of Carrara, and the men had to walk all night to get there. They're a peaceful lot these days.'

They walk up to look at Lucio's old school, which he remembers as a rather run-down building with wonderful seventeenth-century frescoes on the ceiling. Now it's a bright yellow four storey apartment building. He hopes the frescoes survived the renovation.

They drop in to the Santa Maddelana church to visit Lucio's old teacher, Don Franco, who takes only a minute to remember the dreaming 10-year-old and is surprised to hear Lucio has been able to stay focused for long enough to start a restaurant.

Salvatore points to an altarpiece of the crucifixion by Pieter Brueghel the Younger, and says, 'That's the most important painting in the Lunigiana'. Don Franco says there's something more important behind it. He unlocks a cupboard and points to the church's precious relics, which he says pilgrims travel hundreds of kilometres to see. They are a bone of St Anthony and a hair of St Joseph. They are very dusty. Salvatore and Lucio nod dutifully and say they must be off to an appointment.

Armanda's trattoria is a narrow room that seats 30 people at a squeeze. On its white walls are framed prints of local foodstuffs. From the kitchen Armanda's 14-year-old granddaughter can be heard practising her French.

Possibly to balance this outbreak of informality, Salvatore says this is a very historic room, because the first *presidio* (official meeting) of the Slow Food movement was planned here, and more recently, the *tavola rotonda* (round table) of the food critics from *L'Espresso* magazine met here to allocate the scores for every good restaurant in Italy.

Lucio asks how he became a food critic.

Salvatore: 'My family is from Sicily but we moved up here when I was small. My mother used to do cleaning and chores in the homes of the rich, and take me with her. Sometimes they would invite us to join them for lunch. It was nothing like what we had at home.

'I learnt the important lesson that food varies from place to place and from family to family. The first time I saw prosciutto was when I was a teenager, in one of those rich houses. I realised that the rich eat differently from the poor, but not always better.

'I was studying geology at university but I drifted into journalism because I was interested in the different ways people approach food and it was an opportunity for me to earn money while eating. Now I check 96 restaurants a year in the north of Italy for the

Near the entrance to Castelnuovo, Salvatore waits to meet Lucio for lunch.

Luciana makes
panigacci, and, opposite,
Valerio offers *lattughe
ripiene* (stuffed lettuce);
rolled rabbit with
braised fennel;
polenta with *baccalà*;
chestnut mousse with
persimmon jelly; and
scarpazza (greens pie).

Espresso guide. Our score out of 20 is based on food only. We are not allowed to formally take into account atmosphere or service, but good bread is important, and the use of local wines. The more expensive they are, the tougher I am on them.

'I'm friends with a lot of restaurateurs, but that doesn't stop me being critical. No restaurateur has ever tried to take revenge on me, because they know I am from Sicily.'

Armanda Ponzanelli is 84, so most of the serving is done by her son Valerio and most of the cooking is done by her daughter-in-law Luciana. There is a small handwritten menu, but the ordering is always by discussion. The lunch is spectacular. It begins with a chicken broth containing a kind of ravioli wrapped in lettuce leaves instead of pasta. There's an assortment of savoury tarts, including what Lucio considers an impeccable torta d'erbi. There's rabbit rolled around pistachio stuffing, and grilled lamb chops with herbs. And kidneys. And tripe.

There's polenta with beans and spinach stirred through. (Lucio asks for olive oil to pour on it, and Valerio asks: 'From Fosdinovo or Calstelnuovo?' Answer: local, of course – even if Fosdinovo is just 2 kilometres away.)

Dessert is a chestnut mousse that will single-handedly make the food of the partisans fashionable again, served with a puree of persimmons, just ripe on the nearby trees.

Most fascinating of all, there's a version of testaroli which Armanda insists on calling *panigacci*, even though they are not cooked on hot terracotta plates. When he hears they are coming, Lucio asks if he can go into the kitchen and watch the preparation.

It's as he'd hoped. Luciana rubs a half-potato in olive oil and smears it over the surface of a long-handled black skillet. Then she pours a thin layer of batter over the skillet, tilting it to drop off excess. She sits the skillet on a flame for 50 seconds, flips over the pancake for another minute, then transfers it to a plate and immediately daubs it with pesto. 'Hurry back to your seat,' she tells Lucio. 'You have to eat this fast.'

'This is the real Lunigiana,' he says, not for the first time on this journey. But how can he possibly sell this in Sydney?

trattoria ARMANDA

If you want to see how it's possible to get the balance between tradition and modernisation just right, you have to come up to my town and have lunch.

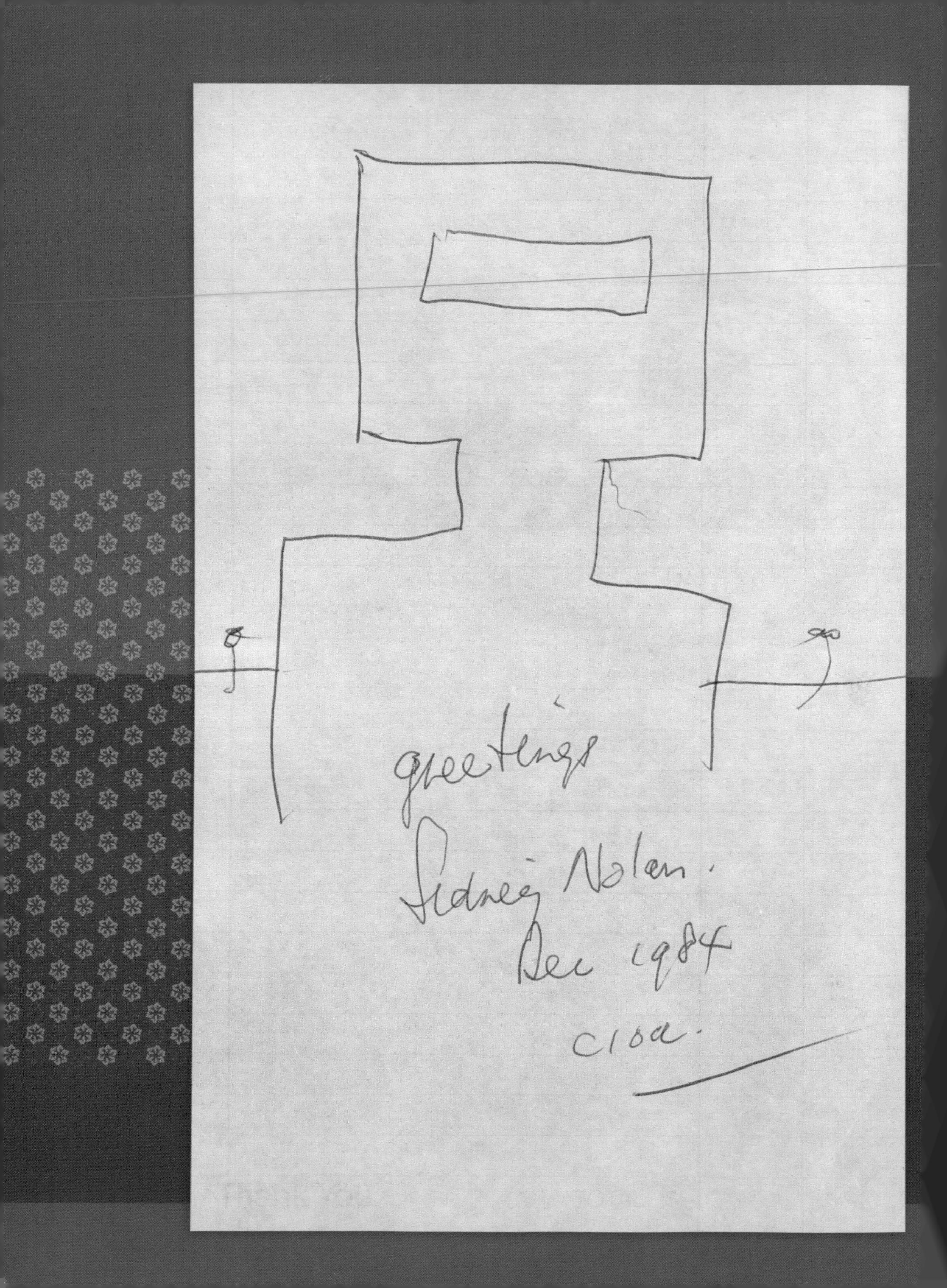

greetings

Sidney Nolan.

Dec 1984

c10a.

—Colin Lanceley, artist, 2003

In Australia

Lucio arrives at his restaurant at about 9.30, six mornings a week. He opens the Venetian blinds and makes sure the wooden slats are level. Usually the cleaners have been by then, and there are encouraging noises coming from the kitchen.

On this morning, the noisemaker is David Wu, pasta specialist. Lucio puts his head in the kitchen, genuflects and intones, 'Master Wu, Master Wu, how are you?' David has a long sheet of green dough in his hand and he's about to put it into the pasta machine to produce tagliolini with spinach flavour. Served with a crab and tomato sauce, it has been one of the restaurant's signature dishes for 20 years.

Lucio is delighted that his pasta maker is Chinese. He sees it as a poetic joining of two cultures. He dismisses the myth that Marco Polo brought the concept of noodles back to Italy from his travels in China (the Romans were making pasta 1,000 years earlier, there were written references to macaroni 100 years before Marco Polo's birth, and Polo probably never went there anyway). But he is prepared to concede that the Chinese developed noodles in a process of parallel evolution with the Italians developing spaghetti.

More to the point, David Wu is the best pasta maker he's ever encountered. He's one of the few cooks with the patience to run the dough through the rollers often enough to get the silky texture Lucio requires.

to day
Lucio became
an
Australian
well done. John Olsen   27.9.01

David Wu: 'I arrived from China in 1985 with my mother, and I worked as a kitchen hand in a French restaurant, then in a Lebanese restaurant, which served spaghetti bolognese and tortellini. Then I got a job as a kitchen hand in Lucio's and I decided I wanted to learn to be a chef. They got me making pasta the first day I was here, and at the time I would take two hours to get it right. Now I can do it in an hour.

'I particularly like making ravioli. It's a challenge to make it strong enough so it will hold the filling when it's boiled, but thin enough so they can taste the filling. It's a matter of texture. You have to keep running it through the rollers till you get that springiness. The balance of salt, egg and flour is vital. I am now at the point where I can just hold it, weigh the sheet in my hands, and I can sense when it's right.'

David is one of an array of specialists Lucio has gathered around him in two decades of running a restaurant in Sydney. We'll flash back over those years in a moment, but for now, let's continue with Lucio's morning.

In the front room, Luke Sciberras, an artist, has a large octopus spread out on a table, and is painting watercolours of it. Discarded sheets lie all over the floor. Lucio arranged with his fish supplier to obtain the octopus for this purpose, but he hadn't expected Luke and the octopus to spread quite so far.

When passers-by look through the windows, they often mistake Lucio's for one of the art galleries that proliferate in the Sydney suburb of Paddington. He's been feeding painters and sculptors ever since he opened in a corner terrace that was formerly an art gallery, and they've kept reciprocating. In 1984 he framed a doodle of Ned Kelly done by Sidney Nolan on the back of a bill. Other artists saw that and began donating their sketches, then watercolours, then oils, then sculptures. And he was proud to squeeze them into every available space.

Today Luke is taking the relationship a step further by using the front room as a studio. Lucio hopes he'll be finished by midday, because he's having a belated twentieth anniversary lunch for some of his favourite artists in the front room. And the longer the octopus lies there, the greater the residual smell.

Lucio sits at the table called Bar One, which is only used when every other table is full. He is studying the bookings book for that day, trying to allocate seating. Most customers don't specify a particular position in the restaurant, but some of the businessmen among his clientele have formed theories about which are the 'top tables' and will be disappointed, even resentful, not to be seated there.

Today he has Lachlan Murdoch, who never cares where he sits, and some executives from the rival Packer empire, who do. Their tables should not be in any position to overhear each other. And they shouldn't be near a birthday party of Ladies Who Lunch, since that will be noisy.

Waiter Charles (born in Holland) arrives to start his shift at 10 am and offers Lucio his first macchiato of the day (four more will follow before sunset). Charles reports that the

espresso machine is producing a nasty brown liquid that can't really be called coffee. The water temperature seems to be down. 'Phone Segafreddo and get them to send someone this morning,' says Lucio.

Bar One puts him in the perfect position to observe and greet the stream of suppliers and artisans who scurry through to the kitchen all morning. Most of them are Italian. Often they stop and chat over coffee.

First comes the bread, in the form of rolls and long loaves in big brown paper bags. Marco, the baker, used to work in Rome. As Lucio confides to David Wu: 'He's such a nice guy – not like a typical Roman at all. Usually they are arrogant.'

Giovanni, an engineer from Sardinia, pops in to check the thermostat on the airconditioning. He arrived in Sydney in 1968 and says he made a lot of money repairing bar refrigeration systems for the illegal gambling casinos that thrived at that time.

Piero, from Sicily, sells wines and deli items. He is always immaculately dressed in Italian brand names, and is inclined to point to his new shoes and say, 'Who made those, come on, tell me, who made those?' Piero developed his taste in clothes while working as a black marketeer of cigarettes in Genoa, where, he says, the girls used to flock around him: 'I was a handsome *figlio di puttana*' (son of a bitch).

Piero keeps trying to interest Lucio in odd pasta shapes and it's become a running gag that Lucio studies the catalogue carefully, and then says, 'But Piero, you know we make our own', to which Piero replies: 'But you never know'.

Mario, from Calabria, represents an importer of European wines. He and Lucio like to sit and compare life experiences. Mario recalls seeing a man killing a pig in his town square and letting the blood run into a bucket to make black pudding. Lucio is glad blood pudding is not part of the Lunigiana culture.

Gianmarco trained as a marine biologist in Milan, and now imports exotic sea products. He produces samples of various forms of *bottarga* (fish roe). The dried tuna roe is dark with an intense flavour that burns the back of the throat. Gianmarco suggests it would work with ricotta and mandarin. Lucio rejects it and instead orders the fresh roe, which is pink and mild.

In his truck, Gianmarco has big cardboard boxes of dried porcini. 'They're from Yugoslavia,' he says apologetically. Lucio says, 'Well, we have to be flexible,' and orders half a kilo.

They discuss olive oils. Gianmarco has a wonderful one from Puglia, from a company that only makes 4,000 bottles a year. But Lucio needs Ligurian olive oil for the artists' lunch today. 'Ah, I'm getting a great one,' says Gianmarco, 'handpicked taggiasca olives, crushed within six hours of picking. But it's not in the country yet.' Lucio may have to go to the local providore, Simon Johnson, for 'il vero Ligure olio' today.

Gianmarco is also offering aged balsamic vinegar made by a company called Cavedoni since 1860. Lucio is craving that caramel nectar he was given by Italo Pedroni, and Gianmarco's samples don't come close.

Lucio's wife Sally comes down from the office upstairs to report on a phone conversation: 'There's a woman who claims she spoke to you about a birthday dinner where you would make 30 individual tiramisus. She wants to put a picture of the birthday girl, made of icing, on the top of every tiramisu, and she needs to know the size so she can get the pictures made.'

'Sheet,' says Lucio, and scurries into the kitchen. He comes back carrying a metal ring. 'This big,' he tells Sally. They work out it's about 4 centimetres across. Another caller has requested a round table for her lunch today, for a party of eight that might grow to ten. 'Can't do it,' says Lucio. 'Our round tops only work for six. It will have to be rectangular.'

'For future reference, we should get Tony to make a top for eight,' says Sally. Antonio (Tony) Dorigo, originally from Udine in north-east Italy and now semi-retired, is a friend who does any carpentry task that arises in Lucio's, and sometimes suggests renovations. He's currently up a ladder at the back, adjusting the shade cloth over the glassed-in courtyard. Lucio doesn't like the patchy way the sunlight filters through.

'The first rule of restaurants, Tony, is the light must be uniform, because it sets the mood,' he says.

Tony replies: 'I thought you told me the first rule of restaurants is hot food on hot plates and cold food on cold plates'.

Lucio: 'Yes, that is the other first rule of restaurants. And the other one is, "Always say goodbye to the customer".'

Lucio wonders if there's a phrase in Italian for Tony's role, which would be 'Jack of all trades' in English. Charles says there's a phrase in Dutch: *manusje van alles* which literally means 'little hands for everything'. When Tony comes down from the ladder, Lucio asks him what he would call himself. 'Factotum' he says immediately. Lucio is mightily amused. 'That's because you do fuck-all,' he says, hoping that's a Latin pun.

That reminds Tony of the problem English speakers have when Italians say, 'It's hot'. Hearing '*Fa caldo*', they are inclined to react: 'What have you got against Aldo?' (which happens to be the name of another of Lucio's waiters).

Tony and Lucio try to reconstruct an old joke that requires a knowledge of English and of Naples dialect. The Italian expression *fa più* (do no more) is pronounced *fa kiú* in dialect. So the joke is about an old couple from Naples who are visiting New York. They go to the movies, and are annoyed because 'a big black guy a few rows behind' keeps throwing popcorn. The wife asks the husband to tell him to stop. Nervously, the old man speaks to the guy and returns to his seat. 'Did you tell him to stop?' asks the wife. 'Yes,' says the old man. Wife: 'What did he say?' Husband: 'He says he won't do it any more'.

One regular conversational topic when participants in the morning parade through Lucio's stop for coffee is 'How I came to Australia'. Lucio is happy when the discussion takes this turn, because it enables him to say 'Well, I came for love,' stretching out the vowel in the final word for as long as he can manage.

Tony came for adventure – and money. In 1959, as a youth in Udine, inland from Venice, he saw an advertisement in his local paper inviting farm workers to come and pick fruit in Australia. He'd never worked on a farm – his hands were used mostly for turning the pages of books – but he was unemployed at the time, with dreams of becoming a draftsman or an engineer if he could afford the training.

His grandfather put him through a crash course in physical labour, making him dig a series of unnecessary holes in his vegetable patch, and sure enough, when Tony turned up for his interview at the Australian immigration office in Trieste, the first thing they did was look at his hands for calluses. He also had to provide a police report declaring his family had "no taint of communism".

Apparently the need for fruit pickers had faded by the time Tony stepped off the ship in Melbourne. He built houses and painted fences in the expanding Melbourne suburbs; he made coaxial cables for TV networks; he worked for an importer of Italian products; he ran a wine shop; and he moved to Sydney and set up his own business erecting blinds and awnings.

When Lucio shifted his restaurant to the suburb of Paddington in 1983, he invited the neighbours to a drinks party to introduce himself. Tony was one of those neighbours, and as tends to happen with Italians abroad, they quickly worked out how they could be of assistance to each other.

Winewaiter Giorgio (born near Venice), who works the night shift, phones to see how much he's allowed to spend on restocking wines for the coming week. Lucio does some calculations based on a proportion of the previous week's takings. 'Not a cent more than $3,000,' he says, 'otherwise it comes out of your wages'.

Jules arrives with the fish delivery. His company is called JOTO, which stands for Jewels Of The Ocean. He's from London, and has been sourcing specialised seafood for top restaurants for four years.

What's he got that's unusual today? Fat scallops from Queensland. 'Okay,' says Lucio, 'but have you got *triglie*?' This is the small sweet pink fish that proliferates around Bocca di Magra, that's called babunya by the Greeks, rouget by the French and, unromantically, red mullet by Australians. Lucio wants to use it as a special for the artists' lunch today – crisped and sitting on rolled pancakes smeared with mascarpone and finely sliced radicchio, surrounded by a saffron sauce. Yes, Jules can do triglie.

Patrice, the Greek printer of Lucio's menus, drops in to discuss Lucio's plan to create a little folder in which to place the bill or the credit card receipt. 'Will you want an Olsen on it?' asks Patrice, since the menu covers display a painting by John Olsen.

'I'd like to do something tacky, some cartoon, after all the tastefulness of the art everywhere,' says Lucio. It takes Patrice a minute to realise he is joking.

The repairman from Segafreddo arrives. 'Ah, it's my twin,' shouts Lucio. Salvatore is short and dark and from Sicily. Once before when he came to fix the machine, they worked out they were born on the same day. He opens a tool box of tiny compartments and starts to strip down the 15-year-old machine.

Then comes the highlight of Lucio's month – the delivery of the wheel of parmesan. The rule in this restaurant is that only Lucio can make the first cut, so he has the deliveryman dump it on a wooden table next to the bar, and heads into the kitchen for an apron and his wedge-shaped knife.

He scores the cheese across the middle and down each side, plunges in the knife and works his way along the scoremark, turning the wheel over to do the other side. Then he plunges the knife into the centre again, twists it sideways, and the wheel falls neatly into two halves. He puts one half away and cuts the other half into eight big wedges. And now it's ready to be served with fruit at the end of the meal, or grated over the pasta.

It's ten to twelve and suddenly Lucio remembers a vital detail. He puts his head into

the kitchen and shouts: 'Do the garlic, guys'. This ritual has been performed from the first week he opened in Paddington, more than 20 years ago. Chopped garlic is set sizzling in olive oil and then one of the cooks walks through the restaurant, waving the pan back and forth like an incense pot in a church.

The restaurant then has the smell of Italian home cooking – in fact, the smell of the kitchen in which Lucio grew up. Normally David Wu does the garlic about 12.15, but today, the first customers will be here at 12, and the garlic ritual is something no customer must ever see – the smell must register unconsciously. Lucio intones random priestly Latin words, as the garlic wafts by.

He checks that the salt and pepper grinders are perfectly aligned with the edge of each table, and goes to fix the music. When there are no customers, Lucio plays 1960s rock such as Creedence Clearwater Revival, or Italian folk and rock singers such as Zucchero, Lucio Dalla, Fabrizio de André. Now he changes to opera. He thinks arias in Italian are suitable for lunchtime, while cheerful classical music without singing is suitable for dinner.

The Segafreddo man can't find anything wrong but has cleaned the parts. Giovanni has sorted out the airconditioning. Tony has adjusted the flow of sunlight. Charles and Aldo have put on their blue shirts and bright ties.

A young man in a dark suit pokes his head uncertainly through the door, wondering if this is an art gallery or the appointed site of his lunch meeting. And it's showtime.

At the artists' lunch that day, there's an outbreak of passionate speechmaking, to Lucio's deep embarrassment. These are some examples …

Salvatore Zofrea: 'I was born in Calabria but I've been in Australia from the age of nine. Lucio comes from Liguria, which is a very different part of Italy, but it has the same spirit. We're lucky to have him here in Sydney as an enrichment of our way of life.

'I met him in 1993, when my agent brought me here. It was an enlightenment to see how generous he was of himself. The atmosphere was light and friendly, and I liked the

Fernando, one of the chefs, does the noon garlic ritual; right, a signature dish at Lucio's – *tagliolini* (tajarin) with blue swimmer crab.

food. I'm into fish, and it's always fresh and delicious. Lucio captures the Italian quality of freshness and diversity. He's an artist with food, which is just as important as painting. Lucio is one of the few who has been able to blend art and food. Other people get bogged down in wanting money money money, sometimes they cut corners or they're aggressive. Lucio has been able to build himself a lifestyle that he enjoys without doing that.'

Fred Cress: 'I started coming here in the mid '80s. I'm a mad eater, equally interested in almost all cuisines. But this restaurant tends to answer all my tastes. I particularly look forward to it when I come back from France. When service is almost invisible, that's a good sign. I'm greeted as if I'm a member of the family.'

John Beard: 'Lucio's is the place you always compare the others to. Generosity is at the core of what art is all about. That's one of the reasons why so many artists have enjoyed being part of Lucio's, not only for the generosity of Lucio, or for the food, but because it sets you in a frame of mind that one should always be about anyway.'

John Coburn: 'I know I've always come here as the leading restaurant of Sydney because I just like the food. Lucio seems to like artists and I'm very inclined to help him in that respect.'

Colin Lanceley: 'My association with this building goes back to the early 1960s, when there was a gallery upstairs, I had my first one-man show above where we're sitting now and there's a famous photograph taken on the balcony.

'We need this atmosphere because it's something we can't create for ourselves, though we've talked about it for years. Lucio has given us a place to meet and talk about the things we need to talk about, like our dealers, our money or the lack of it.

'Lucio has provided us with the most wonderful, warm familial place. We come here with the expectation that we're likely to see someone we know, someone we can talk to.

'In the world that we all inhabit, which is so political and problematic, we can walk in here and we feel at ease. There's touching going on from the moment we walk in the door, which is very Italian and I love it. Whether you're female or male, or you're gay or you're not, you come to Lucio's and it doesn't matter. It's about this tremendous relationship Lucio has with artists where he gives his most passionate self to what he does for them. He's a warm person who brings together feeling, thought and action.'

The chief protagonists will now explain how they got to this point …

Sally: 'We were met at the airport by my parents who took us immediately to Centennial Park. That was because I had said how ugly all those red roofs of Sydney looked from the plane, compared to the beauty of Bocca. I had a real case of Australian cultural cringe.

'I had come from a background where food was just a necessity, and you never thought about it. So I go to Italy and I am won over by the food, and I come back in 1977 disgusted by the Australian approach to eating at the time. I was horrified you couldn't get fresh bread on a Saturday, and people were still serving tinned spaghetti and people didn't know the difference between a fresh pasta and a dry pasta and didn't know how to cook a fish properly – all things I never would have thought about before.

Olsen was inspired by Lucio's tales of learning about food at the kitchen table.

When I phoned my mother to tell her I was opening a restaurant, she didn't sound surprised. She just said 'Treat your staff well'.

'My parents let us stay in a flat they had in Double Bay. My mother got out a *Women's Weekly* cookbook and made Lucio a lasagne so he'd feel at home. He was polite about it.

'I went back to work at the ad agency. Lucio was qualified as a geometra, but we found he would have to do a four-year conversion course. So he got a job as a waiter at a German restaurant while he did an eight-week intensive English course, then got a job at one of the top Italian restaurants where he had to wear a green vest and velvet bowtie. He was enjoying that.

'We started eating out in a lot of restaurants in Sydney – it was the first time Lucio had tried Chinese or Greek or Middle Eastern. We found most of the Italian places boring because they believed they had to cater for Australian tastes. And we started thinking we had to be able to do better. We looked around and the cheapest restaurant for sale was in Balmain, which we got for $12,000 with my parents' help. We cleaned it up ourselves, my parents and friends scraping wallpaper. Two years later we moved to Paddington.

'What we knew about restaurants came from Ciccio, so we did some of the dishes from there: fritto misto. We also had scaloppine, whole fish, fish in cartoccio, prawns and calamari spiedini (on skewers), home-made fresh pasta, home-made icecream.

'I was working at the ad agency by day and at night I was either washing dishes, making zabaglione or doing the bills. We had a great write-up in a newspaper and my parents said: "Lucio's really going to make something of himself, isn't he?"'

Lucio: 'I missed coffee very much when I first came to Australia. In restaurants if you wanted an espresso, you asked for a "demi-tasse".

'After a few weeks working in a German restaurant, I applied to an Italian restaurant where Sally and I had eaten a reasonable meal. The boss asked, "Do you drink?" I said no. He said: "You've got the job".

'The place was hilarious. The chef was always out placing bets at an illegal gambling joint, the waiters were drinking on the job all the time. When a customer appeared, it was a race for the door, knocking each other out of the way for the tips.

'We spent most of our money eating out in the first few months I was here, and I didn't like most of the Italian places and we decided to open a restaurant. I'd met a guy from Bocca di Magra who had been a chef on cruise ships and he'd married an Australian girl. He said he would be a partner with us.

'So it was very much a Bocca way to begin. When I phoned my mother to tell her I was opening a restaurant, she didn't sound at all surprised. She just said: "Treat your staff well".

'We didn't want to change the world, but we wanted to do good food, something different, and to have the pleasure of our own place. I realised it was my way of life. I never planned to work in the food business and I never consciously studied it. But in my blood was the growing and the cooking and the serving. I am contadino, after all.'

Above, Mario and Wendy join Sally, Lucio and children Michela and Matteo during a visit from Bocca di Magra (opposite above). Opposite below, a Lunigiana hill town painted by Orti, the commander of Mauro's partisan unit.

'To constitute Italy, to fuse together the
diverse elements of which it is made, to
harmonise the north with the south, offers
as many difficulties as a war against Austria
and the struggle with the Vatican.'

—Camillo Benso di Cavour, prime minister of Piemonte, 1859

'COSTITUIRE L'ITALIA, FONDERE INSIEME GLI
ELEMENTI DIVERSI DI CUI SI COMPONE,

Into Piemonte

The brothers are on the highway heading north-west towards Turin, the city where the nation called Italy was born and where the Slow Food movement is holding its biannual 'Salone del Gusto', an exhibition that displays foods that are becoming endangered by modern tastes and technology.

But those scholarly details are just excuses. In fact, the brothers are making the journey because they want to eat truffles. It's the season. Every November, the hills around Alba are alive with men and dogs seeking out round brown lumps that are amazingly light for their immense cost.

Lucio has returned for a second visit in Autumn, and when the brothers were having a welcome-back dinner at Il Cantinone in Sarzana, chef Mario brought a surprise dish of what he called fonduta (warm melted cheese and egg yolk) and grated a white truffle over it. The brothers exclaimed together, 'It's the season!' The way the warm fonduta brought up the smell of the truffle was so extraordinary they decided they needed to get to the source. Until that moment Lucio had been in two minds about using up his limited time by visiting the Slow Food exhibition. But the realisation that he was only three hours away from the world's finest fungus clinched it.

Aulo is excited that they'll also be in the territory of Italy's greatest red wine, barolo. As a white exclusivist, Lucio doesn't care.

In the car, Lucio is playing a Beatles CD and trying to convince Aulo of its importance. Every song seems to have personal relevance. In 'Get Back', the line about getting back to where you once belonged is what Lucio has been doing. In 'Yesterday', when Paul McCartney sings about not being half the man he used to be, Lucio pats his belly and says, 'That's right – I'm twice the man I used to be'. 'Maxwell's Silver Hammer' reminds him of

Ciccio testing for air pockets in the wheels of parmesan. The whole CD reminds him of the time he skipped a Sunday shift at Ciccio's and sneaked off with Sally to see Paul McCartney performing in Venice. This caused Mario to declare, with cold fury, that Lucio had no future as a waiter.

Aulo is recalling when Lucio, aged 19, did his national service near Turin, and at the end of the first week phoned his parents complaining about the army food. 'And then our father calls me and says "Lucio can't eat the food they are giving him in the army. You have to take him something he can eat." I'm saying he has to eat the food – that's why he is in the army, to suffer. He can't be spoiled all his life.'

But Mauro couldn't stand the idea that his boy was eating badly. He convinced Aulo, then a newlywed with a small baby, to pack a hamper and drive for four hours to the army base with some decent Lunigiana tucker – roast chicken, a cooked rabbit, salami, cheeses, home-made bread.

Lucio tries to distract Aulo from these embarrassing reflections with the theory that the army used to put drugs in its food to reduce the libidos of the trainees. 'I think they put bromuro in our caffelatte in the morning,' he says. 'At least you had coffee,' says Aulo.

Lucio was too cunning for the army. He was assigned to work in the communications room, where the ten trainees secretly organised a roster system whereby they could each go home three days a week, while those remaining covered for them. Lucio went back to Bocca di Magra and worked at Ciccio's.

They got into big trouble – a *cazzettone* (dressing-down) from the sergeant: 'The army is not anarchy. You are not supposed to organise your own working times. You are supposed to sleep in the barracks every night. You are a disgrace.' Lucio draws on that experience whenever he has to chastise one of his waiters. Grudgingly, he must admit the army may have pulled him out of his teenage dream world and prepared him for his ultimate career.

The brothers speak in a mixture of Sarzana dialect and Italian, with Lucio occasionally throwing in English words without realising it. Their dialogue is peppered with '*che casino!*' (literally 'what a brothel', meaning what a mess) and '*cazzo*' (literally 'dick' but used more as English-speakers would use 'shit' as an exclamation).

With Aulo unimpressed by the Beatles, Lucio puts on a CD of their favourite folk singer, Fabbrizio de André, whose greatest hit was about a gorilla who escapes from the zoo and is kept by an old lady as her sex slave.

They pass the town of Cuneo, which reminds Lucio of a favourite expression of their father's: '*Chi in mette to pescio o mette o limon o o l'è de Cuneo o l'è un belinon*', which means, 'Whoever puts lemon on fish either is from Cuneo or is a dickhead'. They debate its meaning. Is it saying that people from the inland town of Cuneo are contadini, and therefore would not know how to treat a fish, or is it just saying the Cuneans are stupid? 'Since I've been in Australia I've been putting lemon on my fish all the time,' says Lucio.

On the outskirts of Alba they pass a row of stalls selling torrone, and remember that the town's other speciality, after truffles, is nougat confectionery. Alba isn't quite the quaint village they'd expected – bigger and more industrial, and they're having trouble finding a hotel with a vacancy because hundreds of other delegates to the Salone del Gusto have also hit on the idea of visiting truffle-town on their way to Torino.

The sex life of the truffle

WHAT'S THE APPEAL OF TRUFFLES? WHAT CAUSES A LIGHT BROWN LUMP THE SIZE OF A TESTICLE TO BE WORTH 100 EUROS AND THE DOG THAT CAN DIG IT UP TO BE WORTH 3,000 EUROS? THE CURRENT THEORY IS THAT TRUFFLE FANCIERS DON'T ACTUALLY WANT TO EAT THE TRUFFLE. THEY WANT TO HAVE SEX WITH IT.

The truffle is a fungus that attaches itself to the root of a tree and sucks the sap (oak roots supposedly nurture the strongest-smelling truffles, but you get pretty good results with poplars, lindens, willows and the hazelnut bushes). About 80 per cent of it is water, and the rest is tiny quantities of trapped nitrogen, proteins, fats, sugars and fibre. Round and smooth ones come from softer soil, gnarled ones from hard soil.

The Alba area has the ideal conditions for the white truffle (actually light brown on the outside and light grey on the inside). The less pungent black truffle grows further south, around Norcia in Umbria.

The hunters and their dogs are looking for moist soil in shady woods, between October and December. Truffle dogs are mongrels, trained for three months. The dog runs around, nose close to the ground, then backtracks to a particular spot and starts pawing the ground. The trifolau (hunter) rewards the dog with a piece of bread and then gently digs out the fungus with his sapin, a long curved hoe. He then wraps the lump in a blue-and-white check hanky and puts it in his pocket.

At the market in Alba, no truffles are visible. The trifolaus stand around waiting to be approached by a buyer. Then they pull their cloth-wrapped bundles out of the pockets of their jackets. One of the proliferation of documents released by Italy's National Truffle Study Centre says:

> Scholars have discovered that steroidal compounds similar to sex hormones and with a special scent are present in animals, man and some vegetables. Celery, for example, contains 8 nanograms, white truffles contain 26–62 nanograms per gram …The complex aroma of truffles, therefore, is a chemical code that goes unnoticed by the rational part of the brain, straight to the limbic system, which controls our emotions and feelings, and reveals itself as an invitation to life.

So this explains why we like them so much – it's not the obvious garlicky cheesy slightly rotting smell, but sexual undertones we detect subconsciously. That's why truffles can sell for as much as 4,000 euros.

The Study Centre says 10 grams are enough to enrich one serving of pasta, but you must use a truffle grater which produces fine sheets – the maximum surface area means the maximum aroma. The warmth of the dish pushes out the smell.

Two rules with truffles: 1. Never wash them. Brush off the dirt or wipe with a cloth. 2. Never cook them – with high heat they lose all smell rapidly.

They find space at the small modern Hotel Le Langhe, where they ask for advice on a restaurant that might do interesting things with truffles. The owner suggests Ca' del Lupo, which is 'just up the hill'. This turns out to require driving for half an hour along country lanes in darkness to reach what seems to be a convention centre with a swimming pool and a huge crowded restaurant.

Their doubts are dispelled when the waiter arrives at the table with a tiny weighing machine and a basket with two truffles wrapped in a blue-and-white check cloth. He explains that he will weigh the truffles before the meal, grate them over any dish they like, weigh them again at the end and charge by the amount they have consumed. Lucio says: 'We'll have truffle with everything'.

One truffle is smooth and almost white, and the other is grey and lumpy. The waiter explains that truffles vary according to soil. The ugly one with the strong perfume comes from an area called Le Langhe, where the soil is hard. The pretty one comes from Roero where the soil is soft.

The truffle goes particularly well with a *carne cruda all'Albese* (tartare of veal), and with the Piemonte version of tajarin noodles, which have been dressed only with butter and parmesan because any sauce would distract from the truffle aroma.

When the waiter goes, Lucio grates more truffle over the tajarin, saying, 'We're not in Alba every day'. The truffle proves unnecessary with a dish called *Agnolotti del plin all'olio e rosmarino* – small meat-stuffed pasta parcels with oil and rosemary. The term *del plin* means the parcels are pinched together at the top by the chef's fingers. Lucio: 'I don't think rosemary works with pasta, but this!'

During the meal Lucio discovers that rarest of phenomena: a new wine. It's a white called arneis, which in local dialect means 'little rascal'. Until 1988, arneis grapes were used only for eating, and the grape type, unique to the Piemonte region, was on the verge of extinction. You could say it was the Cinta Senese pig of the grape world.

Then a winemaker from Roero, west of Alba, found a way of turning the grape into a pale yellow, slightly sweet wine with an alcohol content of 11 per cent (most wines are at least 12 per cent). That's ideal for reluctant consumers like Lucio. So now there are three wines that don't remind Lucio of his childhood nausea in his uncle's barrels: pinot grigio, vermentino, and arneis. He rejoices in his flexibility.

The waiter is shocked to hear that Lucio does not drink red. He turns out to be Stefano di Dricco, part of the family that owns the restaurant (his brother and sister are in the kitchen). He points out that the Langhe part of Piemonte is a twin province with Lunigiana, but sadly that doesn't mean discounts for people who come from there. It does, however, mean an invitation to the cellar to try a new vintage of barolo that has just arrived.

Stefano explains that the rules for barolo are strict. It must be 100 per cent nebbiolo grapes from a defined area south-west of Alba, and the juice from those grapes must have been aged for at least two years in oak barrels and a further one year in the bottle. Its alcohol content must be 13 per cent. Winemakers who don't want to follow those rules can call their wines barbaresco or nebbiolo, but then they can't charge as much for them. Lucio sips politely.

Next morning they stroll down Via Vittorio Emanuele, Alba's main drag, which is lined

with food shops selling porcini, cheeses, and various forms of pasta del plin. Furtive looking men stand on street corners with their hands in the pockets of heavy jackets. They might be truffle hunters, waiting for an offer.

In a glittering store called Ponzio, Lucio learns that the latest fad in Sydney restaurants, truffled olive oil, is always flavoured with an artificial chemical, because the scent of genuine truffle doesn't last. 'Okay, we'll never use it again,' he declares.

They follow a battered 'tartufi' sign down a lane to a little shop devoted to sausages and truffles, where a small scholarly woman begins explaining how her husband hunts truffles with their dog named Doc (a pun on 'Denomination of Origin Controlled', which is used to certify wines). She is interrupted by her husband, who has been asleep in the back room but now enters to prevent his wife revealing his secrets to these strangers. What if they were other truffle hunters?

Lucio explains his purposes, and the man, slightly mollified, introduces himself as Ettore Forte: 'I hunt with a group. We did badly last night. Not cold enough. There were 14 of us, set off at 1 am, found only 11 by 4 am.'

Seeking lunch on the way to Torino, they stop at the town of Monforte, where Al Giardino, recommended in *L'Espresso* guide, turns out to be closed. Chosen at random, the nearby La Collina is a fascinating experience. The chef, Federico Ricatto, is going through an enthusiasm for cocoa beans. He has sprinkled them over the appetiser – a strong 'high mountain ricotta' with olive oil, and joined them with a sage sauce on roast duck. Lucio is willing to concede that cocoa beans might be The Next Big Thing.

Federico has also put his pinch on some excellent agnolotti del plin, and a risotto with onion and capsicum, and of course, tajarin with generous gratings of truffle. But it's the wine waitress, Ivana Fozzi, who has the brothers riveted. She expounds upon various forms of barolo and finally opens one which, she warns, is a challenging experience:

Truffles vary in shape according to the soil they're in, and must be finely grated with a special tool, says hunter Ettore Forte.

Ivana warns that barolo is a challenging experience: tight at the beginning but after 20 minutes 'it will reveal its secrets'.

tight at the beginning, but after 20 minutes, 'it will reveal its secrets'. She couldn't be more right. Lucio's first sip confirms his negative expectations about reds. A second sip half an hour later has him demanding a whole glass.

They reach Turin about 5 pm, and find that their tiny Hotel Liberty is a short walk from the palaces of the former kings of Italy. Torino was the nation's capital from 1861 to 1865, and the nobles of the House of Savoy, who were lifted from obscurity to sovereignty over a brand new nation, felt compelled to awe the populace with the splendour of their architecture. Italy threw out its royal family in 1946, and the palaces stand as monuments to decadent excess.

But Italy's post-war shift to a republic did not lessen Turin's commitment to pomp and splendour, as is immediately apparent when Lucio and Aulo walk into their dining target for the evening, Ristorante del Cambio. They could be in eighteenth-century France – gilded mirrors, crystal chandeliers, towering floral arrangements and solemn waiters in complex uniforms with small variations to indicate gradations in status. The customers are equally magnificent, and the brothers realise they are the only men in the room not wearing ties.

The food is stuffy too. The specialities of the house are *La Finanziera del Cambio* – chicken guts in a white sauce – and chateaubriand, a long slab of fillet steak with foie gras sauce, fennel, and cauliflower.

One table for four stays empty all night, and the reason for this is revealed by a metal plaque on the wall behind it. This was the favourite table of Count Camillo Benso di Cavour, first prime minister of Italy.

Aulo can picture Cavour plotting and scheming at that table, figuring out how to provoke Austria into attacking Piemonte in order to get the sympathy of rest of Italy. In the 1850s Cavour was the brains behind a plan to unite a bunch of argumentative city states into one nation under the royal family of Piemonte. The brawn was Giuseppe Garibaldi, who travelled around the peninsula with 1,000 red-shirted supporters convincing the populace to get with the strength. It's a matter of debate whether Cavour or Garibaldi has the greater number of streets, piazzas, sportsgrounds and public buildings named after him.

Aulo doubts if Garibaldi would have joined Cavour at the table in Ristorante del Cambio. The two national heroes didn't like each other, and Garibaldi would probably have preferred the contadino food of Lunigiana. 'And he wouldn't have met the dress code,' suggests Lucio.

Next morning, the brothers take tram 18 to Turin's convention centre and the Salone del Gusto. The Slow Food movement was born out of the death of the Italian communist party in the 1980s. A bunch of idealistic lefties realised they were getting nowhere with traditional political action, and decided to focus on a key factor in human happiness: the growing and distribution of food. What started as a protest movement against the standardisation imposed by multinational companies captured the public imagination and became hugely influential in European government policy formation.

Outside the convention centre, men in folkloric costumes are roasting chestnuts and using shovels to throw them high in the air. Inside are 500 stalls displaying rare, endangered, and downright peculiar foodstuffs. It's hard to get near any of them because

At La Collina, Federico and Ivana offer *tajarin* with truffles, ricotta with cocoa beans, *agnolotti del plin* and capsicum risotto, and a wondrous barolo.

Roasting chestnuts in Turin and the truffle market in Alba; opposite, the 19th century glitter of Ristorante del Cambio.

of the crowds, but Lucio manages to sample a type of corn from Mexico, a type of rice from Malaysia, a type of wild salmon from Ireland, black beans from Spain and dried llama meat from the Andes.

Then Lucio sees a familiar face. It's Simon Johnson, an Australian importer of Italian products whose shop is close to Lucio's restaurant in Sydney. Simon has come to Italy and set up a stall offering Tasmanian rainwater. Nobody is going near it. Aulo observes that he'll never get anywhere trying to sell water to Italians if he doesn't put a sticker on it listing its chemical composition and health benefits, with a certifying signature by a tame professor of biological sciences.

The adjoining stall, which is generating a little more interest, is labelled 'Big Country – Sapori d'Australia' and is offering kangaroo prosciutto. Lucio is not a big fan of kangaroo himself, but enjoys the idea that a food exchange now exists between Australia and Italy. Previously the traffic went only one way.

In the next aisle, devoted to pork products, they see a noisy crowd gathered around a tall man whom Lucio suddenly recognises as Fausto Guardagni, the maker of lardo he met in Carrara. Now dressed in an expensive leather jacket, but still dishevelled, Fausto's been taken up as a hero of the Slow Food movement, and is at the Salone del Gusto to celebrate 'Lardo di Colonnata' receiving certification from the European Union.

For dinner they walk to a restaurant called Capannina, which was recommended by their hotelier in Alba. As it turns out, Capannina is run by the hotelier's father, a charming white-haired man who looks like the actor Anthony Quinn. The walls are covered with black-and-white photos of cabaret performers from the 1950s. The owner chats about what they might eat and the 50-year history of his establishment, scribbles their order on post-it notes which he puts in several pockets, then delivers a plate of small salamis, which are delicious.

They can picture Count Camillo Benso di Cavour plotting and scheming at that table, figuring out how to provoke Austria into attacking Piemonte.

At Turin's Capannina, the antipasto plate and the *bollito misto*; opposite, the bridge in the town of Varese Ligure.

Then a waiter comes over and asks: 'What did you order?' He apologises that the boss has a habit of losing his notes and forgetting what customers have said, so would they mind going through it all again? Lucio wonders, 'Will I be like this in 20 years?' 'More like next year,' says Aulo.

The best part of the meal is a bollito misto – various simmered spiced meats trundled to the table on a trolley and sliced before their eyes. When it comes to bill time, the owner pulls scraps of paper from his pocket, stares wildly at them, tosses them on to the cashier's desk and just estimates 50 euros a head.

On the way back from Torino they take the inland route through forests and mountains instead of the coast road. They stop at a tiny roadside stall where a farmer is selling home-made salami and pecorino. He tells them that he calls his one-year-old cheese Viagra, because it's hard and strong. The brothers hope they don't seem like wimps if they prefer the five-month cheese, which is softer and milder tasting. 'These cheeses have never been in a fridge,' boasts the farmer, 'because that would spoil the flavour. They invented cheese before they invented refrigeration.' He has run this stall, on a road he calls *strada dei vini e sapori* (route of wines and flavours) for 25 years.

'We're in deepest Liguria here,' says Aulo. 'The Etruscans cut down all the trees around here for their iron mines, then collapsed as a society. The Romans planted chestnut trees.'

The salami and cheese provides a picnic that keeps them going till they reach the town of Varese Ligure, where Aulo has promised to show Lucio a different way of constructing pasta. Varese turns out to be a tiny cobbled town of two-storey pink buildings with green shutters and trompe l'oeil ornamentation, built in a crescent around the town square, with a squat stone tower in the centre. In aerial photos, it looks like the lower case 'e' shape of the euro symbol.

They dine at a country tavern called Locanda del Goloso (inn of the glutton). The downstairs bar is empty except for two teenagers playing on a soccer machine, but in an

By the road, a farmer sells his salami, pecorino and mushrooms. In Varese Ligure, Pietro carves stamps for pasta called croxetti.

upstairs room full of locals, a teenage girl serves them stuffed onions and artichokes, herb pie, prosciutto, lardo, salami, gnocchi with tomato and eggplant sauce, and tortellini in chicken broth, brought to the table in a big earthenware pot from which they can help themselves. 'This beats del Cambio any day,' says Lucio. 'Well, of course,' says Aulo. 'We're in Liguria now, not Piemonte.'

Next morning Aulo asks direction from locals and they go in search of this mysterious new pasta technology he's promising. They knock on a blue door and it's opened by a ruddy-faced, plump man who introduces himself as Pietro. He invites them into the workshop, where he is the last person in Varese – and possibly in Italy – to carve wooden pasta stamps called croxetti. You roll out your sheet of dough, cut out a disc, put the disc between the two halves of the stamp, press hard and there is a beautifully embossed white coin, which keeps its imprint when boiled. It is best served with pesto sauce.

Far from being new, it's an ancient custom, and it's disappearing. Pietro says lords and bishops used to commission their crests in croxetti, and amaze their guests with personalised pasta. Now he hopes families and businesses might take up the idea. But he has nobody to whom he can pass on his carving skills.

Lucio buys five stamps and wonders if he should get stamps made for his restaurant – perhaps carved in an ornate 'L' insignia. Would Master Wu have time to stamp out croxetti? Pressing the discs is labour intensive. More to the point, isn't the very idea of having pasta with a personal crest pretentious – the kind of thing a Piemontese would do, not appropriate for a contadino from Lunigiana?

Lords and bishops used to commission their crests in croxetti, and amaze their guests with personalised pasta.

'Society is changing. Families are fragmenting. Now the restaurant must become what the family used to be.'

—Giuseppe Nucera, head waiter, 2004

'LA SOCIETÀ STA CAMBIANDO. LA FAMIGLIA SI STÀ FRAMMENTANDO. OGGIGIORNO IL RISTORANTE

Farewell to Lunigiana

The dark green waistcoat won't button up. The waiter's uniform which Lucio shunned at 14, wore with pride at 18 and left behind at 23 is now too small to fit around his enlarged frame. Giuseppe observes, straight-faced, that Australians must have a different body shape from Italians.

Lucio is back in Bocca for the mid-summer madness, and he has volunteered to help Giuseppe out by doing a Sunday lunch shift. He wants to recapture one of the happiest and most hectic times of his life, when he'd swim in the morning, work a lunch shift, grab a short nap, work a dinner shift, and then stay up most of the night talking, singing and, if he was lucky, kissing.

There won't be any kissing this time, because Sally's in Sydney, but he has already attempted a swim. Because of the boat marina, it's no longer possible to jump into the river outside Ciccio's and let the current sweep you around to the beach. Instead, Lucio has rented a tiny changing room at the Debi-Ross beach club at the end of Via Fabbricotti, jumped off the club's deck into the ocean, and swum around to emerge onto the grey sands.

This act marks him as thoroughly Australianised. No adult Italian would do this. They remain stationary in the water, or lie on deckchairs slathered in oil. Only children and Australians swim.

Lucio starts singing a song he knew as a kid: '*Tutti al mare per vedere le chiappe chiare*', 'Let's all go to the beach to see the pale buttocks'. He is delighted when a girl swimming nearby finishes the verse.

On Via Fabbricotti, he keeps bumping into kids he swam with 40 years ago. They used to come with their parents, and now they bring their children – though the holidays are shorter these days. One is a doctor, one a dentist, one a teacher, one a TV comedian.

There's still a flea market along the street. Lucio overhears a man at a clothing stall saying he would double the price if he was selling this stuff at Forte dei Marmi, down in Tuscany. So Bocca hasn't been entirely yuppified. A gift stall reminds Lucio of how he would cry in the kitchen of Ciccio's for a toy from the flea market. Mario found this so entertaining he would sometimes pay Lucio to cry, to watch the effect on his parents.

At the other end of the promenade from Ciccio's, a pancake stall is doing a roaring trade with the tourists. The locals don't go near it, because the owner is a *pentito* – a man who gave evidence against some supposed members of the Red Brigade. He was moved to Bocca by the police as his reward, but the locals think it was all a frame-up. His wife tried to set up a fortune-teller's stall using tarot cards, but nobody in Bocca di Magra would want their future predicted by a pentito's wife.

Lucio notices that every surrounding village now performs some form of historic tourist attraction. Up in Castelnuovo they're doing a re-enactment of Dante's reconciliation of the Bishop of Luni and the Malaspina family. The tall man playing the poet wears a kind of leather helmet and a crown of bay leaves. He kisses the bishop on both cheeks, reads a proclamation about peace and prosperity for all, and then welcomes a parade of drummers, flag hurlers, stilt walkers, trumpeters and fire eaters. Presumably this is just as it was in 1306.

More exciting is the food festival held every evening in Sarzana's Piazza Matteotti, with stalls offering *scarpazza* (vegetable pie), testaroli, torta d'erbi – all the dishes Lucio is contemplating for his Lunigiana night next month. They're a bit short on flavour in this mass feeding environment, but intriguing to the Milanesi holidaymakers. For their

Because of the boat marina, it's no longer possible to jump
into the river and let the current sweep you around to the beach.

*Most Italians are like me – if you ask where we are from,
we don't say Italy, we don't say our region, we say our town.*

grandparents this was the food of poverty. Driven by the Slow Food movement, Italians are reimagining the roots they never quite lost.

The Sarzana streets are crammed with people till midnight and Fiammetta Gemmi can't stop to chat because she is rushed off her feet selling freshly made cannoli stuffed with lemon cream.

In a local record store, Lucio has found a new album called Bluesugar, by one of his teen pop heroes, Zucchero, which has this credit line: 'Conceived and written at Lunigiana Soul – Pontremoli'. The concept of 'Lunigiana soul' has set him wondering if his area is about to become The New Umbria, and if he's happy about that.

He's also reading in the local paper about a move to create a new political region in Italy, extending in a rectangular shape from Parma and Modena in the north-east to La Spezia and Carrara in the south-west – pretty much the old assumed boundaries of Lunigiana. They are proposing to call this region 'Lunezia'.

Mario thinks it's a brilliant idea: 'I think of myself as from Sarzana, because I was born there. When I was young, I knew everyone in town. I'm like a tree with my roots there. Most Italians are like me – if you ask where we are from, we don't say Italy, we don't say our region, we say our town.

'People who live in Carrara don't feel Tuscan, and their capital, Florence, doesn't care about them. People in Parma don't feel Emilian, and Bologna doesn't care about them. People in Sarzana don't feel Ligurian, and Genoa doesn't care about them. In mentality, those towns have much more in common with each other than with their regions. They are all part of Lunigiana – or call it Lunezia, if you like.'

On this particular Sunday, people are sunbaking all over the grass in front of Ciccio's. One of the women is topless, which never would have happened when Lucio was a teen, more's the pity. Taking her daily promenade, Zia Anna is unshocked. She's seen worse than that in her 82 years.

Anna strolls outside Ciccio's and observes the summer crowds, while Lucio relives his waiter days inside.

Conceding that Lucio can wear the waistcoat open – just this once – Giuseppe demonstrates how they toss a salad these days (the leaves must be turned 36 times) and how there are three copies of every order – one for the kitchen, one for the cash desk and one for the waiter. 'You don't just go and shout to the chef,' he warns.

During lunch, Giuseppe has to reprimand Lucio for spending too much time talking to the customers. Lucio has slipped into host mode. And anyway, he knows half the people in the place. He served them or their parents 30 years ago.

One of them is Dino Pastorelli, a former truck driver who hit upon the brilliant idea, early in 1969, of making gold medallions to commemorate the American moon landing. It was a big gamble, but they made him rich. He used to drive to Bocca di Magra in a Lamborghini. One day, he gave a small medal to Mauro, instead of a tip. 'Before, I was too overawed to say a word to him,' Lucio remembers.

After lunch, Giuseppe finds time to chat with Lucio about what they have learnt in their 30 years of restauranteering in two countries. Giuseppe notes how society has changed since they last worked together. On a Sunday in the 1970s, tables mostly had eight or ten people at them. Now they are threes and twos and plenty of ones. The big family meal is a disappearing tradition.

Each man has independently come up with 'the coffee curve' of customer satisfaction: the restaurateur should keep a graph of the number of coffees people are ordering at the end of their meals. If the number goes down, something has changed in the atmosphere or the service which is discouraging people from wanting to linger. You'd better find out what that is.

Giuseppe says: 'You and I could be so big here. We could run 20 restaurants in Ameglia.' Lucio: 'Maybe, but you'd never leave Ciccio's'.

Last night Lucio dined in Mario's Latest Project, which has finally opened, under the title Ciccio Marina (because it's at the port called Marina di Carrara). It's very glamorous, with three floors, connected by glass lifts. Downstairs the transparent plastic chairs are the work of American designer Philippe Starck. In a nod to Ciccio's, the back patio has a roof made of the leafy river canes that formed the original ceiling for the shack on the sand.

The view is less peaceful than at Bocca – the dining room overlooks the cranes and warehouses of Carrara's port. It's noisier than Bocca too – trucks loaded with white blocks roar past all day. But for people in the marble business, it's a dream. They can entertain clients in style within a ten-minute drive of the quarries, instead of making the 40-minute haul down to Forte dei Marmi. Lorenzo will be jealous.

The architecture magazine *Abitare* did a feature on Ciccio Marina which described it thus:

> The simplicity of the exterior is mirrored in the unfussy refinement of the interior sculpted by the daylight that floods into the restaurant on the upper floor, illuminates the large ground floor kitchen, and penetrates through a double height mirror-walled lightwell to the basement where the jazz club is situated.
>
> There are two illuminated bar counters (one for drinks, one for food) and, unusually for a jazz club, a spacious reading area stocked mainly with art books that enables the basement to be used at all times of the day. Once again, the materials create a distinctly nautical ambience: oak, white sailcloth, steel, grey tiles, and bar counter lights designed to resemble the stanchions of a ship's rail.

(In the same issue, there's a spread on the Sydney Italian restaurant Iceberg's, which is described as 'a virtual space of natural light to enhance the magic of a restaurant designed to welcome in the ocean and offer a convivial domestic dining experience'. That could almost be said of the original Ciccio's.)

Although Mario keeps telling him not to make comparisons, Lucio feels Marina doesn't yet have the welcoming warmth of Ciccio's. He's not excited by 'modern' dishes such as scampi on sliced pineapple and melon, or sole with guacamole, or smoked swordfish and raspberry vinegar with grated carrot and lettuce (Lucio splashed olive oil on top to Ciccio-ise it). But he had a great time with the 'retro' crepes suzette flamed at the table by Giorgio, a veteran of the cruise ships.

What delights Lucio is that Wendy is an active partner in Ciccio Marina. She was never a big participant in Capannina Ciccio, because she didn't want to get lost in the Guelfi family womb. But the new place is her passion.

On these hot nights she's been sleeping in a deckchair in the garden of the Ameglia

How to be a great waiter

1. Act as if it is your restaurant, so its successes are your triumphs, and its failures are your embarrassments, from which you learn.

2. Control the chefs – otherwise they will control you. You are the customers' ambassador to the kitchen, and you must never let the kitchen say, 'It can't be done'.

3. Prepare yourself to be able to talk on any subject. A good waiter spends the first half-hour of his working day reading the latest papers and magazines, because you never know when a customer will want to discuss politics, sport or gossip.

4. Know the back story of everything in the restaurant – not only the menu, but the wine, the oil, the mineral water, the paintings, the owners and the regular customers.

5. Know when to shut up. Some customers may be too polite to tell you the conversation is over.

6. Don't make customers look like imbeciles in front of their friends. 'If someone comes in with a group and says, "Ciao Giovanni", then I am Giovanni for that table for the night.'

7. The serving of food and wine is a performance, not just a delivery. A waiter must be able to carry, carve, compose, explain and entertain, while simultaneously analysing what else the customer needs.

8. Smile. It doesn't cost you anything and it will increase the tips. If you look relaxed, the customer feels relaxed.

9. Eat out often in your own time, to learn from other restaurants.

10. It's better to serve a smaller quantity of top quality ingredients than a large helping of something the customer will remember as second rate. That way the restaurant has bella figura (a good image) and so do you.

Every customer has a story, and the supreme pleasure of a restaurateur's life is piecing those stories together, through conversation and imagination.

house, watching the asteroid showers in the sky as she dozes off, and waking at first light to open up at Marina di Carrara and welcome the first coffee drinkers of the day. Then she has time to read the papers and observe the tides of humanity that wash up on the island she and Mario have created.

She has discovered what saved Mario's soul when his father's death made him a boss at 19 – that it's like directing a movie, because every customer has a story, and the supreme pleasure of a restaurateur's life is piecing those stories together, through conversation and imagination.

One customer, Paolo, has been sitting at a sunny table most mornings tapping away at a tiny laptop and turning the pages of a pile of Italian–English dictionaries. Wendy's speculations on what he was writing were nowhere near the truth. It turns out he is translating the sonnets of William Shakespeare into Italian. And although his spoken English is basic, his understanding of Elizabethan English seems impeccable.

The first verse of Shakespeare's 'Sonnet XVII' goes like this:
Shall I compare thee to a summer's day?
Thou art more lovely and more temperate.
Rough winds do shake the darling buds of May,
And summer's lease hath all too short a date.

In Paolo Cucurnia's Italian, it becomes:
T'accosteró a un caldo dǐ d'estate?
Sei dolce e più piacevole di questo:
Tenere gemme, in Maggio, son squassate
Dai venti; eppoi, l'estate muore presto.

The bar, the dining room and the barista in Mario's gleaming new project.

A local builder named Gino Lucetti told her proudly his great-uncle tried to assassinate Mussolini in 1926 by throwing a grenade at his car. Another regular, an artist named Claudio, suddenly stopped coming. Then Wendy read in the local paper that his 83-year-old father had been charged with his murder, allegedly because the father had discovered Claudio was gay.

Another morning coffee drinker, Adolfo Guegliemini, recognised her Australian accent and told her, over several mornings and many macchiatos, an amazing tale of adventure on the high seas.

She invites Adolfo to Lucio's farewell lunch, held in the garden of her house at Ameglia, so Lucio can hear the story. As they listen, Andrea, a friend of the family who used to be a baker in Sarzana, cooks a meal the way it would have been done 100 years ago – entirely in a stone oven with logs burning inside. It includes hand-made focaccia bread with sausage meat embedded in the dough; a *farinata* (flatbread) made with chickpea flour; and *castagnaccio* – a dense cake of chestnut flour, rosemary, pine nuts and sultanas, which would have been familiar fare for the partisans in the winters of 1943 and 1944.

Adolfo: 'In 1953 I went to Australia as an assisted immigrant, and worked as a bricklayer in Melbourne for a year. I loved it. For breakfast, I used to eat a steak as big as a

cushion. But I got an ear infection, and I didn't trust the Australian hospitals to operate, so I came back to Italy.

'When I got here I cried for two weeks. I realised what an idiot I was. Two months after the ear operation, I went to Genoa, found out which ship was leaving for Australia, got a boarding pass to see off passengers, and stowed away. It was called the *Oceania*.

'They started checking tickets in Naples, but I managed to avoid them. I stocked up on foods from local sellers in the ports on the way, and I made friends with the captain and the priest. I slept in the bathrooms, sitting on the toilet.

'One day out of Perth they collected passports. The captain said "Adolfo, where is yours?" I turned purple, confessed, and he was very angry.

'They wouldn't even let me onto the land. They put a gangway across to another ship that was leaving Perth, and locked me in a cabin all the way back to Naples. They handed me over to the police there, but they just congratulated me on surviving 60 days as a stowaway and sent me home. That was 50 years ago and I've been homesick for Australia ever since. My son is promising to take me one day.'

At the lunch, Mario expands on his dreams for the Latest Project. He never goes to Capannina Ciccio any more. He feels Marina needs his presence in order to grow, while Ciccio's can coast on its reputation and Giuseppe's professionalism. He is training his niece Silvia to run the nightclub and his nephew Tommaso to run the restaurant.

'For four or five years I've been working to ease myself out of Ciccio's, so they are not dependent on me being there all the time. The artists like to see me, but the other family members are good at talking to them.

'I'm lucky to have Tommaso and Silvia. They read about the industry, they study the science of hospitality. When I started, I had to make it up as I went along.

'Tommaso does not have confidence, he is too worried because it's a big place, so I have to work with him, but he gets better every day, a little bit more confident. It may take one or two years. Silvia is excellent, but she has a law degree and we don't know if she will become a lawyer or stay with us. I'm inclined to think the future of this family may lie with her and her sister Roberta.'

Silvia: 'I started helping in the bar at Ciccio's during the summer season at the age of 14, and slowly, slowly I grew into it – just like most of us in this family. During university I worked at Ciccio's every Friday, Saturday and Sunday, and full-time when I graduated.

'Now I'm here, some people may be surprised at how a lawyer knows all these things about food, but it's been part of my life since I was small. Living in that atmosphere, it comes to you naturally. And to prepare myself I did a wine appreciation course and a cocktail making course.

'Personally, I prefer traditional dishes which I learnt from my grandmother. Some are so old they would seem new if I tried them in a restaurant.

Adolfo the stowaway; opposite, Andrea demonstrates the right way to make focaccia and chickpea farinata.

I prefer traditional dishes which I learnt from my grandmother.
Some are so old they would seem new if I tried them in a restaurant.

'Mario wants to keep the two restaurants separate, with a more modern style at Marina. The clientele here is *ricercata* – they have money, they like to go out often, they are open-minded about new dishes. The clientele at Bocca is more traditional. At Marina we are aiming for the bosses of the quarries, not the miners, who would probably prefer Bocca.

'The family taught me to work, not to go out and have fun. It doesn't matter how many hours you've been working, if there are still customers, you stay around. I'm in the club till 3 am most days.'

Mario: 'I have to change the menu every 20 days, because Carrara people want to try the new. The style is modern but comfortable, so they don't want to leave. I spent three times what I intended on Marina, and it will take 15 years to pay off. But I think it is going to work.

'I'm getting a new chef who can do banquet food – ice sculptures, big displays. I want to start that theatrical kind of thing because people don't remember it. It's possible to do that because at Marina we have many different spaces.

'We're doing crepes suzette again with Giorgio, who is technically fantastic. He is too friendly, because he has the mentality of those guys from Ameglia who were working on the cruise ships. When those guys try to put in the humour, and stand around your table with a cigarette in the hand, it's terrible. I have to retrain him.

'I think what we are doing here is the future of looking after people. It's a big space with lots of small spaces in it, so people can come here for many different experiences – a big formal meal, or just a *panino* [bread roll] and a coffee, or a drink and listen to music.

'You know what was wonderful the other day: a couple came in to book their wedding party, and the girl told me her grandparents had held their wedding party at Ciccio's, 48 years ago.'

Mario remarks that the architect of Marina has suggested they can now franchise the format around the world: Ciccio Roma; Ciccio New York; Ciccio Sydney. But he wonders what is the essence of Ciccio that would be translated to these other environments. Food? Art? Service? View? Generosity? The family? Italianness? How much of this can be exported?

'Hang on, I thought I was already doing Ciccio Sydney,' says Lucio, not entirely joking.

On Giuseppe's recommendation, Lucio has tried out Ciccio's two main competitors in the neighbourhood, and had spooky experiences in both of them. Just across the river, Il Pilota is still going strong after 80 years. It's the place where the writers drank and danced before Ciccio won their hearts in 1951, but it survived the arrival of the ambitious newcomer.

Nowadays it's a small hotel and trattoria run by Carla Germi, granddaughter of the river boatman who founded it. Framed on the wall are newspaper clippings about how her grandfather rescued a 4 year old from drowning and rowed the empress of Germany across the river. Projecting over the river is a peeling rotunda with a sign that says 'Dancing'.

Lucio has always had a powerful memory for sounds, smells and tastes. The clinking of a spoon in a coffee cup always reminds him of his mother waking her sons on winter mornings, bringing milky coffee to their room; the smell of red wine puts him inside his uncle's mouldy barrels; and at Il Pilota the slightly iodine taste of the seafood sauce on the spaghetti and on the risotto sends him back to the family table at Ciccio's when he was ten years old.

'They're using the same soffritto,' he's thinking. 'It's garlic, parsley and cuttlefish. This place has never changed.'

There's a similar flashback in the antipasto – local anchovies marinated in oil and lemon. The seafood salad differs from the Ciccio 1962 version only by the addition of borlotti beans. The dessert – a fresh peach in a bowl of ice – reminds him of the time he reached for a peach in the kitchen and Ciccio gently slapped his hand away, saying, 'The best fruit is only for customers.' Then Ciccio relented and let Lucio take the perfect peach – 'but just this once'. The lesson in kitchen etiquette became more memorable with the happy ending.

A time warp of a different kind awaits him when he has dinner with Sandro, Ciccio's most consistent customer for 30 years, at the Hotel Garden. The dining room, which has been operating as a restaurant for only five years, is painted bright yellow. It has blue cloths on its tables and red nets hanging from the ceiling. The food is modern and interesting – little gnocchi with stingray sauce, tajarin noodles with lobster.

The best looking dish is a circular slice of octopus in its own jelly that shimmers like a purple and white rockpool. When Lucio speculates on how it's made, Sandro asks a waiter if they could talk to the chef, a burly guy in his 30s named Francesco Bologna. He explains the procedure for 'Polpi in bottiglia' – clean the octopus, cut it into small pieces, poach it for half an hour with carrots, onion and celery then shove it into a plastic mineral

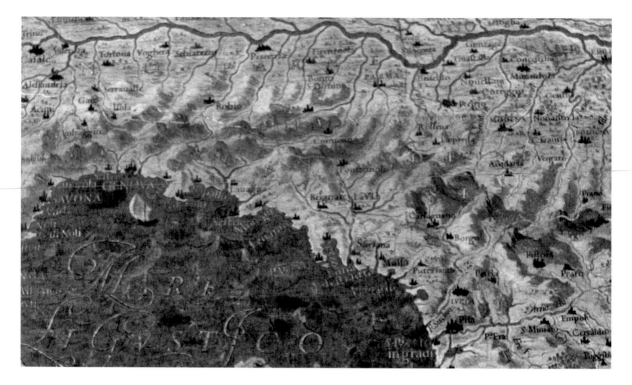

A 17th century map in the Vatican shows Lunigiana has barely changed; Luke Sciberras's painted map showing Lucio's journey.'

water bottle with the end cut off, so it forms a sausage shape. Deep freeze it, and when you're ready to serve, cut off the plastic bottle and slice the sorpressa into discs.

When he's finished the recipe, Francesco looks at Lucio and says: 'I knew your father. When I was a kid I used to hang around the kitchen of Ciccio's watching them cook. Mauro was always kind to me. I used to call him Babbo [daddy].'

It appears that after Lucio left for Australia, Mauro 'adopted' Francesco and gave him an education in restaurant life. What Lucio absorbed unconsciously in Ciccio's kitchen, Francesco learned conscientiously. He has clearly benefited from the experience.

Lucio feels as if he's meeting the younger brother he never knew. It's the first time he's thought about how life in Bocca di Magra went on without him. And will again.

The August madness is over, and Lucio is packing his bags in Mario's pink house in Ameglia. Next week the contadini around here will start preparing for the grape harvest and the wine pressing, and right after that, the olive harvest. He'll have to miss it.

On the way to the airport he stops by Capannina Ciccio to say goodbye to Zia Anna. It's 10 am and Mario's sister Giovanna tells him she has already made 60 espressos and 40 cappuccinos. The pastries to go with them were served by her 14-year-old daughter Giulia.

Giuseppe is looking tired. He tells Lucio he's about to go on two weeks' holiday – the first time he's taken more than a few days off in 30 years. Lucio asks: 'Where will you spend your holidays?' Giuseppe replies, with enthusiasm: '*A casa*' (at home).

On the car radio, Lucio hears a couple of talk jocks discussing strange dishes they had during the August holidays. One of them nominates *carne di canguro* (kangaroo meat) and

the other responds: '*Che schifo!*' (how disgusting). Maybe the food exchange that started Lucio speculating at the Slow Food fair won't happen so easily.

Staying a day in Rome before catching his plane for Sydney, Lucio wanders through the Vatican museums, and discovers, on the wall of the map room, a seventeenth-century fresco that shows everywhere he's reached in his recent journeys around north-western Italy, from Siena on the bottom right to a city called Trino, which is presumably Turin, on the top left. It's even possible to make out Luna in the centre.

In Rome, he goes for dinner at a two-Michelin-star restaurant called Convivio Troiani. This is about as upmarket as it gets in Italy, serving reinventions of traditional dishes in tiny portions, with fastidious presentation.

As he sits in the elegant bar waiting for his table, Lucio glances along a shelf crammed with cookbooks from every country in the world. He notices a copy of the Australian food bible, *The Cook's Companion* by Stephanie Alexander, and then, with a leap of the heart, a copy of a recipe book he published four years earlier, *The Art of Food at Lucio's*. It's out of print in Australia, so he's surprised to see it here.

When the head waiter appears, Lucio asks where the Australian books came from. He replies: 'They were left here by a woman who had dinner and came back the next day to give us those books for our collection. I have no idea of her name.' A pleasant mystery for Lucio, and support for his sense of an accelerating flow of ideas between two countries. Now he's about to find out if he can translate one of the oldest food cultures of Italy into Australian dialect.

The other dinner

This story ends, as everything should, with a meal. It was served to the Sydney chapter of the Slow Food movement, a gathering of 24 gluttons and Italophiles (if there's a difference), in the spring of 2004.

The planning for it started two weeks earlier, immediately after Lucio flew back from Rome. Or, depending on how you look at it, three years earlier, when Lucio made his first research trip to Lunigiana, or 50 years earlier, when Lucio started absorbing the kitchen customs at Ciccio's.

You know the 50-year story, so let's focus on the immediate planning. At 10 am on a Tuesday, Lucio and his chefs, Tim Fisher and Logan Campbell, are having coffee in the sun-filled front room of the restaurant, discussing what they should do for the Lunigiana night. Lucio is filled with the joy of the journey and eager to show his customers everything he has rediscovered. Tim is filtering this enthusiasm through the realities of a kitchen that has never cooked this stuff before and a Sydney audience accustomed to light, modern food.

While Lucio is talkative, Tim is taciturn, signalling his opinions mostly by small movements of the mouth and eyebrows. He looks particularly grim when Lucio is talking about testaroli. Lucio is not about to be inhibited by practical concerns, because he knows the kitchen can do anything.

When Lucio talks about his chef, he pronounces the name 'Team', so that the listener may think he's talking about a brigade of helpers rather than an individual. In effect he is. Lucio has built a team who seem to need only a few words of backgrounding to replicate the cooking of Milan, Bologna, Genoa, Venice, Rome, Naples or Palermo. The kitchen workers come from China, Britain, New Zealand, Afghanistan, Argentina and Australia, but, as Lucio says, their souls are Italian. So he's confident they'll have no trouble reproducing 2,000 years of Lunigiana history.

'Do you know what Team did yesterday?' he asks Logan, who had the day off. 'The butcher brought a whole baby lamb from Tasmania, and Team made the legs into a stew with beans, and stuffed the body with chestnuts, thyme and parmesan and roasted it for three hours at low temperature.

'It's a bit of an inconvenience in our tiny space, but you really know the chefs are in the kitchen when you get offered a special like that. That's the real Slow Food. We sold all 15 portions within an hour.'

But much of the success of any dish is in how it's described. Logan asks how Lucio sold it to the customers. 'It's a bitch to explain this kind of preparation,' he replies. 'You can't go on too long, or you'll lose them, but you want them to know what's involved. We said it was deboned baby lamb, stuffed with chestnuts and herbs, served on a light stew of white beans and lamb leg. Now, guys, should we do that for the Lunigiana night?'

They toss the question around. Yes, lamb is part of the cooking of the high Lunigiana, and so are chestnuts. But having chestnuts in the main course means they couldn't really put them in the dessert, where Lucio is hoping to do that castagnaccio cake made by Andrea at Wendy's farewell lunch. The ingredient that kept the partisans alive through the bitter winter of 1944 deserves a more prominent role than mere stuffing.

In any case, lamb was never part of Lucio's childhood diet. So for the meaty main, they decide to stick with his first inclination – rabbit, more appropriate for the peasant style the scholars are expecting. Lucio explains how it was done at Armanda – deboned, rolled around pine nuts, pancetta, and rosemary, and served with a black olive sauce. Tim says he'll experiment.

Lucio wants to start the meal with tartina, in celebration of its inventor, Ciccio, and its maker, mamma Bruna. Small problem: the base is supposed to be deep-fried bread. The kitchen does not possess a deep-fryer. Okay, they agree, let's make a bruschetta instead – a thick slice of bread, baked in the oven, with a little oil and garlic rubbed on (to replace the flavour contributed by the frying). Then add a salad of mussels, calamari and prawns and a thread of mayonnaise – just like mamma used to make, only lighter.

On the same plate, Lucio says, there should be three olives and a slice of prosciutto, because that's how it was always served. He acknowledges that the prosciutto won't be as good as he'd get in Italy, and the chefs are dubious about how ham will match with seafood salad, but the memory of Ciccio will be duly honoured. They're off to a great start.

Now, a true Lunigiana meal must include testaroli, he says. What's that, the chefs ask. 'Just flour, salt and water,' says Lucio. 'You cook it like a pancake. It's easy.' Tim's eyes narrow.

Lucio has seen testaroli or panigacci made three ways: baked between hot terracotta plates in the mountains, fried on an iron skillet in Castelnuovo and at home with his mother, and boiled in a pot in Pontremoli. The kitchen possesses neither terracotta plates nor a roaring fire, so the mountain method is out. He has experimented at home with the second method: cutting a potato in half and using the exposed surface to rub oil onto a frying pan, then pouring on a thin layer of batter. The result was pretty good – thin crunchy discs that went well with pesto – but Lucio can't really imagine the team doing this 50 times on a busy night. So Armanda's thin panigacci are not an option.

That leaves the method from Trattoria da Bussé. First bake your batter in a pot, extract

the pancake thus formed, cut it into diamond shapes and boil just before serving. The result is not crispy, the way Lucio likes his panigacci, but it has been hallowed by hundreds of years of tradition.

Lucio's first inclination is to dress the testaroli only with parmesan and oil, but he's sure the customers will expect pesto sauce, which is, after all, a speciality of Liguria, and he knows Logan will make a definitive version. Tim is sceptical about the whole idea of testaroli – their grossness goes against all his inclinations as a twenty-first century chef. So that's another experiment he must start today.

Lucio wants a mixed antipasto, including something with farro, and capsicums stuffed with anchovies like his mother used to make. And there should be ravioli, because that's the festive food of his area. 'Before weddings the women would make thousands of ravioli – their arms must have been so tired,' he reflects. He outlines a recipe with a stuffing of silverbeet, veal, pork sausage, breadcrumbs and parmesan, with a meat ragù. He warns they might have to make the wrapping a bit thicker than normal to stand up to the sturdy ingredients. This goes against the grain in a restaurant famed for its delicate hand-made pasta, but history makes its demands.

'This meal feels like an old-style wedding feast, where you had lots of antipasto, then two primi, maybe ravioli and tortellini, and then two secondi – maybe a roast and a boiled chicken with salsa verde; then fruits and cheese and then a cake. We'll do rabbit instead of the chicken. And our roast should be the pesce al sale.'

Clockwise from left, the antipasto of mushroom salad, farro cake, polenta with kale and beans, and stuffed capsicums.

This is emotional for me. I was interviewed soon after I opened here and I said I wanted to do this food of my region. But then I forgot about it.

The guys are looking alarmed. Yes, the pesce al sale is a real crowd-pleaser. Customers cheer as Lucio lifts the salt lid and the fragrant steam gushes out. But can the ovens cope with pesce al sale for 24 and simultaneously meet the needs of the 60 other people who'll be eating from the normal menu that night? Lucio is arguing with himself: 'I know this is not meant to be a Ciccio dinner, it's meant to be a Lunigiana dinner, but this is emotional for me'. They compromise on snapper fillets that can be plated in the kitchen. The fish will sit on a classic Ligurian stew called *inzimino*, with spinach, pine nuts and slices of cuttlefish.

Lucio would like to do a spungata for dessert, in honour of Gemmi, but worries that the crisp top will shatter if they try to cut it into pieces small enough for the end of a meal. Logan will take Lucio's specifications and see what he can develop.

For wine, Lucio has found a distributor in Melbourne who imports a vermentino called Santa Caterina, which happens to be the name of the village with the dance hall where Anna first met Ciccio. Lucio enjoys the poetry of that. To go with the rabbit, he should serve a sangiovese, since that's the main red grape around Lunigiana, but he's decided to use a Nebbiolo, because it reminds him of drinking barolo with truffles in Alba, and because he'll be able to say to his customers: 'It will reveal its secrets'.

The next day they reconvene to discuss the kitchen's experiments. Tim has bad news: 'The farmed rabbit we normally get has no flavour done this way. When it's cooked on the bone it tastes all right, but when it has to be wrapped around the filling it becomes tasteless.' He'll try to find some wild rabbit, which will have more flavour, or think of a way to marinate the farmed rabbit with garlic for a couple of days before the event.

'Oh, forget about rolling it,' says Lucio. 'It's too fussy anyway. We'll just do it the way my mother did, with black olives.'

Now Tim presents his first attempt at testaroli. The fried and boiled dough is cut into small triangles about half a centimetre deep, and sprinkled with oil, pepper and parmesan. They look a bit like the Roman form of gnocchi. Tim is embarrassed, but Lucio shovels them in with delight. 'They're just stodge,' says Tim. 'No, they're great,' says Lucio. 'Just put more water in the mix and make them thinner.

'I'm so happy to be finally doing this. You know, it's taken me 20 years to get around to testaroli. I remember I was interviewed by a food writer soon after I opened here and I said I wanted to do this food of my region. But then I forgot about it till now.'

Tim can see how important this is to Lucio, but he wants to go lighter. If Lucio is determined to stick with the testaroli, the ravioli must be sacrificed. 'It's too much – tartina then testaroli then ravioli,' says Tim. 'Then rabbit then fish. They'll never eat the dessert.'

'Small servings, Team, small servings,' says Lucio. Even so, they'll be groaning. 'Okay, we dump the ravioli,' Lucio concedes, waving his hands in mock despair.

Another day, another testarolo. Next morning Tim produces a batch which are thinner, with lighter texture. 'I've been thinking about these overnight and I think they need to be cooked longer the first time, so they are not so floury,' he says. 'What if we fry them, finish them off in the oven, then cut them up and boil them?'

'Good idea, but these are too salty,' says Lucio. It takes four more batches over three more days before he is satisfied. 'After 2,000 years,' says Lucio, 'this is going to be the new big thing in Sydney'. Tim is clearly pleased, but keeps his frown.

Clockwise from top left: tartina alla Ciccio with prosciutto; snapper on cuttlefish inzimino; rabbit with black olives; Logan's spungata; and chestnut cake with ricotta.

The evening turns into a triumph. Lucio gives the Slow Foodies a souvenir menu which says this:

DISCOVERY OF THE ANCIENT LUNIGIANA

Lunigiana is a geographical region in the north-west of Italy, between Tuscany, Liguria and Emilia-Romagna.

It takes its name from the ancient Roman town of Luna (the moon goddess), which was an important sea port, shipping the white marble (used by Michelangelo) from the mountains of Carrara to Rome.

Lunigiana is my birth place, and is the location of our family restaurant Capannina Ciccio, founded 53 years ago by my parents, Bruna and Mauro, and my uncle and aunt, Ciccio and Anna.

'About rich cooking, we talk and debate. With the food of the poor, we fall in love. The best example: the testaroli.' — *Salvatore Marchese*, Enogastronomo

Buon Appetito
Lucio Galletto

Opposite, *testaroli*, somewhere between pasta and a pancake.

MENU

TARTINA AI FRUTTI DI MARE
Seafood bruschetta with mayonnaise
Our interpretation of Tartina alla Ciccio, a speciality of my family's restaurant.

ANTIPASTO LUNIGIANESE
Polenta incatenata con baccalà mantecato (polenta with
beans and cavolo nero, with cod mousse)
Torta di farro (cake of farro grains with parmesan)
Insalata di funghi (raw sliced mushroom and celery salad)
Peperoni sott'olio (roasted capsicums stuffed with anchovies)
Small tastes from the mountains to the sea

TESTAROLI AI DUE MODI
Mountain pancakes served with traditional pesto
and with Ligurian olive oil and parmesan
This dish is prepared as the shepherds have been eating it for centuries

DENTICE SU SEPPIE INZIMINO
Snapper on a stew of cuttlefish, silver beets, pine nuts and tomato
A favourite Australian fish with a favourite of Ligurian fishermen

CONIGLIO AL VINO BIANCO E OLIVE TAGGIASCHE
Rabbit sautéed with rosemary, vermentino and black olives
The 'Sunday roast' of the farming families

SPUNGATA DI ALBICOCCHE
Apricot and pine nut tart with green apple sorbet
Logan's take on the dessert speciality of Sarzana

CASTAGNACCIO
Chestnut cake with ricotta
The particular dessert of the mountain people, with fresh cheese

CAFFÈ E BISCOTTI TRADIZIONALE DI SARZANA
Coffee and almond biscuits
The biscuits of Sarzana, Lunigiana's 'capital'

The hit of the night are the testaroli. The Slow Foodies keep describing them as 'the ultimate comfort food'. They applaud Lucio's Lunigiana pesto, made with less garlic and smaller leaves than most pestos they've experienced. His joy is enhanced by the presence of his daughter Michela and his son Matteo, both studying at university but here to help with the serving and discuss the dishes with the guests.

The following Monday Lucio puts testaroli on his menu as a daily special. He goes from table to table explaining them, never failing to laugh whenever male customers pretend to think they have something to do with testicles.

As a joke, his waiters draw up the kind of blackboard you might see outside a trattoria in rural Italy to entice travellers. It translates as, 'Today testaroli with pesto'. It will have no meaning to passers-by in Paddington. Not yet.

One of the first to try the new special is Bob Carr, former Labor Party leader and former premier of the state of New South Wales. He's lunching with Leo Schofield, a retired restaurant critic who congratulates Lucio on getting back his 'two hat' award in the latest *Good Food Guide*.

Lucio says: 'We have a special today that is called testaroli. We serve them with our own pesto. They are very ancient, something between pasta and a pancake. When the Romans came upon my people in the north-west of Italy, they found them eating testaroli.'

This gets Carr's attention. He's a history buff and a fan of the emperor Marcus Aurelius. He stops Lucio's recitation and asks: 'What do you mean — your people? You were there before the Romans?'

'The Liguri Apuani,' Lucio replies, channelling Sara the Luni guide and Alma-Vittoria Cordiviolia, and moving just slightly into the realms of fantasy. 'We were invaded by the Romans in 200 BC, and we lost our land. We took our pots up into the mountains and cooked our testaroli.'

'So what you're telling me,' says Carr, 'is that you are an Italian Aborigine?'

'Yep, that's about it,' says Lucio. All three laugh. The politician and the critic order the testaroli.

Afterword

It was with great enthusiasm that I went back to my native Lunigiana with the intention of showing David Dale around and sharing the secret places of this mysterious region. But I soon realised that it was still very mysterious to me. So as David was discovering Lunigiana, I was too.

When I was growing up, I had other priorities. As a child I was playing on the beach and swimming in the river during the summer months, and kicking a soccer ball in the winter. As a teenager I was playing guitar and writing songs and worrying about the length of my hair. Then I realised that there had to be more to life – girls! I met Sally, fell in love at first sight, woke up from what I now call my 'dreamtime' and at 23 went 'walkabout' to Australia.

I had never really had time to know my neighbourhood, its people and its food. David and I went up and down this region of amazing beauty, talking to the people in the villages, eating and analysing their food in trattorias and homes. We found an extraordinary hospitality and pride of belonging to the land and to their trade.

The fishermen of the village of Bocca di Magra became real people to me, not just shadows that I used to meet in the early mornings on my way to bed, or figures putting their heads out of their bedroom windows, screaming at us teenagers when we were making too much unnecessary noise during the night. These were the people who found the seafood that we used to sell the next day in Ciccio's restaurant.

I realised what was behind the pecorino (sheep's milk) cheese that we used to serve, and the wheels of parmesan that I so much enjoyed watching my father or Zio Ciccio cut open, and the prosciutto that was so good people used to queue at Ciccio's to buy slices to take home instead of going to the delicatessen in the village. And I also realised what it takes to produce all those crates full of beautiful fruits and vegetables at the markets.

The rich masters who once ruled the region have gone, leaving behind only the ruins of their castles. What remains is the traditional cooking of the poor, passed orally from generation to generation. I think now that hospitality is Lunigiana's culture. After all, so many travellers passed through this land over the centuries – Greeks, Etruscans, Romans, Saracens, Normans, pilgrims, merchants, poets, painters – and each of them left an influence. That is why the food of my area is so different from the food of the rest of Italy. And this is the first book in English about it.

David jokes that the meals in Lunigiana taste good because of MSG. That does not stand for monosodium glutamate, a chemical often added to Chinese dishes to boost flavour (although, as it happens, there is natural monosodium glutamate in parmesan and tomatoes). MSG stands for Modesty, Sincerity and Generosity – humble ingredients prepared with care and served with love. That is what I learned in my mother's kitchen and between the tables at Ciccio.

A note from Lucio about the recipes

THE DISHES WE CHOSE FOR THIS BOOK ARE THE ONES THAT BEST EXPRESS THE PERSONALITY OF THIS AREA, FROM THE SEA, THE RIVER VALLEY AND THE HILLS TO THE HIGH MOUNTAINS. THEY ARE SIMPLE RECIPES AND YOU MIGHT FIND SOME OF THEM QUITE STRANGE, BUT WE WOULD LIKE YOU TO TASTE SOMETHING OF THE PAST THAT IS ALSO THE FUTURE OF LUNIGIANA.

We've divided the recipes into four sections – the favourites served at Capannina Ciccio since it opened in 1951 (mostly based on local seafood); the dishes made by my mother when I was growing up (mostly from the farm); the traditional dishes from the mountains around Pontremoli; and the dinner I served to the food scholars when I returned to Sydney.

Most of the cooks we spoke to in Lunigiana do not use written recipes. They simply know what goes with what, because they grew up watching their parents catch, harvest and prepare food in all its forms.

To write down these instructions for the first time, I had to make my best guesses about quantities and cooking times, based on my own preferences. But please don't feel restrained by the precise measurements. This is not a chemistry lesson, where disaster can follow from the smallest deviation. Lunigiana cooking is flexible and comfortable. You may need to be careful with the pasta and the pastry, but for the rest, you can vary these recipes according to your personal taste and creativity.

The more you play, the nearer you'll come to finding your own *soffritto*.

The Lunigiana Pantry

BASICS:
olive oil (cold pressed extra virgin) – *olio d'oliva*
onions – *cipolle*
garlic – *aglio*
eggs – *uova*
wheat flour – *farina bianca*
chestnut flour – *farina di castagne*
cornmeal – *polenta*

HERBS:
basil – *basilico*
bay leaves – *alloro*
capers – *capperi*
marjoram – *maggiorana*
nutmeg – *noce moscata*
oregano – *origano*
parsley – *prezzemolo*
rosemary – *rosmarino*
sage – *salvia*
thyme – *timo*

SEAFOOD:
anchovies – *acciughe*
bream – equivalent of *orata*
calamari – *totani*
clams – *vongole*
cuttlefish – *seppie*
dried cod – *baccalà*
eels – *anguille*
whitebait – *bianchetti*
mullet – *muggine*
mussels – *muscoli*
octopus – *moscardini*
prawns – *gamberi*
red mullet – *triglie*
sardines – *sardine*
scampi
snapper – equivalent of *dentice*
trout – *trota*

MEAT:
beef – *manzo*
chicken – *pollo*
lamb – *agnello*
pork – *maiale*
rabbit – *coniglio*
tripe (and livers, kidneys, hearts) – *interiora*

FRUIT AND VEGETABLES:
apples – *mele*
apricots – *albicocche*
artichokes – *carciofi*
asparagus – *asparagi*
beans (borlotti, canellini, fave) – *fagioli*
cabbage – *cavolo*
capsicums – *peperoni*
carrots – *carote*
celery – *sedano*
chestnuts – *castagne*
chickpeas – *ceci*
farro
figs – *fichi*
leeks – *porri*
loquats — *nespole*
mushrooms – *funghi* (porcini, galletti, pioppini)
olives – *olive*
peas – *piselli*
persimmons – *cachi*
pine nuts – *pinoli*
potatoes – *patate*
silverbeet – *bietole*
spinach – *spinaci*
tomatoes – *pomodori*
tuscan kale – *cavolo nero*
walnuts – *noci*

CHEESES:
parmesan – *parmigiano-reggiano*
sheep's milk cheese – *pecorino*
fresh curds – *ricotta*
soft creamy cheese – *stracchino*

TOOLS:
mezzaluna (two-handled chopping knife with crescent blade)
sharp slicing knife – *coltello affilato*
frying pans – *padelle*
deep pots – *pentole*
baking dishes (round and rectangular) – *teglie*
whisk – *frusta*
wooden spoon – *cucchiaio di legno*
rolling pin – *mattarello*
sieve – *setaccio*
slotted spoon – *schiumarola*
strainer – *scolapasta*
mixing bowl – *terrina*
chopping board – *tagliere*
Mouli (food mill) – *passatutto*

The Dinner at Ciccio's

Carpaccio di branzino
Fish carpaccio

600 g fish fillets
lemon juice
extra virgin olive oil
  (a lighter style,
  preferably Ligurian)
white pepper
flat-leaf parsley, chopped

Branzino is a white fish not available in Australia, but tuna, salmon, ocean trout or kingfish are suitable replacements. The fish must be very fresh.

Immediately before you are planning to serve this, slice the fish into thin fillets (like smoked salmon) with a long flat knife, and arrange them on a flat plate. Squeeze lemon juice over the entire surface, zigzag a little olive oil over it and sprinkle with white pepper and parsley. SERVES 4

Tartina alla Ciccio
Crostini with seafood salad

SEAFOOD SALAD:
300 g octopus
2 medium calamari
1 cuttlefish
400 g prawns
1 kg mussels
½ kg clams

BOUILLON:
3 litres water
2 carrots
1 onion, peeled
2 stalks celery
2 tomatoes
½ glass white-wine
  vinegar
½ tsp white pepper
salt

SEAFOOD DRESSING:
2 cloves garlic
juice of 1 lemon
extra virgin olive oil
1 handful flat-leaf
  parsley, chopped

FRIED CROSTINI:
½ litre fish stock
3 eggs
200 g flour, sieved
thick slices of white
  bread, crusts removed,
  one slice per person
mayonnaise
black olives, to serve

Clean and wash the octopus, calamari and cuttlefish and leave the prawns in the shell.

Prepare the bouillon by filling a pot with about 3 litres of water, the carrots, whole onion, celery, tomatoes, vinegar and pepper and bring to the boil for 20 minutes. Then simmer the prawns for 5 minutes in this broth, take them out, shell and devein them and put to one side. Then simmer the octopus for 15 minutes, and finally the cuttlefish for 10 minutes.

While the octopus or cuttlefish is cooking, wash the mussels and the clams, put them into a hot pan with a little olive oil and stir until they open. Remove immediately, take out of the shells and put to one side with a little of the cooking juice to keep them moist.

Roughly chop all the seafood together and place into a bowl that has been rubbed with cut garlic. Dress with the lemon juice, olive oil, parsley and a pinch of salt.

TO PREPARE THE TARTINA:

Prepare 3 bowls: one with warm fish stock, one with beaten eggs and one with sieved flour.

Heat the oil for frying to 180°C.

Dip the bread first into the stock for a few seconds, then the egg mixture and finally the flour. Fry immediately, turning as necessary until golden. Remove and drain on paper towels to remove any excess oil. The resulting crostini should be crispy on the outside and soft on the inside.

Place one crostino on each plate and top with the seafood mix, leaving a small border. Fill a piping bag with mayonnaise and make a zigzag pattern on and around the tartina. Surround with 3 olives and serve immediately. It must be eaten hot. SERVES 4

Gamberi e fagioli
Prawns with cannelini beans

300 g dried cannelini beans
1 carrot
1 celery stalk
½ onion
1 sprig rosemary
2 sprigs thyme
600 g prawns, peeled
   with tail intact
juice of ½ lemon
¼ cup extra virgin olive oil
salt and pepper
1 small jar black caviar or
   red salmon roe

1 clove garlic, peeled
½ red onion, thinly sliced

FIRST METHOD:

Gently boil the cannelini beans in salted water, scented with carrot, celery, half onion, rosemary and one sprig of thyme for about 45 minutes. Drain and place cannelini beans in a bowl, discarding everything else.

Bring 1 litre of water to the boil with the remaining thyme and gently poach the prawns for about 3 minutes. Drain and keep warm.

Whisk the lemon juice, olive oil, salt and pepper together lightly to dress the beans. Place a little caviar or roe and a splash of olive oil on top, mix well and divide onto each serving plate, like a little mountain.

Place the prawns on top with a dollop of caviar on top of each prawn.

SECOND METHOD (WITH RAW ONION):

Place the cooked cannelini beans in a bowl that has been rubbed with the cut garlic clove and dress with the lemon juice mixture. Add some of the finely sliced red onion and mix well. Pour the beans onto a serving platter, arrange the prawns on top and add more slices of red onion. Dress with a little more olive oil and put it in the centre of the table for your guests to help themselves. SERVES 4

Zuppa di farro e moscardini
Farro and octopus soup

extra virgin olive oil
1 clove garlic, finely chopped
½ red onion, finely chopped
600 g baby octopus
   (smallest possible)
½ glass white wine
chili to taste
marjoram
400 g ripe tomatoes,
   processed through
   a Mouli
fish or vegetable stock
400 g farro
1 carrot
1 celery stick
1 onion
salt and pepper
crusty Italian bread, to serve
olive oil, to serve

In a pot (preferably terracotta) make a soffritto with the oil, garlic and onion. Add the baby octopus, cut in halves or quarters according to size, and sauté over a high heat for about 5 minutes. Pour in the wine, cook until it evaporates and then turn down the heat. Add the chili, marjoram and tomato and simmer slowly for about one hour, adding some stock from time to time.

In the meantime, cook the farro in plenty of boiling salted water with the carrot, celery and onion for 15 minutes. Remove the vegetables, drain the farro and add it to the octopus soup. Mix well, season and let it cook for a further 5 minutes.

Serve in individual bowls with a slice of toasted bread and a drop of olive oil on top. It tastes even better the next day. SERVES 4

Cacciucco
Fish soup

2 cloves garlic
handful flat-leaf parsley
5 ripe tomatoes
½ kg mussels
2 cuttlefish
2 calamari
300 g baby octopus
2 kg whole fish (5 different
    types, such as red mullet,
    rock cod)
1 cup extra virgin olive oil
1 cup dry white wine
salt and pepper
crusty Italian bread,
    toasted, to serve
garlic, to serve

Chop the garlic and parsley together very finely and put to one side.

Wash the tomatoes and, with a sharp knife, cut a cross through the skin at the top of each tomato. Plunge into boiling water for a couple of minutes and then plunge them into ice-cold water. When the skin starts to wrinkle, remove tomatoes from the water and peel the skin off. Seed and dice them and put to one side.

Under running water, scrub mussel shells with a hard brush and remove the 'beard' that sometimes protrudes from the shell. Put mussels to one side. Clean and wash the cuttlefish, calamari and baby octopus, then cut them into thin strips. Cut the bigger fish into pieces, but leave the red mullets whole.

Make a soffritto by heating some oil in a high-sided pan and adding three-quarters of the garlic–parsley mix. Let it fry for 1–2 minutes, stirring with a wooden spoon, being careful not to let the garlic burn.

Add the cuttlefish, calamari and baby octopus and cook on a medium heat, stirring often to mix all the flavours for about 9–10 minutes. Add the wine and continue cooking until it evaporates, then add the tomatoes, mix well, cover the pot and cook for another 10 minutes. Next add the fish to the pan, cover it well with the sauce and cook it for 6–7 minutes. Finally add the mussels. When the shells open, sprinkle with the remaining garlic and parsley.

Mix gently, taking care not to break the fish, for another couple of minutes and then place the whole dish in the centre of the table for your guests to help themselves. Serve with small slices of toasted bread rubbed with cut garlic. SERVES 6–8

Muscoli alla marinara
Mussels marinara

2 kg mussels
extra virgin olive oil
2 cloves garlic, chopped
    finely
1 chili, cut in half
½ glass white wine
1 lemon, juiced
handful flat-leaf parsley,
    chopped
pepper
extra lemon juice, to serve
crusty Italian bread,
    toasted, to serve

Wash the mussels under running water. Scrub the mussel shells with a hard brush and snip off the 'beard' that sometimes protrudes from the shell by pulling in a downward motion (towards the base of the shell). In a high-sided pan, heat the oil and fry the garlic and chili for one minute, then remove the chili. Add the mussels, white wine and lemon juice.

As the mussels open, remove them to a serving dish. Reduce the pan juices over a high heat and then pour over the mussels with a squeeze of lemon and a sprinkle of parsley and pepper. Serve immediately with crusty toasted bread. SERVES 4

Fritto misto
Tempura seafood

200 g baby calamari
8 prawns
4 red mullets
4 small garfish or other
   small fish available
   at the market
salt
enough flour for
   tossing the fish
1 litre vegetable oil,
   for frying
salt
2 lemons, cut into
   wedges, to serve

Clean and wash the calamari and cut the body into rings, leaving the tentacles whole. Peel the prawns. The rest of the fish should be cleaned and scaled when you buy it, with heads and spines removed.

Mix some salt with the flour, then quickly roll the seafood in it, and shake off any excess.

In a heavy high-sided pan, heat vegetable oil to 180°C and fry the seafood in small batches. When the seafood is golden and rises to the surface, it is ready. Remove from the oil with a slotted spoon and drain on paper towels to absorb any excess oil.

Serve hot on a platter, sprinkled with salt and with lemon wedges. Cook fast and eat fast is the principle here. SERVES 4

Spaghetti alla Ciccio
Spaghetti with seafood

2 calamari
4 scampi
4 medium prawns
40 clams
20 mussels
extra virgin olive oil
1 clove garlic, chopped
   finely
1 chili, chopped finely
½ glass dry white wine
400 g spaghetti
handful flat-leaf parsley,
   chopped finely

Clean and wash the calamari and cut into strips, leaving the tentacles whole. Cut the scampi and prawns in half lengthwise (still in their shells) and put all to one side. Wash the clams under running water. Wash the clams and the mussels under running water. Scrub the mussel shells with a hard brush and snip off the 'beard' that sometimes protrudes from the shell by pulling in a downward motion (towards the base of the shell). Put clams and mussels to one side.

In a big pan, slowly heat 6 tablespoons of oil and fry the garlic for about a minute, being careful not to let it go brown. Then add the chili, calamari, scampi and prawns. Cook for a few minutes, stirring with a wooden spoon and pressing down on the heads of the prawns and scampi to release all their flavours. When they have changed colour, add the wine and let it evaporate.

In the meantime, cook the spaghetti until it is very al dente – at least one minute less than the recommended cooking time on the packet, because it will continue cooking in the pan.

Add the mussels and clams to the pan and when they are all open, add the spaghetti and toss. Sprinkle with parsley and serve. SERVES 4

Pesce al sale
Whole fish baked under rock salt

4 kg rock salt
1 glass water
1 whole snapper or whole Murray cod, weighing about 1.8kg
black pepper
2 tbsp extra virgin olive oil
½ lemon
lettuce or steamed baby vegetables, to serve

Preheat oven to 200°C.

Place the rock salt in a bowl with a glass of water and mix – this allows the salt to adhere to the fish much better. Lay the fish in a baking dish and cover it with a 2-centimetre layer of the rock salt mix, making sure to completely cover the fish all over and around.

Bake for 45 minutes (add 8 minutes for every half-kilo above 1.8 kilos)

Remove from the oven and carefully break the salt crust off. Fillet the fish and plate individually. Grind some black pepper over the fish and dress with a little olive oil and lemon juice.

Serve with tender lettuce leaves or with steamed baby vegetables. SERVES 4–6

Rombo al vermentino
Whole fish with white wine and pine nuts

2 cloves garlic, peeled
a few sprigs marjoram
a few sprigs rosemary
1 x 800 g whole flounder or snapper or bream, gutted and scaled
110 ml dry white wine
3 tbsp extra virgin olive oil
½ cup pine nuts
110 g small black olives
½ cup sultanas
about 12 small cherry tomatoes
⅓ cup flat-leaf parsley, chopped
salt flakes, to taste

Preheat oven to 180°C.

Put the garlic, marjoram and rosemary in the fish's belly cavity. Place the fish in an oiled baking dish. Combine the wine and olive oil in a bowl and pour this over the fish. Sprinkle on the pine nuts, olives, sultanas and tomatoes. Cover with aluminium foil and bake for about 20 minutes, or until the eye of the fish is completely white.

Fillet the fish and place on serving plates, pour some of the cooking liquid over and arrange the pine nuts, olives, sultanas and tomatoes on top. Salt to taste and serve with a sprinkle of parsley. SERVES 4

The Unveiling of the "Pesce al Sale"

for Lucio
John Olsen '04

Bruna's kitchen

Fave con pecorino
Fava beans with pecorino cheese

1 kg small fava beans,
 in their pods
3 pinches of sea salt
½ cup olive oil
200 g pecorino cheese,
 sliced into 1 cm wedges

Your antipasto begins here. Fava beans are the first sign of spring (March in Italy, September in Australia). If you can get them small enough and fresh enough, you can just pull them out of the pod, put them in a bowl, sprinkle on sea salt and oil, mix and eat with a spoon, accompanied by wedges of pecorino. If the beans are bigger than the nail of your little finger, you'll need to peal off their skins before you salt, oil and eat them. SERVES 4 OR MORE

Carciofi sott'olio
Artichokes preserved in oil

1 kg artichokes
½ lemon
1 litre water
½ litre white wine vinegar
peppercorns
salt
several bay leaves
extra virgin olive oil,
 as needed

Clean the artichokes by trimming the stems and peeling them. Remove the tough outer leaves. Cut off the sharp pointed leaves, leaving only the tender heart, which is a pale colour. Cut them in half lengthwise and scrape off any coarse hairy bits. If they are large, cut them in half again. Immerse immediately in a bowl of water with half a squeezed lemon. This stops them from going black.

Pour the water and vinegar into a deep pot and add the artichokes and a few peppercorns, a pinch of salt and the bay leaves. Bring the pot to the boil and cook until the artichokes are soft but still al dente – approximately 20 minutes. Drain the artichokes in a colander and let them dry, then place in a very dry glass container with a few more bay leaves and peppercorns. Cover them completely with extra virgin olive oil, and after 2 hours put the lid on the container and store in a dark place for about 2 weeks, when they will be ready to serve as part of an antipasto. SERVES 4 OR MORE

Peperoni sott'olio
Roast capsicums

10 red and yellow
 capsicums
20 anchovy fillets in oil,
 drained
2 handfuls capers
1 handful fresh oregano
salt and pepper
1 cup olive oil

Burn the capsicums over an open flame until the skin is black (or burn them under a griller), allow to cool and peel off the blackened skin. Cut the capsicums in half, remove all the seeds and pat dry with a clean cloth.

Lay the capsicums on a workbench. On each half, place one anchovy, a few capers, some oregano and season with salt and pepper. Fold the other half over and secure in place with a toothpick. Arrange in a deep dish or glass container and cover the capsicums with olive oil. Allow them to soak in the oil for a few hours (ideally, overnight) before serving. SERVES 4 OR MORE

Cipolle ripiene
Stuffed onions

2 medium white onions
inside of 1 large bread roll,
  soaked in milk and then
  squeezed
3 eggs
pinch oregano
pinch marjoram
1 clove garlic, chopped
  finely
salt and pepper
olive oil
1 tsp breadcrumbs
1 tomato, chopped roughly
3 tbsp grated parmesan
  cheese

Preheat oven to 180°C.

Peel the onions and scald them in boiling salted water. Drain and cut them in half, scooping out the centre to make a cavity for the filling.

Chop the scooped-out part of the onions and place in a bowl with the bread. Mix with a wooden spoon and add the eggs, oregano, marjoram, garlic, salt and pepper. Mix well with a little olive oil. Fill the prepared onions with this mixture, sprinkle with breadcrumbs and a little olive oil.

Grease the bottom of a baking dish with olive oil and cover it with the chopped tomato. Place the onions on this tomato bed and cook in the oven for 25–30 minutes.

Serve as part of a hot antipasto or as a side dish. In some parts of Lunigiana chopped mozzarella and spinach are added to the filling. **SERVES 4**

Sedano al forno
Baked celery

1 kg celery sticks,
  trimmed and washed
½ cup olive oil
½ cup grated parmesan
black pepper
250 g ricotta
4 eggs
salt and pepper

Preheat oven to 180°C.

Cut the celery stalks into 10-centimetre pieces, boil them in salted water until tender (about 5 minutes). Drain and allow to cool.

Oil the bottom of a baking dish and make a layer of celery. Sprinkle with grated parmesan and black pepper. Continue layering in this manner and finish with a top layer of celery only.

With a wooden spoon, beat the eggs and ricotta together with a little salt and pepper, making sure to mix well. Spread this mixture over the top layer of celery to form a crust and sprinkle with parmesan.

Bake until the surface is a golden colour (about 30 minutes) and serve immediately. **SERVES 4**

Crostini di fegatini
Chicken liver crostini

½ onion, chopped finely
40 g butter
½ cup olive oil
½ kg chicken (or rabbit)
  livers, chopped
parsley
½ glass white wine
½ cup small capers
salt
crusty Italian bread,
  toasted, to serve

Gently fry the onion with the oil and butter. Add the livers and cook for about 10 minutes, stirring them carefully. Remove the livers from the pan, allow to cool slightly, and finely chop them with the parsley. Return this mixture to the pan and add the wine. Season and complete the cooking. Add the capers, season to taste and spread on the toasted bread. **SERVES 4**

Focaccia sarzanese alla salvia
Sage focaccia

40 g yeast
600 g white flour
1 glass warm water
240 ml olive oil
8 sage leaves, 4 of them
   finely chopped
sea salt

Melt the yeast with some water. Mix the flour with the water, a pinch of salt, about 150 ml of the olive oil, the yeast mixture and the chopped sage. Work the mixture with your fingers until it forms a soft dough, then cover it with a cloth and let it rest in a warm place for about 2 hours.

Preheat oven to 200°C. Put the dough in an oiled baking dish, ideally a round one 20–25 centimetre in diameter, and flatten dough to cover the whole dish. Then with the tips of your fingers, make imprints all over the dough, pressing lightly on the surface. Sprinkle with sea salt, place the four sage leaves on top and finally pour over the remaining olive oil. Bake until golden (about 20 minutes).

Tajarin
Tagliolini pasta

500 g white flour
3 eggs
water as needed

Sieve the flour into a mound on a table or benchtop, form a well and break the 3 eggs into it. Add a little water and mix in the eggs with a fork, incorporating a little flour at a time until the dough starts to form. Then, using your hands, work the dough until you have a smooth mixture.

Cover with a cloth and let dough rest for 10 minutes, then knead it for about 10 minutes or until little bubbles start to appear on the surface. Form the dough into a ball, and, first with the palm of your hand, and then with a rolling pin, flatten the dough into a rectangular shape until it reaches a thickness of about 2 millimetres. Keep folding it over and rolling it out until the dough feels elastic.

Sprinkle the dough with flour and carefully roll the sheet into a cylinder from the longest edge. Then cut this cylinder into 2-millimetre wide sections. Unroll each section and you have your tajarin noodles. Sprinkle with more flour if necessary to stop them from sticking together.

Boil the ribbons in salted water until they float to the surface (about 2 minutes). Drain and dress with your favourite sauce. **SERVES 4**

Sordei
Ravioli

RAGÚ (SAUCE):

1 small onion
1 clove garlic
5 leaves sage
a few sprigs rosemary
5 tbsp olive oil
300 g beef mince
250 g peeled tomatoes
1 ladle broth (chicken, beef
　or vegetable stock)

FILLING:

1 bunch silverbeet
200 g spinach
3 tbsp olive oil
salt and pepper
½ handful breadcrumbs
5 eggs
200 g parmesan, grated
pinch of salt
nutmeg
1 clove garlic
handful of mixed fresh
　herbs (thyme, sage and
　rosemary)
150 g beef mince
150 g veal or pork mince
100 g peeled tomatoes
½ ladle broth

PASTA:

300 g plain flour
3 eggs
2 tbsp warm water
Parmesan, grated to serve

RAGÚ (SAUCE):

Chop the onion, garlic, sage and rosemary together finely. Heat the oil in a high-sided pan and fry over medium heat until the garlic starts to colour. Add the minced beef and cook for 10 minutes until browned. Add the tomato and broth and let it simmer for one and a half hours or while you are preparing the other elements.

FILLING:

Wash the silverbeet and spinach and put into boiling water for 2 minutes. Drain, squeeze dry and chop finely. Heat 1 tablespoon of the olive oil in a pan and sauté the greens with salt and pepper for 3 minutes. Remove to a mixing bowl and add the breadcrumbs, eggs, cheese, a pinch of salt, a grating of nutmeg and some thyme, mix well and put to one side.

Chop the garlic, parsley, sage and rosemary and make a soffritto in a frying pan with the remaining oil. When the garlic starts to change colour, add the minced meats and continue frying for 10 minutes, stirring often to make sure all the meat is browned.

Add the tomatoes and broth and simmer for 15 minutes. Remove from heat and let it cool, then add to the spinach mixture and mix well. The filling is ready – keep it to one side until you need it.

PASTA:

Make and roll out a large sheet of pasta as in the Tajarin recipe (page 227). Place it on a floured surface. Use a spoon to deposit small dollops of the filling mixture (each about the size of a walnut) across one half of the pasta sheet. They should be in parallel lines, about 3 centimetres apart. Fill one side of the sheet in this manner, then fold the other half of the sheet over the top of the dollops. Using your fingers, seal around the dollops where the two halves join. Press lightly around each raviolo making sure not to leave any air pockets. Then place a glass or small cup over each mound, press down, twist and cut out each raviolo. When all the ravioli are separated, arrange them on a floured tray until ready to cook.

Bring the water to a boil in a large pot, add 3 pinches of rock salt, then delicately drop in the ravioli and boil for 7–8 minutes. Remove them with a slotted spoon (do not drain in a colander, as they might break) and arrange in a serving dish, dressing each layer with the sauce and plenty of parmesan cheese. Serve immediately. **SERVES 4–6**

Lasagnette al sugo di coniglio
Rag pasta with rabbit sauce

SAUCE:

1.5 kg rabbit, cut into
   about 10 pieces
1 clove garlic
1 medium onion
1 stalk celery
5 tbsp olive oil
50 g butter
1 tbsp flat-leaf
   parsley, chopped
salt
1 glass white wine
40 g parmesan, grated

Chop the rabbit into about 10 pieces. Finely chop the garlic, onion and celery all together. Heat the oil and butter in a heavy pan, add the mixture and cook for about 3 minutes. Then add the rabbit pieces and the parsley and season with salt. Cook over a low heat for about 15 minutes, stirring regularly so the rabbit incorporates all the flavours.

Add the glass of wine and cook for about 90 minutes until the meat is so tender is easily separates from the bone, adding water if it looks like drying out. Remove the rabbit pieces from the sauce, debone them and chop the meat into small cubes. Return to the sauce and mix well. The sauce is now ready to use.

PASTA:

Use the Tajarin recipe (page 227) and when you have the round thin sheet of pasta, cut it in square pieces of 5 centimetres x 5 centimetres. Sprinkle with flour so that the pieces will not stick to each other.

Cook the pasta pieces in boiling salted water for 5 minutes and drain. Arrange them in layers on a serving dish, topping each layer with sauce and parmesan. Shake the dish a little, so that all the pasta is covered by the sauce, and serve.

This recipe can also be made using hare if you like a stronger flavour. The procedure is the same, except you begin by washing the hare with white wine to moderate the gamey smell. SERVES 4

Four sauces for pasta …

Pesto
Pesto sauce

30 small-to-medium
   basil leaves
1 clove garlic, peeled
pinch sea salt
handful pine nuts
2 tbsp parmesan, grated
1 tbsp mild pecorino,
   grated
1 cup olive oil, or as much
   as the pesto will absorb

Carefully wash the basil leaves and dry them gently between two paper towels without pressure. If you want to use the mortar (which must be made of marble and the pestle made of wood), begin by putting in the garlic with a pinch of salt (this helps to keep the basil green). Crush the garlic, then add the basil leaves and continue crushing. Then add the pine nuts, the two cheeses and a little oil. When the mixture is reduced to a very fine consistency, transfer it to a glass jar or bowl with a lid, stir in more oil and then cover the mixture with oil. The pesto must stay covered by olive oil at all times to maintain the colour and stop it from going black.

If you prefer to use a blender, put all ingredients in at once and use the pulse action until it reaches the desired creamy consistency. The pulse action is necessary so as not to damage or overheat the basil.

When using the pesto with pasta, it is best to put the pesto into the bowl first, moisten with a little of the pasta-cooking water, then add the noodles and toss the pesto through. SERVES 4

Sugo di funghi freschi
Fresh mushroom sauce

400 g mushrooms
5 tbsp olive oil
2 cloves garlic, peeled
  and crushed a little
1 tbsp white wine
400 g peeled tomatoes
some flat-leaf parsley
salt and pepper
grated parmesan, to serve

Clean any dirt off the mushrooms with a brush, wash them and slice thinly. In a pan, heat the oil with the whole garlic for 3 minutes, taking care not to let the garlic burn. Remove the garlic from the pan and add the mushrooms. Mix them well for 3 minutes over a moderate heat.

Add the wine, tomatoes, chopped parsley and season to taste. Cover and cook over low heat for about an hour.

This sauce is very good with fresh pasta or on top of ravioli. Serve it sprinkled with grated parmesan. SERVES 4

Sughetto
Pork sausage ragù

5 tbsp olive oil
1 onion, finely diced
4 small pork sausages,
  skin removed and
  roughly chopped
500 g ripe tomatoes,
  peeled, seeded and
  crushed
sea salt and pepper
pecorino cheese, to serve

Heat the oil in a heavy-bottomed frying pan with high sides and gently fry the onion until soft but not coloured. Add the sausage meat and cook for about 5 minutes, stirring often. Add the tomatoes, season with salt and pepper and cook on a gentle heat for 20 minutes.

This sughetto is best enjoyed with short dried pasta like rigatoni or orecchiette, or with fresh fettuccine or pappardelle. Pecorino cheese works better with this sauce than parmesan. SERVES 4

Sugo al pomodoro
Tomato sauce

5 tbsp olive oil
800 g ripe tomatoes,
  chopped
1 onion, chopped
some basil leaves
salt

Heat a little oil in a pan and toss in the chopped tomatoes, chopped onion, basil and a pinch of salt. Cook over a moderate heat. When everything softens (about 10 minutes) and becomes thick, put it through a Mouli. Heat the rest of the oil in the pan and pour puree back in the pan. Simmer for another 5 minutes.

This sauce is very good for dressing any type of hard pasta, especially spaghetti. Add a bit of chili if you like, or more basil, or even pesto. SERVES 4

Gallina bollita
Boiled chicken

1 large chicken
2 onions
2 carrots
2 stalks celery
3 bay leaves
sea salt

Traditionally, this was the way hens that had reached the end of their laying life were cooked, but you can use a large chicken from the supermarket.

In a big pot, cover the chicken with cold water, bring it to the boil and add one whole onion, one carrot and one celery stalk. Boil for 15 minutes.

Prepare another large pot of boiling water to transfer the chicken into. Discard the first broth as it will be fatty. Add the remaining ingredients and simmer for about an hour, or until a fork will easily penetrate the meat. Remove the chicken from the broth, cut into serving pieces and serve with salsa verde (below).

Strain the liquid to remove the vegetable pieces and make a broth which can be served as a consommé (light soup) or used as a stock (in which you can boil small pasta such as tortellini). SERVES 6

Salsa verde
Green sauce

20 g pine nuts
2 or 3 anchovies
1 bunch flat-leaf parsley,
  leaves only
4 tbsp olive oil
2 tbsp white wine vinegar
20 g capers, rinsed
  and drained

Put the pine nuts, anchovies and parsley in a blender. Mix well, then add the oil, vinegar and capers, and mix a little – it should not be too fine. Put the sauce in a glass container adding a little more oil if necessary. This will keep for one week in the refrigerator.

This is best served with boiled meats, poached or grilled fish and chicken.

Torta di riso
Rice pudding

150 g white rice
10 eggs
500 g sugar
1 litre milk
grated zest of 1 lemon
butter
flour

Preheat the oven to 190°C.

Cook the rice in a big saucepan of salted water for 8 minutes, drain and let cool.

Break the eggs into a large bowl, add the sugar and beat energetically with a wooden spoon until you obtain a smooth texture. While still mixing slowly, add the milk and the lemon zest. Reserve about a quarter of the egg mixture to use later and mix the remaining three-quarters with the rice.

Grease a 40-centimetre baking dish with the butter, sprinkle with white flour and shake out the excess. Pour in the rice mixture, pour over the reserved egg mixture and bake for 45–50 minutes or until it is golden-brown on top.

Up-end it onto a board, and then up-end it again onto a plate, so the eggy top is visible. Serve at room temperature, in triangles. Great with sliced fresh fruit. SERVES 8

The high Lunigiana

Lattughe ripiene in brodo
Lettuce parcels in chicken broth

2 large iceberg lettuces
  (five leaves per person)
200 g lambs' brains
50 g butter
200 g veal, finely chopped
15 g dried porcini
  mushrooms, soaked for
  20 minutes in water,
  then chopped
50 g prosciutto
few leaves of fresh
  marjoram
100 g parmesan, grated
1 egg
pinch of nutmeg
salt and pepper
1 litre chicken stock

Choose the white inner leaves of the lettuce and wash them. Dip them for a minute in salted boiling water, drain them and put them to dry on a cloth.

Clean the brains, removing any skin and blood vessels, and cook them in boiling water for about 3 minutes. In a frying pan, melt the butter and sauté the veal for 2 minutes, then add the brains and the mushrooms. Cook together, stirring continuously, for another three minutes.

Empty the contents of the pan onto a chopping board, add the prosciutto and marjoram, and chop everything very finely.

Transfer the mixture to a bowl, add the parmesan, the egg, and a grating of nutmeg. Amalgamate well and season with salt and pepper. Now you have your stuffing mixture.

Bring the stock to the boil. Lay the lettuce leaves on a clean working surface. Put a large teaspoon of the stuffing into each leaf, like a raviolo. Wrap each leaf around its stuffing, and tie it into a parcel with cotton, to keep it closed. Immerse the parcels in boiling stock for two minutes. Fish them out of the stock with a slotted spoon. Snip off the cotton, and place them in soup bowls, five per person.

Pour two ladles of stock into each bowl, sprinkle with parmesan and serve. In some parts of the Lunigiana, the lettuce parcels are sautéed in a pan with a little butter, and served with a tomato and basil sauce (see Sugo al Pomodoro, page 230). SERVES 4

Barbotta
Onion cake

2 large onions
400 g polenta flour
5 tbsp extra virgin olive oil
40 g pecorino or parmesan,
  grated
2 glasses milk
100 g ricotta
salt

Finely chop the onions and sauté in 2 tablespoons of the olive oil until transparent (about 15 minutes).

Preheat oven to 180°C.

Place the onion and all other ingredients in a bowl with a pinch of salt, and stir with a wooden spoon until the mixture is free of lumps. Smear a little oil on base and sides of a round 25-centimetre baking dish and pour in the mixture. Bake in the oven for 40 minutes.

Instead of the onion, you can use chopped zucchini flowers. If you want to add more flavour and a textural contrast, you can spread a soft cheese such as stracchino over the top as soon as it comes out of the oven. This is an excellent accompaniment for salami or prosciutto. SERVES 4

Farinata
Chickpea flatbread

250 g chickpea flour
1 litre water
10 tbsp extra virgin olive oil
salt and pepper

Put the flour and water in a big bowl. Stir well to remove all lumps, add half the oil and a pinch of salt and keep stirring to achieve a homogenous liquid. Rest the mixture for half an hour and skim any foam off the top.

Preheat oven to 200°C.

Pour the rest of the oil into a shallow baking dish with 50-centimetre diameter, making sure it covers the bottom. Pour the mixture in (it should be only about 2mm deep) and sprinkle with black pepper. Cook in oven for 10 minutes, or until the surface forms a golden crust.

This is delicious on its own, sliced into triangles as part of a mixed antipasto, or as a focaccia filling. SERVES 4

Panigazzi di Sarzana
Savoury pancakes

½ litre water
400 g white flour
1 potato
extra virgin olive oil
100 g parmesan, grated
salt

Pour the water into a large bowl and add a little salt. Add the flour while mixing to obtain a runny lump-free batter.

Pour some olive oil onto a flat plate. Cut the potato in half, and stick a fork into the round side of one half, so the fork becomes a handle. Dip the cut side of the potato into the oil and use this to grease a 20–25 centimetre non-stick frying pan.

Heat the pan. Take a ladlefull of the batter and pour it into the centre of the pan. With the back of the ladle spread the mixture evenly using a clockwise motion from the centre to the outside of the pan. The pancake should be about 3 millimetres thick – in other words, very thin. This may take a little trial and error to get the right amount. Cook it for 2 minutes on one side, and then flip it with a wide knife and cook the other side for another 2 minutes. When cooked, remove it to a warm plate and cover with a cloth. Continue until all the batter is used.

Layer the panigazzi on a plate, dressing each one with olive oil and parmesan cheese and forming a tower of about six, which you can cut in quarters and serve. Panigazzi can be enjoyed with pesto as well. SERVES 4

Cipollata
Cheese and onion frittata

6 whole white onions
1 clove garlic
1 handful flat-leaf parsley
5 tbsp extra virgin olive oil
salt and pepper
4 eggs
50 g parmesan, grated

Preheat oven to 180°C.

Peel the onions and slice very thinly. Chop the garlic and parsley together, heat the oil in an ovenproof frying pan and fry the garlic and parsley mix for a few minutes, then add the onions, salt and pepper and mix well with a wooden spoon. Let this cook on a low heat for 20 minutes, adding a little water during the cooking if necessary.

Break the eggs into a bowl and beat them with the parmesan and a pinch of salt. Add this mixture to the onions, and mix well. Put the pan in the oven and cook for 6 minutes at 180°C. Remove and serve immediately. SERVES 4

Sgabei
Puffs

400 g white flour
20 g yeast
1½ glasses warm water
salt
500 ml vegetable oil,
   for frying
sea salt

Sieve the flour onto a work surface and make a well in the centre. Melt the yeast in some of warm water and pour it in the centre of the well. Add the remaining water and some salt. Knead the dough until it becomes smooth and soft. Let the dough rest in a warm place for 1 hour.

On a floured work surface, roll the dough out to a thickness of 1.5 centimetre. Cut into rectangles approximately 3 centimetres x 15 centimetres. Let these pieces rest for about 20 minutes in a warm place.

Heat the oil until very hot and cook the sgabei until golden. Remove them with a slotted spoon and drain on kitchen paper to remove excess oil. Sprinkle with sea salt and serve immediately.

Sgabei are excellent filled with peas or steamed spinach (not silverbeet) and stracchino, gorgonzola, prosciutto or hot salami. SERVES 4

I cian
Chestnut pancakes

400 g chestnut flour
¾ litre warm water
3 tbsp olive oil
200 g ricotta or stracchino
salt

Mix the chestnut flour in a bowl with water and a pinch of salt until it is a lump-free batter.

Heat a non-stick pan, grease with a little olive oil and ladle in enough batter to thinly cover the base of the pan. Fry for 2–3 minutes on each side. Continue with the rest of the mixture, cooking the pancakes one by one and keeping the finished ones hot in a warm oven.

To serve, stack the pancakes on a plate in the middle of the table, with the ricotta or stracchino in a separate bowl, and let your guests help themselves. SERVES 4

Scarpazza
Vegetable pie

PASTRY:

250 g white flour
1 ½ glasses warm water
2 tbsp extra virgin olive oil
salt

FILLING:

500 g silverbeet
2 large leeks
4 tbsp extra virgin olive oil
6 eggs
60 g parmesan, grated
35 g pecorino, grated
salt

PASTRY:

Preheat oven to 200°C.

Knead the flour with a little water, the oil and a pinch of salt until you achieve a uniform elastic dough, adding water as necessary. Divide the dough into two balls, one bigger than the other.

Using a rolling pin, roll out both balls of dough in a circular shape on a floured surface, to a thickness of 1–2 millimetres. Using the larger sheet of dough, line the base and sides of a round 35-centimetre pie dish. The smaller sheet is used for the top.

FILLING:

Remove and discard all stalks of the silverbeet. Wash the leaves, drop them in boiling water for a few seconds, strain, squeeze out any excess moisture and set to one side. Peel off and discard the outer layers of the leeks and then cut into thin discs. Heat the oil in a medium pan and cook the leeks for 5 minutes, stirring with a wooden spoon. Remove them and set to one side. In the same pan, gently sauté the silverbeet for about 10 minutes. Put the silverbeet, leeks, eggs and both cheeses in a bowl, and mix well.

Pour the leek mixture into the lined pie dish and shake the dish to make sure it is spread evenly. Fold any excess pastry from the base onto the top. Cut the smaller sheet of dough into strips and lay in a lattice pattern over the top of the filling.

Bake for 40 minutes. SERVES 4

Zuppa in padella
Vegetable soup

400 g potatoes
1 onion
4 medium-sized zucchini
2 stalks celery
2 tomatoes
1 clove garlic
1 handful flat-leaf
  parsley leaves
6 tbsp extra virgin olive oil
½ litre water
8 slices crusty Italian
  bread, to serve
garlic
40 g parmesan,
  grated, to serve

Peel the potatoes and onion, and rinse them under running water. Cut the onion, potatoes, zucchini and celery into cubes.

Wash the tomatoes and cut a cross through the skin at the top of each tomato with a sharp knife. Plunge into boiling water for a couple of minutes, then plunge into ice-cold water. You will then be able to peel the skin off easily. Remove the seeds and dice into small pieces.

Finely chop the garlic and parsley. Heat the olive oil into a high-sided pan and add the mix of garlic and parsley. Stir well with a wooden spoon, add the potatoes, onion, zucchini and celery and cook on medium heat for 10 minutes, stirring occasionally. Add the tomatoes and fry for 5 minutes. Add the water and simmer for a further 15 minutes, stirring occasionally.

Meanwhile, toast the bread, rub with cut garlic and place a slice in the bottom of each serving bowl. Pour the soup on top and serve with a sprinkling of grated cheese.
SERVES 4

Zuppa della Lunigiana
Vegetable soup

1 white onion
1 medium leek
2 tomatoes, peeled
  and seeded
2 carrots
3 potatoes
300 g fresh borlotti beans
200 g silverbeet
400 g cabbage
2 stalks celery
salt
8 tbsp extra virgin olive oil
½ litre water
1 clove garlic
1 small bunch basil,
  whole leaves
1 small bunch flat-leaf
  parsley, whole leaves
crusty Italian bread,
  to taste

Clean all the vegetables and wash them. Chop the onion and the leek together very finely. Dice separately the tomatoes, carrots and potatoes. Shell the beans. Roughly chop the silverbeet, cabbage and celery.

In a high-sided heavy-bottomed pan or pot, heat half the oil and fry the onion and leek for a few minutes until they become translucent, then add the tomatoes, carrots, potatoes silverbeet, cabbage, celery and beans. Add some salt and stir well with a wooden spoon to mix all the ingredients and let it cook for about 3 minutes until the vegetables are just starting to soften. Cover with cold water and simmer over a low heat for 2 hours.

When it is ready, remove from the heat, scoop out half of the vegetables, pass them through a Mouli and put the resulting puree back into the pot.

Meanwhile, heat the rest of the oil in a pan and fry the garlic, basil and parsley for a few minutes. Strain the oil, pour it into the soup and mix well. Pour into a soup tureen and serve with toasted bread. SERVES 4

Tagliatelle alla contadina
Pasta, peasant style

400 g tagliatelle
500 g dried borlotti beans,
  soaked overnight
2 potatoes, peeled and
  diced
1 quantity of sauce
  (see note)
pasta (see note)
3 leaves sage
a few sprigs rosemary
salt
parmesan, grated

Use the sauce from recipes for Sughetto, Sugo al pomodoro or Sugo di funghi (page 230). Use store-bought fresh pasta or you can make your own, using the Tajarin recipe (page 227).

Boil the borlotti beans with the sage and rosemary in a large pot of salted water for 15 minutes, then add the potatoes and boil for another ten minutes. When the beans and potatoes are almost ready, add the pasta and cook until it is al dente (not more than 5 minutes). Drain the pot, making sure the contents are still quite moist.

Cover the bottom of a bowl or large serving dish with some of the sauce, and then make a layer of the pasta mixture, add sauce again, and sprinkle with parmesan. Top this with a layer of pasta, sauce and parmesan, finishing with sauce and parmesan on top. Shake the dish gently and toss very delicately (while enjoying the smell and sound it makes) and serve. SERVES 4

Armelette
Chestnut pasta

400 g chestnut flour
200 g plain flour
salt
1 ½ glasses warm water
8 tbsp extra virgin olive oil
100 g pecorino or
  parmesan for grating
salt

Sieve the two flours together with a pinch of salt, and make a mound on your benchtop or table. Form a well in the mound and pour in half the water. Start mixing with your hands, adding more water as needed to form a smooth dough. Using a rolling pin, flatten out the dough to a 3-millimetre thickness. Allow it to dry for a few minutes, then cut it into squares about 5 centimetres wide. Sprinkle with plain flour to avoid sticking.

Bring a pot of water to the boil, add salt and drop in the squares a few at a time. Stir delicately so the squares don't stick together and boil for about 8 minutes. To serve, drain and layer the pasta squares carefully on a serving dish, splashing each layer with olive oil and some grated pecorino or parmesan. Armalette is excellent served with pesto as well. **SERVES 4**

Agnello fricandò
Leg of lamb, Lunigiana style

1.3 kg leg of lamb
3 tbsp extra virgin olive oil
1 tsp butter
2 cloves garlic, finely
  chopped
1 handful flat-leaf parsley
  leaves, finely chopped
2 leaves sage, roughly
  chopped
a few sprigs rosemary,
  finely chopped
pepper
1 glass dry white wine
150 g breadcrumbs
100 g parmesan, grated
5 eggs

Cut (or have your butcher cut) the lamb into chunks about 3 centimetres square and salt them. Heat the oil and butter in the pan, then fry the garlic, parsley, sage and rosemary for 2 minutes. Add the lamb and a generous grind of pepper, mix with a wooden spoon to let the herbs and garlic flavour the meat and cook for 10 minutes. Pour in the white wine and cook on a low heat for 30 minutes.

Mix together the breadcrumbs and parmesan and add to the lamb. Lightly whisk the eggs in a bowl, add them to the lamb and mix well again. Cook for another 40 minutes. Pour into a serving dish. This dish is traditionally prepared in a terracotta pot, but a high-sided pan will do. **SERVES 4**

Fichi secchi
Dried figs

12 figs
sunshine
1 litre water

Try to use figs that are all equally ripe (soft to the touch, more purple than green). Sit them in a tray or flat basket, not touching each other and with their stalks pointing up. Leave them in the sun for two days, covering them at night. Then immerse them in boiling water for two minutes. Put them back out in the sun for two more days. Keep them in a cool place, wrapped in a cloth with bay leaves between them, until you are ready to eat them. They can be served with other dried fruits and nuts, but they must be the star. Best eaten with an Italian dessert wine. **ALLOW 3 FIGS PER PERSON**

The Luni Dinner

Tartina alla Ciccio

Follow the recipe for the Crostini with seafood salad (page 220), but instead of the fried bread, rub a litle garlic on thin slices of toasted Italian bread, splash on a little oil, and top with seafood salad and mayonnaise.

Peperoni

Follow the recipe for Peperoni Sott'Olio (page 225).

Polenta incatenata
Polenta with beans and cavolo nero

3 litres water
rock salt
200 g fresh borlotti beans
500 g cavolo nero
  (Tuscan kale)
150 ml olive oil
200 g polenta
50 g parmesan, grated

Bring the water to a boil with one tablespoon of rock salt, add the borlotti beans and boil for 10 minutes.

Meanwhile, wash and cut finely the cavolo nero and add it to the beans. Add the oil and cook for a further 40 minutes. Lower the heat and, stirring continuously, add the polenta slowly. Cook for about 40 minutes, stirring regularly, and adding more water if it becomes too thick and dry. If using instant polenta, cook for the time specified on the packet.

Spoon into individual bowls and generously grate parmesan over to serve. SERVES 4

Insalata di funghi crudi
Raw mushroom salad

500 g button mushrooms
  (not too small)
½ bunch celery
sea salt and ground
  black pepper
100 g parmesan,
  finely shaved
2 tsp olive oil
juice of half a lemon

Peel off the mushroom skin and discard the stalks. Slice mushrooms thinly and put in a bowl. Use only the tender stalks in the middle of the celery (the yellow-white bits) with the leaves still on if possible. Slice them very thinly and add to the mushrooms. Season with salt and pepper and mix gently. Add the finely shaved parmesan. Dress with the olive oil and lemon juice, toss and serve immediately. SERVES 4

Spungata
Fruit pie

FILLING:

120 g apricot jam
30 g pine nuts, chopped finely
20 g blanched almonds, chopped finely
30 g candied fruits, chopped finely

PASTRY:

250 g plain flour
salt
1 egg
100 g sugar
150 g softened butter
cream or ice-cream, to serve

Preheat the oven to 180°C.

In a bowl, mix the jam, pine nuts, almonds and candied fruit with a wooden spoon and put to one side.

Sieve the flour onto a clean flat surface and add a pinch of salt. Make a well in the middle, break in the egg, add the sugar and softened butter and mix well with your hands until it is uniform. If the mixture is too stiff, add a tablespoon of water.

Divide the mixture into 2 parts (one a bit bigger than the other). With a rolling pin, flatten out the dough in a circular shape so that the larger one can cover the bottom and sides of a greased 30-centimetre baking dish. The other piece of dough will become the 'lid' of the pie.

Pour the jam mixture directly on to the bottom layer of pastry and spread evenly. Cover with the other pastry sheet, sealing the two sheets together around the edges and slicing off any excess dough. Bake for 30 minutes.

Spungata is best served cold, with a few fine slices of apple (dried in the oven for five minutes) on the top for decoration. Serve with cream or ice-cream. SERVES 4

Torta di castagne e ricotta
Chestnut and ricotta tart

½ litre milk
400 g chestnut flour
salt
100 g sugar
50 g sultanas
50 g pine nuts
2 tbsp olive oil
3 sprigs rosemary
300 g fresh ricotta

Preheat oven to 200°C.

Put the milk in a bowl and slowly add the flour, whisking all the time to avoid lumps. Mix well, add a pinch of salt and the sugar, sultanas and pine nuts. Stir and mix well again.

Grease a 30-centimetre cake tin with oil or butter. Pour in the mixture. Sprinkle the olive oil on the surface, arrange the 3 sprigs of rosemary on top and bake for 50 minutes. When ready, the surface should be crispy and cracked, and an intense brown colour. Serve warm with spoonfuls of fresh ricotta. SERVES 8

Biscotti di Sarzana
Sarzana biscuits

600 g plain flour
200 g sugar
grated zest of 1 lemon
⅓ tsp yeast
salt
100 g butter
½ cup white wine
   (ideally muscat style)
3 tbsp olive oil
50 g pine nuts, toasted
50 g almonds, toasted
   and chopped
½ glass milk

Preheat the oven to 200°C.

Sieve the flour into a bowl with sugar, grated lemon zest, yeast and a few pinches of salt and mix well with a wooden spoon. Using your fingers, squash the butter into the mixture and blend it through. Put this mixture onto a workbench and form a well into which you pour the white wine. Start kneading with your hands and gradually add the olive oil, pine nuts, almonds and the milk while still kneading. When the mixture has become an elastic and soft consistency (approximately 20 minutes), it is ready.

Prepare strips of baking paper the length of a 40-centimetre baking tray and 9 centimetres wide. Grease these strips with oil and arrange them on the tray.

Divide the dough into four equal pieces and shape each piece into a cylinder about 5 centimetres in diameter and the length of your tray. Place the cylinders on the paper and press them down slightly with your hands. Let them rest for half an hour, and bake them for 15 minutes.

Remove from the oven and slice diagonally into 2-centimetre biscuits. Lay these back on the tray and cook for another 5 minutes. Allow to cool completely before placing in an airtight container.

These biscuits are better served the day after baking.

Acknowledgements

Many people helped us to make this book. Anna Galletto, Wendy and Mario Guelfi and Aulo and Mariella Galletto were endlessly hospitable and instructive. Salvatore Marchese gave us the benefits of his scholarship. Logan Campbell, chef at Lucio's, advised on the recipes.

Sue Hines saw the possibilities in an idea that looked like six books in one, Andrea McNamara clarified our thoughts with meticulous editing and designers Pfisterer + Freeman brought out the beauty of Paul Green's brilliant images. We're indebted to John Olsen for his drawings and to Luke Sciberras for his painting of Lucio's journey.

Our wives and children – Sally, Susan, Matteo, Michela and Millie – put up with long mental and physical absences and helped us appreciate the importance of family.

We paid for all fares, meals and accommodation (except when we stayed with family) so we don't need to acknowledge any hotels, airlines or tourist bureaucracies.

But we do need to thank the people of Lunigiana for the time they gave us explaining and demonstrating the work which is their life. As the anthropologist Luigi Barzini put it, these people have 'mastered the great art of being happy and of making other people happy, an art which embraces and inspires all others in Italy, the only art worth learning, but which can never really be mastered: the art of inhabiting the earth'.

Bibliography

Bosworth, Richard, Mussolini, Arnold, 2002

Castagno, Dario, Too Much Tuscan Sun, Casa Editrice Imori, 2002

Dante, The Divine Comedy, Oxford University Press, 1980

Farrell, Nicholas, Mussolini, A New Life, Weidenfeld and Nicholson, 2003

Galletto, Lucio, The Art of Food at Lucio's, Craftsman House, 1999

Guglielmi, Laura, Su e Giu per la Val di Magra, Edizioni Agora, 1998

Leitch, Alison, Il Lardo di Colonnata, Fedrico Motta Editore, 2003

Macksey, Kenneth, Kesselring, German Master Strategist of the Second World War,
    Greenhill Books, 2000

McBride, James, Miracle at St Anna, Sceptre, 2000

Marchese, Salvatore, La Cucina di Lunigiana, Franco Muzzio Editore, 1989

Neri, Tiziana and Capponi, Davide, La Vita Lungo La Via Francigena, Edizioni Giacche, 1997

Paracucchi, Angelo, La Cucina della Lunigiana, Longanesi + C., 1980

Plotkin, Fred, Italy for the Gourmet Traveller, Kyle Cathie Ltd, 2003

Puzzo, Dante, The Partisans and the War in Italy, Peter Lang, 1992

Root, Waverley, The Food of Italy, Vintage Books, 1977

Scigliano, Eric, Michelangelo's Mountain, Free Press, 2005

The Eating Places

In Italy, eateries have different labels, according to their degree of formality. In roughly ascending order, they go *osteria*, *trattoria*, *taverna*, *locanda*, *ristorante*. But sometimes a serious (and expensive) restaurant will call itself a *taverna* or a *locanda* or even a *trattoria* to lighten its image – as with Locanda delle Tamerici or Taverna Napoleone.

LUNIGIANA

Angelo, Locanda Del, Viale XV Aprile 60, Ameglia. Tel. 0187 64391 (see Chapter 3) www.paracucchilocanda.it.

Armanda, Trattoria. Piazza Garibaldi 6, Castelnuovo Magra. Tel. 0187 674410 (see Chapters 3, 11 & 15)

Busse Trattoria Da. Piazza Duomo, 31 Pontremoli. Tel. 0187831371 (see Chapters 9 & 15)

Cantinone, Il, ristorante, Via Fiasella, 59, Sarzana. Tel. 0187-627952 (see Chapters 3 & 13)

Capannina Ciccio, ristorante._ Via Fabbricotti 71, Bocca di Magra, Ameglia. Tel. 0187/65568 ((see Chapters 1, 3, 6, 8, 10, 14 & 15)

Caveau del Teatro, ristorante, Piazzetta Santa Cristina, Pontremoli. Tel. 0187 833328 www. caveaudelteatro.it (see Chapter 11)

Chioccia d'Oro, La, trattoria, Via Appia Antica, Luni. Tel. 0187 66689 (see Chapter 3)

Ciccio Marina, ristorante, Viale G. da Verazzano 1, Marina di Carrara. Tel. 0585 780286 (see Chapters 7 & 14)

Da Saine, osteria, Via al Plebiscito, Carrara (see Chapter 5)

Gavarina d'Oro, La, osteria, Via Castello 11, Podenzana. Tel. 0187 410021 (see Chapter 9)

Gemmi pasticceria, Via Mazzini 21, Sarzana. Tel. 0187 620165 (see Chapters 3 & 14)

Hotel Garden, ristorante, Via Fabbricotti 162, Bocca di Magra. Tel. 0187 65086 (see Chapter 14)

Napoleone, Taverna, Via Bonaparte 16, Sarzana. Tel. 0187 627974 (see Chapter 3)

Pilota, Il, trattoria, Via del Pilota 15, Fiumaretta, Ameglia. Tel. 0187 64446 (see Chapter 14)

Tamerici, Locanda delle, Via Litoranea SE, 106, Fiumaretta. Tel. 0187.64262 (see Chapter 3)

Vallecchia, ristorante, Via Vallecchia, Vallecchia. Tel. 0187 674104 (see Chapter 11)

Venanzio, ristorante, Piazza Palestro 3, Colonnata. Tel. 05855758062 (see Chapter 5)

TUSCANY

Lorenzo, ristorante, Via Carducci 61, Forte dei Marmi. Tel. 0584-874030 (see Chapter 5)

Mora, La, ristorante, Via Sesto di Moriano 1748, Ponte a Moriano. Tel. 0583 406402. 88 (see Chapter 5)

EMILIA-ROMAGNA

Cavallino Bianco, Al, ristorante, Via Sbrisi, 2 - 43010 Polesine Parmense, near Parma. Tel. (0524) 96136 (see Chapter 7)

Parizzi, ristorante, Strada della Repubblica 71, Parma. Tel. (0521) 285952 (see Chapter 7)

Rubbiara, Osteria di, Via Risaia, 2, Frazione di Rubbiara, Nonantola. Tel. 059 549019 (see Chapter 7)

Zelmira Ristorante, Via S. Giacomo, 27, Modena. Tel. 059 222351 (see Chapter 7)

PIEMONTE

Ca' del Lupo, ristorante, Via Ballerina 15, Montelupo, Albese. Tel. 0173-617249 www.cadellupo.it (see Chapter 13)

Cambio, Ristorante del, Piazza Carignano 2, Torino. Tel. 011 546690 (see Chapter 13)

Capannina, La, Trattoria, Via Donati Vitaliano 1, Torino. Tel. 011 545405 (see Chapter 13)

Collina, La, ristorante, Piazza Umberto I, Monforte d'Alba. Tel. 0173 78297 (see Chapter 13)

ROME

Convivio Troianni, ristorante, Vicolo dei Soldati 31, Roma. Tel. 06 6869432 www. ilconviviotroiani.com (see Chapter 14)

SYDNEY

Lucio's, 47 Windsor Street, Paddington. Tel. (02) 9380 5996 www.lucios.com.au (see Chapters 1, 3, 12 & 15)

Index